THE WAY THE UNIVERSE WORKS

By
Robin Kerrod and Giles Sparrow

DK A DORLING KINDERSLEY BOOK

Dorling **DK** Kindersley

LONDON, NEW YORK,
MELBOURNE, MUNICH, and DELHI

Project editors Kate Bradshaw, David John, Sadie Smith
Art editors Tim Brown, Sheila Collins, Darren Holt
Senior editor Fran Jones
Senior art editor Martin Wilson
Category publisher Linda Martin
Managing art editor Jane Thomas
Picture research Angela Anderson, Sarah Pownall
Picture librarians Jonathan Brooks, Rose Horridge
Jacket design Dean Price
DTP designer Siu Yin Ho
Production controller Erica Rosen
Special photography Trish Gant
Digital artwork Robin Hunter, John Kelly

Science experiments adviser John Miller

Hardback edition first published in Great Britain in 2002
Paperback edition first published in Great Britain in 2006
by Dorling Kindersley Limited,
80 Strand, London WC2R ORL

A CIP catalogue record for this book is
available from the British Library.

ISBN-13: 978-1-40531-687-3
ISBN-10: 1-4053-1687-X

Colour reproduction by Colourscan, Singapore
Printed and bound by Toppan, China

Discover more at
www.dk.com

CONTENTS

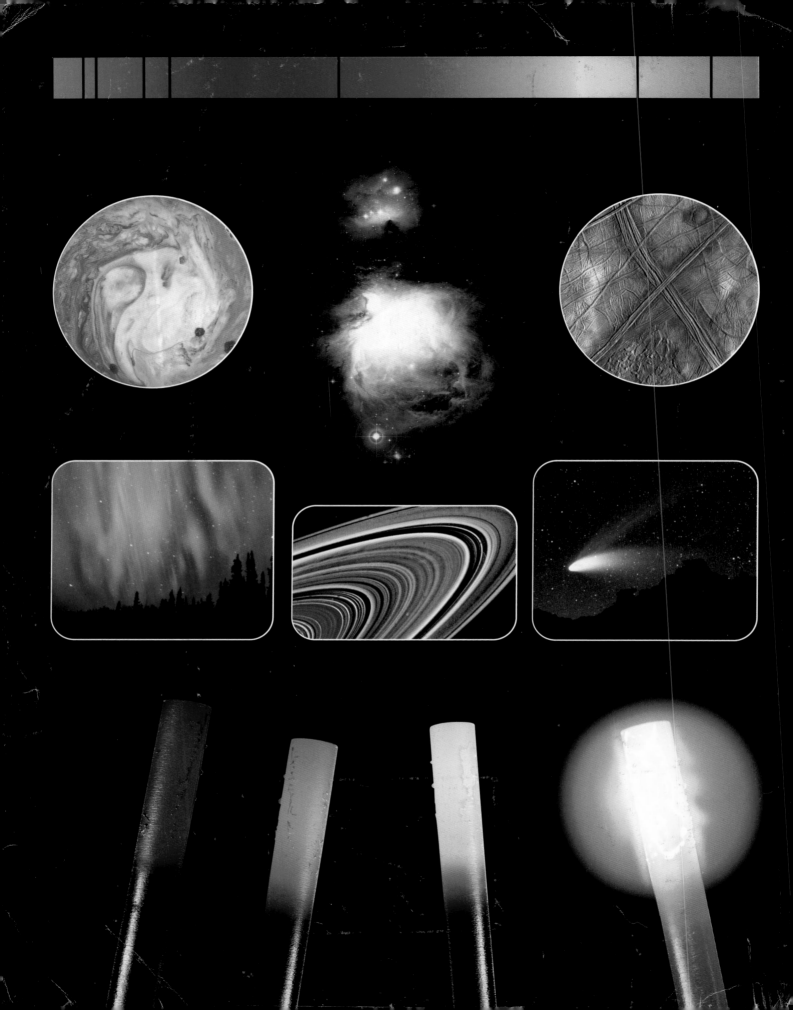

THE WAY THE UNIVERSE WORKS

A SUPERGIANT STAR, hundreds of millions of kilometres in diameter, explodes and blasts itself to smithereens. A black hole, lurking at the heart of a galaxy, tears streamers of gas away from a neighbouring star, and sucks them into its abyssal core. Closer to home, a volcano on one of the moons of Jupiter is erupting and pouring out rivers of molten sulphur. In other words, it's just an average day in the life of the Universe. The Universe means the entirety of all that exists – Earth and everything on it, the planets and their moons, the stars and galaxies, and, of course, space. It is larger than we can ever imagine and was once thought to be a mystery, the truth of which would never be known. But, slowly and surely, over many centuries, astronomers have more or less worked out what makes the Universe tick and why it's the way it is. Even so, many puzzles still remain.

THE ASTRONOMERS' WORK

Astronomers are the scientists who study the objects and phenomena seen in space. They work mainly at observatories – their laboratories. Like other scientists, astronomers investigate the nature of matter and energy. But they do so on the largest scale of all – across the whole Universe in fact. These investigations have gradually allowed them to discover the nuts and bolts of the Universe – from the nuclear source of starlight to the force that keeps planets in orbit, and even the power at

Io, Jupiter's most volcanic moon

EXPERIMENTS – SAFETY FIRST

Before conducting any experiment, be sure to read the instructions carefully. Think of the things that could go wrong first, and be prepared. You should consider whether the experiment could injure yourself or somebody else. This is called risk assessment. Here are a list of things that must be considered before conducting any type of experiment:

General points to remember
- Tell an adult immediately if you have an accident of any kind.
- Do not attempt to clean up any breakages yourself.
- Always follow instructions carefully. Ask if you are unsure.
- Do not use materials or equipment unless you have permission.
- Wear eye protection when necessary.
- Take care when using scissors, a craft knife, or a pair of compasses. Seek immediate help if you cut yourself.

Simulating the stormy surface of Jupiter with milk and food dyes

Electrical equipment
- **NEVER EXPERIMENT WITH MAINS ELECTRICITY.**
- If using electrical equipment, other than battery powered, ensure that the equipment is not near water. Never touch electrical equipment with wet hands.
- Never dismantle electrical equipment.
- Never try to put a plug into a mains socket, or switch on sockets or lamps with wet hands.
- Don't touch the bulbs in lamps when they're lit because they get very hot.

Heating
- When heating anything, always wear safety goggles and tie back long hair and loose clothing.
- If you need to pick up hot equipment use tongs and/or heatproof gloves.
- Always have a fire extinguisher or fire blanket on hand in case of an accident. If burned, hold the burn under cool running water. Tell an adult.

SAFE SCIENCE

In this book symbols are used to indicate whether an experiment is safe to do at home with adult supervision, or should be demonstrated in a school laboratory. If an experiment has no symbol at all, it is safe to do on your own. However, always tell an adult first.

LET'S EXPERIMENT
SOLAR COOKER

Adult supervision
Experiments shown with this symbol must only be done with the help of an adult.

DEMONSTRATING
THE COLOURS OF HEAT

Laboratory experiments
You must not attempt to do these experiments at home. Ask an adult, such as your science teacher, to demonstrate them in a laboratory for you.

work inside black holes. Every branch of science has contributed to our understanding of the Universe. And our knowledge continues to grow. The great scientist Albert Einstein once said, "The most incomprehensible thing about the Universe is that it is comprehensible".

The Universe runs according to physical laws that we can discover. One day, even its full extent may be understood.

SCALE OF THE SUBJECT

Just how large is the Universe? It is so vast that to measure it in in kilometres or miles would be meaningless. So astronomers use other types of units to measure distances in space, such as the light year – the distance light travels in a year. The nearest stars to the Sun lie about four light years away, but astronomers can now see objects that lie more than 10 billion light years away. Their light has been travelling towards us almost from the time the Universe was born in the Big Bang – and that's a subject in itself. The study of the origin and nature of the Universe is called cosmology. Cosmologists try to solve the largest questions of all. How was the Universe created? Will it die or last forever?

OBSERVING THE UNIVERSE

The main tools astronomers use to make their observations are telescopes. Our knowledge about the Universe has grown with each improvement in telescope design since Galileo first looked at the planets nearly four centuries ago. Ground telescopes capture the light and radio waves that stars and galaxies give out. Satellite telescopes are sensitive not only to light but also to invisible rays such as X-rays. These space observatories, such as the Hubble Space Telescope, give us a clearer and often quite different view of the Universe.

Spacecraft have also opened up new windows on the Solar System – the family of the Sun and planets that occupies our little corner of space. These spacecraft, or probes, have now visited every planet except far-distant Pluto. They have revealed that each planet is a fascinating world in its own right, but quite different from Earth.

SKYWATCHING
SHOOTING STARS

TO SEE METEORS, it is best to look after midnight. At this time, our side of the Earth is meeting any incoming meteors head-on, so the meteors approach at high speed and burn up brightly. Several meteor showers repeat every year, and are named after the constellation from which they appear to radiate. The most consistent are the Perseids of early August. A full list of future showers is provided in the space data section (pp. 150–51).

A Perseid shower in British Columbia, Canada

Skywatching boxes
Boxes like these give hints on practical observing. For example, this box on shooting stars gives you hints and tips on where to look for meteor showers. Other boxes help you to locate stars, constellations, and galaxies in the night sky.

DO-IT-YOURSELF

You don't need a giant telescope to become an astronomer. You can simply use the most basic equipment – your eyes! The pages in this book will show you how to follow the constellations and the movement of planets. On most clear nights you should see shooting stars, and from time to time even watch long-tailed, passing comets. Looking at the night sky with binoculars or a telescope is even more rewarding. These can reveal thousands more stars.

Try this book's simple experiments. They'll help you to understand much of the science that governs the Universe.

There are also useful websites that will tell you what's happening in the night sky, and display the latest images. You could even get involved in projects like SETI@home. This uses your home computer to process radio signals from space in the hope of finding intelligent extraterrestrial life. Soon, perhaps, aliens will make contact, and then we'll know for sure that we are not alone in the Universe.

Pleiades star cluster

Cross-reference boxes
Boxes like these cover an aspect of the particular topic discussed, which also relates to subjects on another page. For example, this box about the Moon appears on p. 66 under Earth, but cross-refers you to p. 70, which discusses the Moon in detail.

◄ EARTH'S SATELLITE ►
The Moon has been orbiting Earth for some 4.5 billion years. Its large size and proximity to Earth mean that it has some important effects on its parent planet. The Moon causes strong tides in Earth's seas, and may even protect us from impacts from space.

Moon as seen from space   70

LOOKING AT THE UNIVERSE

Picture: *Comet Hale-Bopp, viewed from Hawaii's Mauna Kea Observatory in spring 1997*

THE STORY OF ASTRONOMY

JUST AS WE DO TODAY, our prehistoric ancestors would have looked up at the night sky and marvelled at what they saw. But it was not until the time of the early civilizations, about 5,000 years ago, that people began to study the heavens seriously. Those early stargazers laid the foundations of astronomy, the scientific study of the heavens and the celestial bodies. These days, astronomers do their stargazing using giant telescopes on the ground as well as instruments carried into space on satellites and probes. Little by little, they are unravelling the mysteries of the Universe.

Stonehenge, near Salisbury in southern England, seems to have been a giant astronomical calendar (built from about 3000 BCE).

ANCIENT STARGAZERS

We don't know exactly when people began stargazing, because no records exist before about 3500 BCE, when writing developed. The Sumerians, Chaldeans, and Babylonians, who inhabited what is now Iraq, were among the earliest astronomers.

The Universe according to Ptolemy, centred on a fixed Earth, in an engraving dating from 1493.

Some of the best-preserved, early astronomical records come from ancient Babylon. Clay tablets and carved stones, dating from about 1100 BCE, show that they were familiar with many constellations, and the zodiac.

EGYPT AND GREECE

Astronomy was also highly advanced in the Nile Valley of ancient Egypt. The pyramid builders (c. 2500 BCE) aligned their great tombs using what was then the north star. People also used a calendar of 365 days a year, not much different from our own. The ancient Greeks inherited many ideas from the Babylonians and Egyptians, but from about 600 BCE they began to develop ideas of their own. In turn, philosophers such as Thales, Plato, Aristotle, Aristarchus, Eratosthenes, and Hipparchus all made major contributions to astronomical science. Most of our knowledge about ancient astronomy comes from a book called the *Almagest*, compiled by Ptolemy of Alexandria in about AD 150.

ARAB INFLUENCE

When the great classical civilizations of Greece and Rome declined, astronomy and most of the other branches of learning declined too. But not everywhere. In the 800s, a school of astronomy was founded in Arabia and the study of astronomy flourished there until the death of ruler and astronomer Ulugh Beigh in 1449.

THE NEW AGE

By this time, the rebirth of learning, known as the Renaissance, was well underway in Europe, and people were questioning age-old beliefs. In 1543, Nicolaus Copernicus challenged accepted thinking by suggesting that Earth circles around the Sun.

Astrolabes, such as this one from Persia, measured the altitude of celestial bodies.

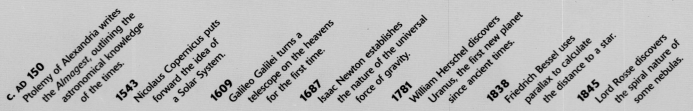

c. AD 150 Ptolemy of Alexandria writes the *Almagest*, outlining the astronomical knowledge of the times.

1543 Nicolaus Copernicus puts forward the idea of a Solar System.

1609 Galileo Galilei turns a telescope on the heavens for the first time.

1687 Isaac Newton establishes the nature of the universal force of gravity.

1781 William Herschel discovers Uranus, the first new planet since ancient times.

1838 Friedrich Bessel uses parallax to calculate the distance to a star.

1845 Lord Rosse discovers the spiral nature of some nebulas.

Timeline

The Arecibo radio telescope (completed 1963), on the island of Puerto Rico in the Caribbean Sea, is built into a mountaintop.

SEEING THE INVISIBLE

Meanwhile, a new branch of astronomy was growing – radio astronomy – which took advantage of the radio "window" in the atmosphere. With the coming of the space age in 1957, spacecraft could be dispatched to observe the planets at close quarters. It became possible to study the heavens at wavelengths blocked by Earth's atmosphere. Satellites like IRAS (infrared), COBE (microwave), and Chandra (X-ray) have shown us how different the Universe looks at invisible wavelengths. But it has been the Hubble Space Telescope, viewing mainly in visible light, that has returned the most spectacular images. Hubble reveals to us a Universe of enormous complexity – and incredible beauty.

This idea went against the teachings of the Church, and astronomers did not accept it for some time. Another breakthrough in astronomy came when Galileo built a telescope (1609) and focused it on the heavens, spotting Jupiter's moons, the phases of Venus, and the mountains of the Moon. The introduction of the reflecting telescope by Isaac Newton (c. 1672) paved the way for bigger and more sophisticated telescopes. They opened up new vistas on the Universe and revealed heavenly bodies never seen before – nebulas, star clusters, double stars, and, in 1781, a new planet (Uranus).

BIGGER AND BETTER

In 1845, Irish nobleman Lord Rosse built a huge telescope 18 m (59 ft) long, with a primary mirror over 1.8 m (5.9 ft) across. Through it he spotted a nebula with spiral arms. But it was not until 1923 that Edwin Hubble established what this, and other spiral nebulas, were. He observed them with another giant telescope, the Hooker at Mount Wilson Observatory in California. These spirals were separate island galaxies. The Universe had suddenly become a much larger place. In 1948, Hubble began observing with the Hale telescope at Mount Palomar Observatory in California, which had a mirror over 5 m (16 ft) across. It would remain the best telescope for decades.

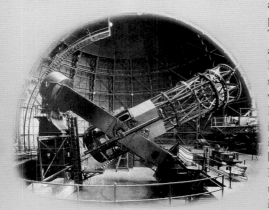

The Hooker 2.5-m (100-in) telescope at Mount Wilson Observatory, first of the giants

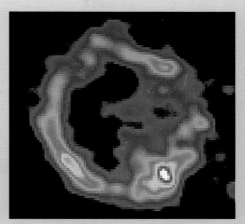

The remains of a supernova, imaged in false colour by the Chandra X-ray Observatory

1905 Albert Einstein introduces his Special Theory of Relativity, in which he shows that mass and energy are related.

1923 Edwin Hubble proves that spiral nebulas are separate star systems, or galaxies, outside the Milky Way.

1931 Karl Jansky detects radio waves from the heavens, laying the foundations of radio astronomy.

1965 *Mariner 4* spacecraft sends back the first close-up images of another planet, Mars.

1969–1972 On six epic missions of discovery, Apollo astronauts explore the Moon's surface.

1990 Hubble Space Telescope is launched and begins to return amazing pictures of the Universe.

Satellite image showing New York, with Manhattan island in the centre

OUR PLACE IN SPACE

THE PLANET EARTH is our home in space. To us, Earth is a very big and important place, but in the Universe as a whole it is actually a tiny, unimportant speck of rock in an ocean of space that is more vast than we can imagine. Earth is one of nine planets that circles around an ordinary star that we call the Sun. The Sun is one of several hundred billion stars that group together to form a great star island in space, the Milky Way. In turn, the Milky Way is one of billions of star islands, or galaxies, that are scattered in clusters through space, and which together form the Universe.

EARTH, OUR HOME

Earth is unique among the planets because it provides just the right conditions to support life. It is just the right distance from the Sun so that it is not too cold or too warm, and water is able to exist in liquid form. Also, Earth is just the right size to hold a reasonably thick atmosphere, of which oxygen is a key component. It is this combination of comfortable temperature, liquid water, and oxygen in the atmosphere that makes life possible on Earth.

Neptune

Giant outer planets

Uranus

Saturn

Jupiter

Rocky inner planets

Mars

Earth

Sun *Venus* *Moon*

Mercury

Light from the Moon reaches Earth in 1.3 seconds.

Light takes 0.08 of a second to travel around Earth.

Our Moon

Earth travels through space with a close companion, the Moon, which is 100 times nearer to us than the nearest planet, Venus. The Moon is a rocky body like Earth, but is only about one-quarter as big across – too small to have an atmosphere. The Moon gets very hot by day and very cold at night. Its surface consists of vast dusty plains, or seas, and rugged highlands. Meteorites have punched craters all over it.

THE PLANETS

The nine planets that circle the Sun (shown above, not to scale) are the main bodies in the Sun's family, or Solar System. Other bodies include moons, asteroids, comets, and meteors. Earth is one of the four small rocky planets that orbits nearest the Sun. They are dwarfed by the four giant planets further out. Jupiter is the biggest planet of all, with more mass than all of the other planets combined. Distant Pluto is in a class of its own.

Centre of the system

Our local star, the Sun, dominates our corner of space. Its enormous gravity holds the Solar System together. Like other stars, the Sun is a great globe of incandescent gas, which produces energy from nuclear reactions. It pours energy into space as light, heat, and other forms of radiation. The other bodies in the Solar System shine only because they reflect sunlight.

The Sun, pictured by SOHO

Pluto, with its moon, Charon

Light from the Sun reaches Earth in about 8.3 minutes.

STARS IN THE SKY

Like the Sun, the stars we see twinkling in the night sky are searing hot globes of gas that produce their energy from nuclear reactions. Stars vary in size and temperature, and in colour and brightness too. The smallest stars live for billions of years and die relatively quietly. The largest live for only a few million years, then blast themselves apart. Light from the nearest bright star, Alpha Centauri, takes about 4.3 years to reach Earth.

Light takes 100,000 years to cross the Milky Way Galaxy.

Stars in the Milky Way

STAR ISLANDS

All the stars we see in the sky belong to a huge star island in space, which we call the Milky Way Galaxy, or just the Galaxy. The Galaxy contains as many as 200 billion stars. There is a dense mass of stars in a bulge in the middle, and other stars are strung into long, curved arms that spiral out from the bulge. There are billions of galaxies in the Universe. Some galaxies have a spiral shape, like the Milky Way. Other galaxies, with no spiral arms, are called ellipticals. Galaxies with no definable shape at all are called irregulars.

Our Galaxy is a spiral, like this galaxy, M100.

Light from the most distant galaxies we can see takes more than 10 billion years to reach Earth.

Space without end

Galaxies are not scattered haphazardly through space, but are instead collected into groups, or clusters, such as the Abell 98 cluster (right). Our own Galaxy belongs to a small cluster called the Local Group, and M100 (above) belongs to the huge Coma cluster. Millions of these galaxy clusters form a loose network that makes up the visible Universe.

BUILDING BLOCKS

EVERY SUBSTANCE THERE IS, every material we find in
the world around us, is made of the stuff we call matter. The
Moon, the Sun, the stars, and all the other heavenly bodies are
made of matter, too. They travel in a vacuum where there is
virtually no matter, the vacuum we call space. The Universe
is made up of matter, energy, and space. There are millions of
different types of matter – rocks and plastics, wood and water,
flesh and blood. But all these things are made up of only about
90 basic "building blocks" – the chemical elements.

ELEMENTS AND COMPOUNDS

The elements are the basic building blocks of matter. Of
the 90 or so elements found on Earth, most are solids, some
are gases, and just two are liquids – bromine and mercury.
Most of the solid elements are metals. Only a few are found
in their pure state. Gold is one of them. The majority
of elements are too reactive ever to be in their pure state,
and instead are found combined with other elements
in compounds. Silicon, for example, is found combined
with oxygen in the compound silicon dioxide. Quartz
is a mineral form of this compound.

Pure gold metal

Gold nugget

*Quartz crystals
(silicon dioxide)*

Where elements are born
Almost all the elements we know were born
inside dying stars billions of years ago. As stars
die, the temperature in their shrinking cores
soars. This triggers a whole series of nuclear
reactions that create heavier and heavier
elements. The heaviest elements are made when
massive supergiant stars blast themselves apart
as supernovas (p. 117). These great explosions
not only create the elements but also scatter
them into the surrounding space. This material
collides with interstellar gas and makes it glow
as a nebula. The Crab Nebula (above) resulted
from a supernova that Chinese astronomers
recorded in 1054.

‹ FIRST ELEMENTS ›

The first two elements formed when the Universe was just a few
hundred thousand years old. They were hydrogen and helium, and they
are still the most common elements in the Universe today. Stars are made
up mostly of hydrogen. They use it as "fuel" in nuclear fusion reactions
to produce the energy they need to keep shining. In these reactions,
hydrogen fuses to form helium. 94

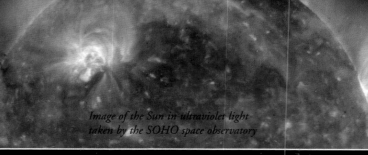

*Image of the Sun in ultraviolet light
taken by the SOHO space observatory*

STATES OF MATTER

Throughout the Universe, matter exists in three states (forms). It is either a liquid, a solid, or a gas. Rock is a typical solid, with a definite size and shape. Water is a typical liquid. It has a definite size, but no definite shape – it takes the shape of its container. Air is a typical gas. It has no definite size or shape and fills completely the space available. However, substances can alter their state when the temperature or pressure changes. For example, a solid, such as rock, can turn into liquid lava (left), and a liquid, such as water, can turn into gas if the temperature rises enough.

Volcano Puu O'o erupts in Hawaii.

At temperatures of about 1,500°C (2,700°F), rock becomes liquid.

Fourth state

Most matter on Earth is made up of combinations of the tiny particles we call atoms. But inside stars, at temperatures of millions of degrees, ordinary atomic matter can't exist. The atoms are stripped of their electrons and become electrically charged ions. Matter becomes a mixture of ions and electrons known as plasma, which is a fourth state of matter. Plasma is ejected from the Sun (right) when flares erupt on its surface.

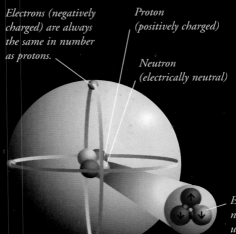

Electrons (negatively charged) are always the same in number as protons.

Proton (positively charged)

Neutron (electrically neutral)

Each proton and neutron is made up from three basic particles called quarks.

Atomic structure for helium – 2 protons, 2 neutrons, 2 electrons

ATOMS AND MOLECULES

Every element is made up of atoms. If you could cut an element into smaller and smaller pieces, an atom would be the tiniest part of the element. The different elements are made up from different types of atoms. Inside every atom is a central nucleus, around which circle tiny particles called electrons. The nucleus is itself made up of two types of particles – protons and neutrons. But atoms are not usually found by themselves. They are found combined with other atoms as molecules.

Subatomic particles

Scientists once thought that atoms were the smallest particles of matter and could not be split up. But the discovery of the electron (1897), proton (1919), and neutron (1930) made them change their ideas. Today, we know of over 200 subatomic particles – ones that are smaller than the atom. Scientists have discovered many of them in "atom-smashing" experiments, such as this one (left), in which atoms and particles collide with one another in a detector. The showers of subatomic particles leave bright trails.

Bombarding gold with sulphur ions creates a shower of particles.

UNIVERSAL FORCES

THE UNIVERSE IS RULED by four fundamental forces, which explain what matter is like and how it behaves. Two of these forces act only within the nuclei of atoms and so are not noticeable in our everyday world. They are the strong and weak nuclear forces. The other two forces are more familiar. They are electromagnetism and gravity. Electromagnetism is what holds atoms together. It is responsible, as you might expect, for electricity and magnetism. Gravity is the force that keeps our feet on the ground and makes things fall when we drop them. On the largest scale, it is the force that holds the Universe together.

THE PULL OF MATTER

Every bit of matter exerts a force of attraction because of its mass – the force of gravity. The greater the mass, or the amount of matter in a body, the greater the attraction. Gravity keeps the Moon circling Earth, it keeps Earth and the other planets circling the Sun, it keeps the Sun circling the Galaxy, and so on. We might think, therefore, that gravity is a very powerful force, but it is not. It is actually the most feeble of all the four fundamental forces – but it acts over much greater distances than all the others.

The gravity of Jupiter, a giant planet, keeps a swarm of moons circling around it, including Io (left) and Ganymede (right).

Newton's apples

A famous story tells that English scientist Isaac Newton was prompted to develop his ideas about gravity by watching apples fall from a tree at his home in Lincolnshire, England. He reasoned that the same force that pulled the apples to the ground was responsible for holding the Moon in its orbit.

Sir Isaac Newton (1642–1727)

EARTH EXERTS a pulling force – gravity – on everything on it and near it. This is what makes things fall. A body's weight is a measure of the force of gravity acting upon it. This is not the same as a body's mass, which is the amount of matter it contains. In this experiment, you'll see how gravity affects falling bodies. **You will need:** metal weight; piece of elastic; clear plastic bottle.

1 Tie the weight to one end of the piece of elastic and drop it into the bottle. Loop the other end around the neck of the bottle and screw on the top. Gravity tugs at the weight, which stretches the elastic. The amount it stretches is a measure of how heavy the weight is.

2 Now drop the bottle. Gravity will tug equally at the weight and the bottle, making them fall at the same rate. The elastic is no longer stretched, so it appears that the weight is weightless. This is similar to the way astronauts appear weightless when they are "falling round Earth" in orbit.

The weight appears weightless as it falls with the bottle.

ELECTROMAGNETISM

Electromagnetism is the force that acts between all substances that have an electric charge. It holds atoms together, binding the electrons (negative electric charge) to the nucleus (positive electric charge). It is also the force involved in chemical reactions, which rely on the interchange of electrons between atoms to form molecules. Electromagnetism consists of two forces, electricity and magnetism, which are related. For example, moving particles with an electric charge create a magnetic field.

A difference in electric charges between clouds and ground causes lightning.

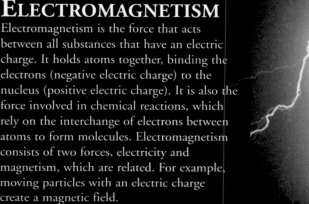

WEAK FORCE

The weak nuclear force is the force involved in radioactivity, in which unstable elements give off radiation. It is stronger than gravity, but weaker than both the strong nuclear force and electromagnetism. It acts only within the nucleus of atoms over a distance of about the diameter of the electron – about one million million millionth of a metre. Electromagnetism and the weak force seem to be related and are sometimes referred to together as the electroweak force.

Testing for radioactivity with a Geiger counter

STRONG FORCE

The strong nuclear force is the strongest of the fundamental forces. It is the force that holds neutrons and protons together in the nucleus of atoms, and has to be strong to overcome the force of repulsion between the positively charged protons. It acts across a slightly longer range than the weak force – over a distance equivalent to the diameter of the neutron or proton. The strong force must be overcome to split atoms in the nuclear fission reactions of nuclear power reactors and atomic-bomb explosions (right).

Nuclear reactions release enormous amounts of energy, providing the destructive power of nuclear weapons.

‹ BIG BANG ›

Scientists think that the four fundamental forces that control the Universe today were once united in a single superforce. This would have happened in the first few moments after the Big Bang. However, as the Universe began to expand and cool, the four forces split off one by one. Today, scientists are trying to come up with a grand unified theory (GUT) to show that the electromagnetic, strong, and weak forces are linked. If they can then unify these with gravity, they will have produced a Theory of Everything (TOE). 142 ▶

RADIATION

THE SUN BATHES OUR WORLD in light, and we see the things around us when they reflect this light into our eyes. We see because our eyes are sensitive to light rays. But the Sun gives off other rays, or radiation, that our eyes can't detect. These include ultraviolet rays, infrared rays, and radio waves. The other stars also give off a range of invisible radiations as well as light. So do galaxies and many other celestial objects. To be able to understand all the heavenly bodies properly, we need to "look" at all the types of radiation they give out.

ELECTROMAGNETIC WAVES

Light and the invisible radiations are very similar to each other. They are all electric and magnetic disturbances, or vibrations, that travel in the form of waves, known as electromagnetic waves. Like a water wave, an electromagnetic wave has crests (high points) and troughs (low points). The distance between two crests is the wavelength. The various types of electromagnetic waves differ from each other because they have different wavelengths. However, they all travel at the same speed – 300,000 km (186,000 miles) per second, the speed of light.

Windows in the atmosphere
Daytime on Earth is bright because light can pass through the atmosphere. Fortunately for astronomers, starlight passes through it too. We see the stars through the atmosphere's "optical window". The atmosphere also has a "radio window", which lets radio waves through. But it blocks almost all other invisible electromagnetic radiations. It is only since the coming of the space age that astronomers have been able to study these other radiations from space properly, by using astronomy satellites.

The atmosphere absorbs most electromagnetic short waves, but long waves pass through.

The range of wavelengths along the electromagnetic spectrum

Gamma rays	X-rays	Ultraviolet rays	Visible light
Up to about 0.01 nm (nanometre – billionths of a metre)	0.001–10 nm	10–390 nm	390–700 nm

SHORT WAVES

Gamma rays have the shortest wavelengths, followed by X-rays and ultraviolet rays. Ultraviolet rays are so called because they have wavelengths just shorter than the shortest-wavelength light rays, which we see as violet. (We see the different wavelengths in visible light as different colours.) The shorter wavelengths carry much more energy than light rays. Gamma-rays and X-rays carry the most energy.

Gamma-ray image of the unstable star, Eta Carinae

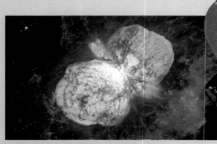

Visible light image of Eta Carinae

The Hubble Space Telescope
The most famous of the space observatories, the Hubble Space Telescope, operates mainly at visible light wavelengths. But it also makes some observations at ultraviolet and infrared wavelengths. It is a reflecting telescope, with a primary (main) mirror 2.4 m (7.9 ft) across. Launched in 1990, it is serviced and upgraded in orbit by astronauts.

LONG WAVES

Infrared rays and radio waves have the longest wavelengths. Infrared rays are so called because they have wavelengths just longer than red light, which has the longest wavelength of visible light. They are also called heat rays because we can sense them as heat. Radio waves cover a vast range of wavelengths, the shortest being microwaves. The 21-cm (8.3-in) wavelength is a good one for "mapping" the Universe. It is emitted by hydrogen, the most common element in space.

Infrared image of Eta Carinae

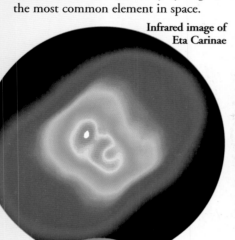

LET'S EXPERIMENT
FILTERING INVISIBLE RAYS

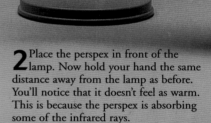

FORTUNATELY FOR US, the atmosphere filters out most of the harmful invisible rays coming from space. In this experiment, you'll see how to filter out invisible rays. **You will need:** an adult to help you; table lamp; a piece of perspex.

1 Ask an adult to plug the table lamp into a wall socket, and switch it on. Hold your hand about 10 cm (4 in) below the lamp bulb. You will feel the warmth of the bulb. The invisible infrared rays given out by the lamp are heating up your skin.

2 Place the perspex in front of the lamp. Now hold your hand the same distance away from the lamp as before. You'll notice that it doesn't feel as warm. This is because the perspex is absorbing some of the infrared rays.

Infrared rays 700 nm–1 mm

Solar arrays power the telescope's equipment.

◄ LITTLE GREEN MEN ►

In 1967, British radio astronomer Jocelyn Bell, working with Antony Hewish, picked up pulsating signals from space never detected before. "Are they signals from an alien civilization?" the astronomers jokingly asked, dubbing the radio source LGM, for Little Green Men. They were not. What Bell had discovered was a strange, flashing star called a pulsar. **118** ►

Antony Hewish inside the radio telescope at Cambridge, UK

Radio waves 1mm–1km+

Radio image of Eta Carinae

Radio sources

Some of the most energetic objects in the Universe are detected by the radio waves they give out. They include radio galaxies and quasars, two types of active galaxies that are powered by black holes (p. 130). Pulsars give out streams of radio waves that sweep around in space like the beams from a lighthouse. Supernova remnants – the remains of stars that exploded long ago – are also strong radio sources.

TOOLS OF THE TRADE

ASTRONOMERS GET MOST of their information about the Universe by studying the relatively weak light that reaches us from space. An astronomer's essential tool is the telescope, an instrument with a light-gathering power many times that of the naked eye. Different types of telescopes also help astronomers to gather invisible rays that come from space. They study radio waves using radio telescopes on the ground. They also send telescopes into space on satellites in order to study rays that cannot pass through Earth's atmosphere.

THROUGH THE TELESCOPE

As the Sun sets and the skies darken, astronomers prepare for a night's viewing. At observatories, they open the domes that house the telescopes and direct the giant instruments at the part of the sky that they wish to study. The best observatories are located high in the mountains. Here, above the clouds and the thickest, dirtiest part of the atmosphere, there is a much clearer view of the heavens. However, professional astronomers do not actually look through their giant telescopes. Instead, they use the telescopes like huge cameras, to record images on photographic film or electronically on chips.

Dome housing the 3.6-m (12-ft) reflector at La Silla Observatory, Chile

MIRRORS AND LENSES

Astronomical telescopes use either glass lenses or curved mirrors to gather and focus light. They consist essentially of two parts, an objective lens or mirror to collect and focus the image, and an eyepiece to view the image. The image is upside-down, but this doesn't matter in astronomy.

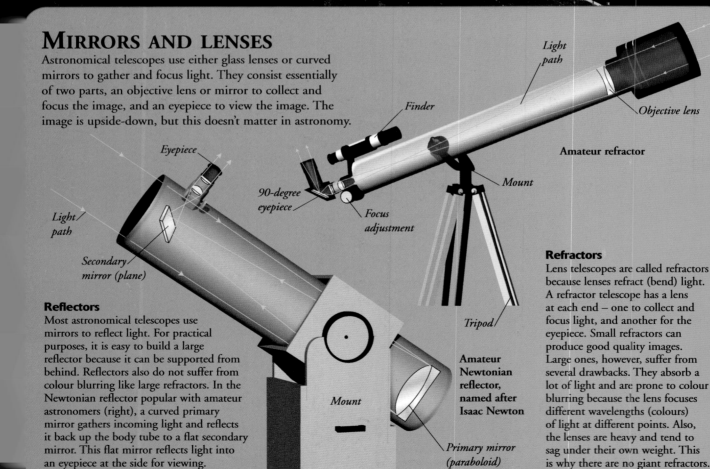

Light path

Finder

Objective lens

Amateur refractor

Eyepiece

90-degree eyepiece

Focus adjustment

Mount

Light path

Secondary mirror (plane)

Tripod

Amateur Newtonian reflector, named after Isaac Newton

Mount

Primary mirror (paraboloid)

Reflectors

Most astronomical telescopes use mirrors to reflect light. For practical purposes, it is easy to build a large reflector because it can be supported from behind. Reflectors also do not suffer from colour blurring like large refractors. In the Newtonian reflector popular with amateur astronomers (right), a curved primary mirror gathers incoming light and reflects it back up the body tube to a flat secondary mirror. This flat mirror reflects light into an eyepiece at the side for viewing.

Refractors

Lens telescopes are called refractors because lenses refract (bend) light. A refractor telescope has a lens at each end – one to collect and focus light, and another for the eyepiece. Small refractors can produce good quality images. Large ones, however, suffer from several drawbacks. They absorb a lot of light and are prone to colour blurring because the lens focuses different wavelengths (colours) of light at different points. Also, the lenses are heavy and tend to sag under their own weight. This is why there are no giant refractors.

ACTIVE OPTICS

The twin Keck telescopes are two of the prime instruments at the Mauna Kea Observatory, located on the 4,200-m (13,800-ft) summit of a dormant volcano in Hawaii. The two giant Keck telescopes each have a light-gathering mirror that is 10 m (33 ft) across. If they were built in one piece, these enormous mirrors would bend under their own weight. Instead, each mirror is made of 36 hexagonal (six-sided) segments measuring 1.8 m (6 ft) across. Computer-controlled supports continually adjust the position of the segments so that they form a perfectly curved mirror for viewing space.

Primary mirror of the Keck 1 telescope, Hawaii, completed in 1992

Very Large Telescope

These four telescopes on a mountaintop in Chile make up the most powerful telescope combination on Earth. They form the Very Large Telescope (VLT) of the European Southern Observatory. Each telescope has a mirror 8.2 m (27 ft) across, with a billion times the light-gathering ability of the naked eye. Working together, the four telescopes are equivalent to a single telescope with a mirror more than 16 m (52 ft) across. The VLT became fully operational in 2001.

DIGITAL IMAGING

Astronomers often use electronic cameras to take pictures. At the heart of an electronic camera is a CCD (charge-coupled device). It is a silicon-chip device, made up of miniature electronic circuits, rather like the microchips used in personal computers. A CCD is made up of a chequerboard array of thousands, or even millions, of light-sensitive squares. These squares, or pixels (picture elements), record the light falling on them as a pattern of electric charges, which a computer displays as a digital image.

CCD camera for Anglo-Australian Telescope

CCD image of Mira, a variable star in Cetus

RADIO TELESCOPES

Most radio telescopes take the form of a huge dish that reflects and focuses incoming radio signals onto an aerial mounted above it. The signals are then fed to a receiver, where they are amplified (strengthened) and processed to produce a false-colour radio "picture". To pick up the faint radio signals from space, the dishes must be huge. The Arecibo radio telescope in Puerto Rico has a dish 305 m (1,000 ft) across. The Very Large Array at Socorro, New Mexico, in the USA, uses 27 dishes working together to produce an effective dish 27 km (17 miles) across.

Radio telescopes at the Owens Valley Radio Observatory, California

BACKYARD ASTRONOMY

PROFESSIONAL ASTRONOMERS carry out spectacular work, using powerful telescopes both in Earth-based observatories and in space. But they are outnumbered many times over by the amateur astronomers around the world, who use more modest instruments. These "backyard astronomers" do valuable work, because collectively they can look at larger areas of the sky than the comparatively few professionals. You can join them, observing the constellations, following the planets, and exploring the Milky Way. Using simple equipment, you can look at meteors, search for comets, and marvel at eclipses.

ESSENTIAL EQUIPMENT

Before you go stargazing, take time to make a few preparations. Gather the equipment you'll need, such as a camera, binoculars or telescope, compass, and torch. You'll also want a set of star maps and a planisphere. A notebook is essential to write down details of what and when you observe, and the viewing conditions. Think about what clothing you'll need – stargazing can be a chilly occupation even on summer nights. Often the clearest nights are also the coldest, so a hot drink and a snack may also be a good idea.

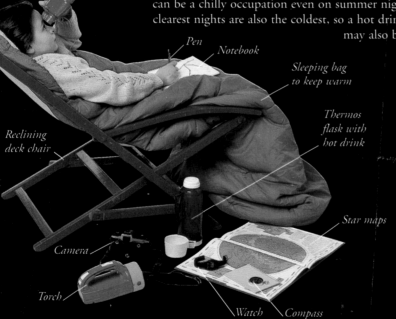

Pair of binoculars

Pen *Notebook*

Sleeping bag to keep warm

Reclining deck chair

Thermos flask with hot drink

Star maps

Camera

Torch

Watch *Compass*

Milky Way, with the naked eye **Milky Way, through binoculars**

Binocular views

Binoculars can gather much more light than our eyes. This allows them to show us many more stars and other objects, such as nebulas, which are too faint for the eye to see properly. To the naked eye, the Milky Way is a vague whitish band in the sky (far left). Through binoculars, it becomes a sea of tightly packed stars and glowing nebulas (left). Useful binoculars for general viewing are 7x50s.

Night vision

When you go stargazing, don't expect to see the heavens in all their glory straightaway. You must first get your night vision – that is, allow your eyes to get used to the dark. This is a physical process in which the pupils of your eyes open wide to let in more light. Your retina – the "screen" at the back of the eye – becomes more light-sensitive. This process takes about 20 minutes. Use a red torch to read star maps, as red light affects your night vision less than white.

Cover a torch with red cellophane, and use it to help read star maps.

ONE OF THE MOST useful aids to stargazing is a planisphere. This device is based on a circular star map. It has a rotating, masking disk over the map with a window in it, which reveals the stars visible at a particular time on a particular date. Different planispheres are available for different latitudes in the Northern and Southern Hemispheres.

1 To use a planisphere, match the time of viewing on the scale on the mask with the date on the scale on the base. The stars that appear in the window show the stars that you would see if you were lying on your back looking up at the sky.

2 To get the window the right way round, hold the planisphere above your head, with its window facing towards you. Use a compass to make sure that North marked on the planisphere's mask actually faces North.

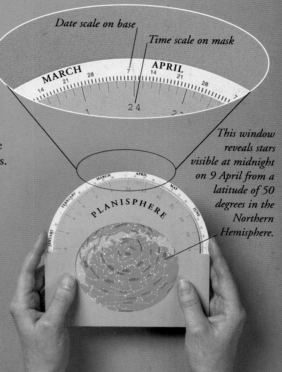

Date scale on base

Time scale on mask

MARCH   APRIL

PLANISPHERE

This window reveals stars visible at midnight on 9 April from a latitude of 50 degrees in the Northern Hemisphere.

Night view of the USA from space

LIGHT POLLUTION

The light from buildings and street lamps lights up the skies of our cities and makes life difficult for amateur and professional astronomers. Even on clear nights, city dwellers are unable to see the fainter constellations and planets. Country dwellers' viewing may also be spoiled by car headlights and the glow of nearby towns. Long-exposure astrophotography is especially affected. Excess light builds up over the long exposure times required, say, to track the movement of stars (p. 30) and ruins the images. There is also natural light pollution, from the Moon.

‹ DAYTIME ASTRONOMY ›

Solar eclipses, when the Moon blocks out light from the Sun, are the most exciting events in daytime astronomy. Total solar eclipses, when the Sun is completely covered, are rare, and can only be seen from a limited area of Earth. Partial eclipses, when the Sun is only partly covered, are visible over larger areas and are much more common. To follow the partial stages of an eclipse, when the Moon is "biting" into the Sun, wear special eclipse glasses that block most of the Sun's rays. Never look directly at the Sun, as this can seriously damage your eyesight. 71 ▶

Eclipse glasses have plastic lenses coated with aluminium. Always follow the safety instructions provided when using them.

THE NIGHT SKY

WHEN WE FIRST GO STARGAZING, the night sky can appear confusing – the stars seem to be scattered around haphazardly in the blackness of space. After a while, we can learn to recognize the patterns that the bright stars make, which stay the same night after night, year after year. We use these patterns, the constellations, to find our way around the heavens. About half of the 88 constellations recognized today were known to ancient astronomers. They named them after figures that they imagined the constellations looked like, which were usually characters in their myths and legends.

Gamma Cassiopeiae (γ) 615 light years

Epsilon Cassiopeiae (ε) 440 light years

True positions of the stars in Cassiopeia, showing their distances from the Sun (not to scale)

Alpha Cassiopeiae (α) 230 light years

Delta Cassiopeiae (δ) 100 light years

W FOR CASSIOPEIA

On star maps, the brighter stars in a constellation are often linked together to form a pattern. This helps us recognize the constellation in the night sky. For example, five bright stars in Cassiopeia form a distinctive W-shape, (shown above, drawn on a photograph of the constellation). As with other constellations, the stars are identified by letters in the Greek alphabet: alpha is the brightest, beta, the next brightest, and so on. Stars are named using these letters and a variation of the constellation name: alpha of Cassiopeia becomes Alpha Cassiopeiae.

Beta Cassiopeiae (β) 54 light years

It's an illusion

To our eyes, it looks as if the five bright stars in Cassiopeia are grouped together in space, forming the W-shape. This is only because the stars lie in the same direction when viewed from Earth. In reality, the stars are widely separated, the nearest being just over 50 light years away, and the furthest more than 600 light years. The same goes for most of the constellations – their stars appear to be quite close together but are, in fact, far apart.

Cassiopeia's stars as we see them in the sky.

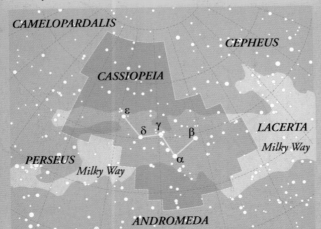

SKYWATCHING
FINDING CASSIOPEIA

CASSIOPEIA LIES IN the northern sky, close to Polaris, the Pole Star. The Milky Way runs through its centre and surrounding it are the constellations named below. Its brightest stars form the W-shape, but the constellation actually extends as far as the jagged boundary lines.

CAMELOPARDALIS

CEPHEUS

CASSIOPEIA

ε

δ γ

β

LACERTA

Milky Way

PERSEUS

Milky Way

α

ANDROMEDA

Lady in a chair

The ancient Greeks pictured Cassiopeia as a vain queen, sitting in a chair admiring herself in a mirror. Queen Cassiopeia was the wife of Cepheus and the mother of Andromeda. She boasted that she was more beautiful than the sea nymphs, which naturally upset them. The sea god Poseidon sent a monster, Cetus, to terrify Cepheus's kingdom, and the king and queen were told that they must sacrifice their daughter. Just as Cetus was about to devour Andromeda, the hero Perseus appeared and killed it. The skywatching box shows that many of these mythical figures lie close to one another in the sky.

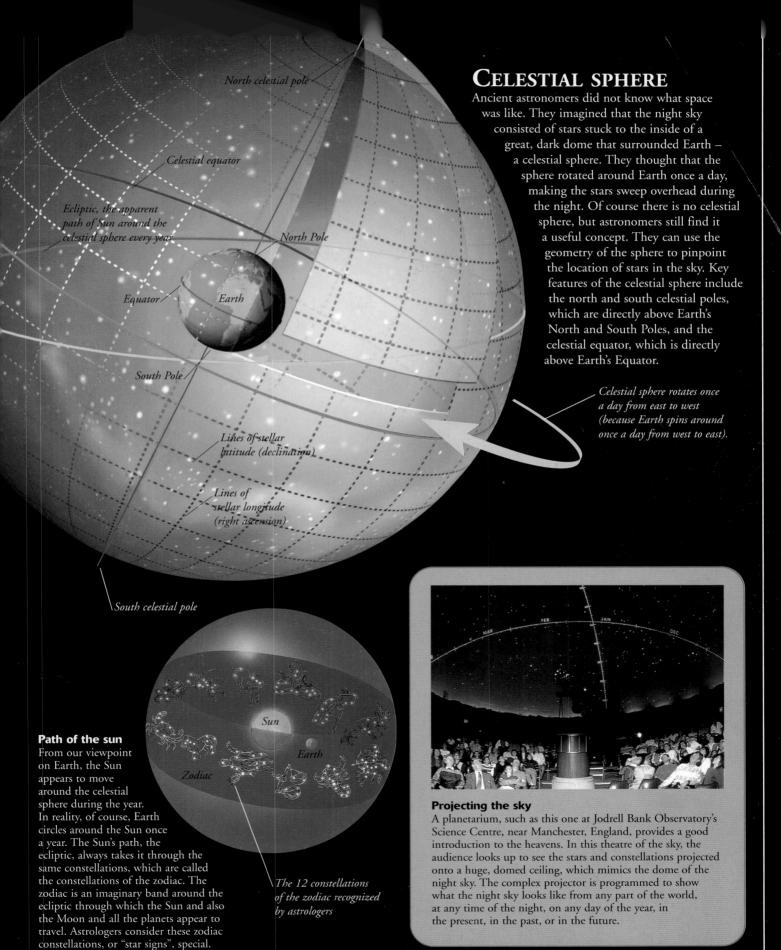

CELESTIAL SPHERE

Ancient astronomers did not know what space was like. They imagined that the night sky consisted of stars stuck to the inside of a great, dark dome that surrounded Earth – a celestial sphere. They thought that the sphere rotated around Earth once a day, making the stars sweep overhead during the night. Of course there is no celestial sphere, but astronomers still find it a useful concept. They can use the geometry of the sphere to pinpoint the location of stars in the sky. Key features of the celestial sphere include the north and south celestial poles, which are directly above Earth's North and South Poles, and the celestial equator, which is directly above Earth's Equator.

North celestial pole

Celestial equator

Ecliptic, the apparent path of Sun around the celestial sphere every year

North Pole

Equator

Earth

South Pole

Lines of stellar latitude (declination)

Lines of stellar longitude (right ascension)

South celestial pole

Celestial sphere rotates once a day from east to west (because Earth spins around once a day from west to east).

Path of the sun

From our viewpoint on Earth, the Sun appears to move around the celestial sphere during the year. In reality, of course, Earth circles around the Sun once a year. The Sun's path, the ecliptic, always takes it through the same constellations, which are called the constellations of the zodiac. The zodiac is an imaginary band around the ecliptic through which the Sun and also the Moon and all the planets appear to travel. Astrologers consider these zodiac constellations, or "star signs", special.

Sun

Earth

Zodiac

The 12 constellations of the zodiac recognized by astrologers

Projecting the sky

A planetarium, such as this one at Jodrell Bank Observatory's Science Centre, near Manchester, England, provides a good introduction to the heavens. In this theatre of the sky, the audience looks up to see the stars and constellations projected onto a huge, domed ceiling, which mimics the dome of the night sky. The complex projector is programmed to show what the night sky looks like from any part of the world, at any time of the night, on any day of the year, in the present, in the past, or in the future.

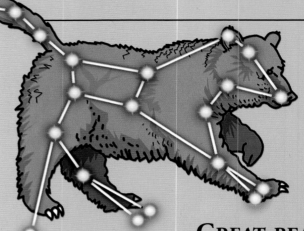

NORTHERN STARS

ASTRONOMERS NAVIGATE THE skies by imagining the stars as a giant celestial sphere around Earth. For convenience, they often divide this sphere into two halves, known as the northern and southern celestial hemispheres. The celestial equator marks the boundary between them (just as the Equator separates the Northern and Southern Hemispheres on Earth). Observers who live in the Northern Hemisphere can see all the constellations of the northern celestial hemisphere at some time during the year. They can also see some of the southern constellations as well. The closer they live to the Equator, the more of the southern celestial hemisphere they will see.

GREAT BEAR

Ursa Major, the Great Bear, occupies a large area of the northern skies. It is best known, not for its bear shape, but for the star pattern at its tail end that we call the Plough. The constellation is called the "Great" Bear because there is a smaller bear (Ursa Minor, the Little Bear) close by. Named by Greek astronomers, Ursa Major is supposed to represent a beautiful nymph, Callisto. She was wooed by Zeus, king of the gods, and bore him a son. Zeus's wife, Hera, found out and turned Callisto into a bear in revenge.

The Plough

The seven brightest stars in Ursa Major form one of the most distinctive patterns in the northern heavens. It is called the Plough because it resembles the curved handle and share (blade) of an old-fashioned, horse-drawn plough. An alternative name is the Big Dipper, because it resembles a ladle used to dip into milk or water. Arab astronomers gave the individual stars their names (right).

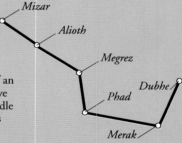

GREAT CLUSTERS

The northern skies show a variety of loose groups of stars, known as clusters, which are easily visible to the naked eye. Cancer, for example, contains the cluster Praesepe, or the Beehive (above), so called because it looks like a swarm of bees buzzing around a hive. Taurus boasts two prominent clusters – the Hyades, scattered around the reddish star Aldebaran, and the Pleiades, further out (p. 110). These loose groups are known as open clusters. One or two more tightly knit groups, called globular clusters, are also visible, such as M13 in Hercules.

SKYWATCHING
SIGNPOST STARS

THE PLOUGH IS an excellent "signpost" to other stars and constellations. A line drawn through Merak and Dubhe leads to Polaris, the Pole Star or North Star. That is why these two stars are called the Pointers. The distinctive W-shape of Cassiopeia is found on the other side of Polaris.

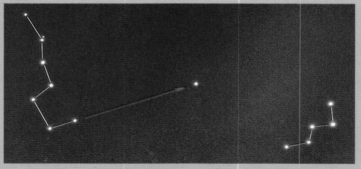

The stars of the Plough, and of Cassiopeia, can be used to find Polaris.

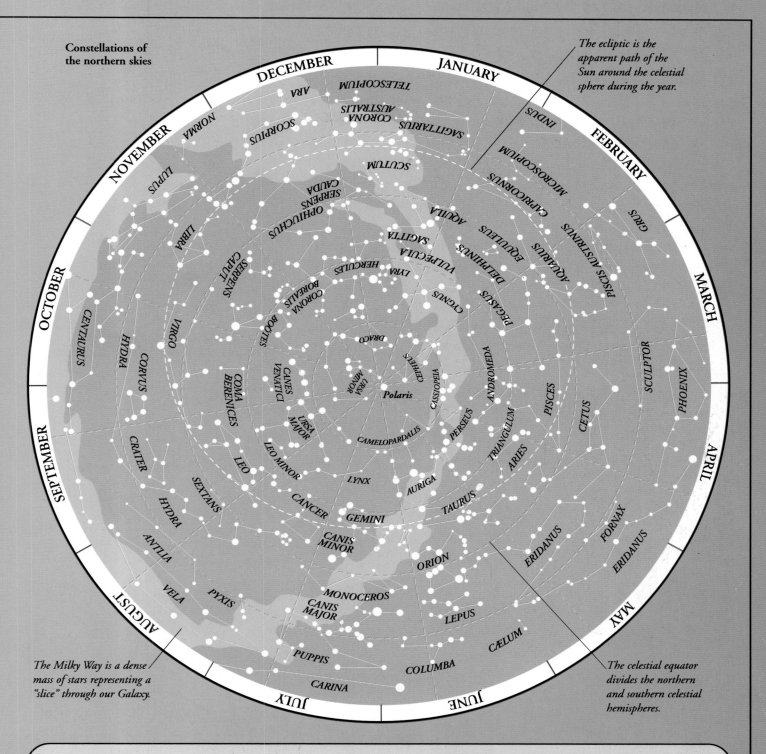

Constellations of the northern skies

The ecliptic is the apparent path of the Sun around the celestial sphere during the year.

DECEMBER
JANUARY
FEBRUARY
MARCH
APRIL
MAY
JUNE
JULY
AUGUST
SEPTEMBER
OCTOBER
NOVEMBER

Polaris

The Milky Way is a dense mass of stars representing a "slice" through our Galaxy.

The celestial equator divides the northern and southern celestial hemispheres.

ARA
TELESCOPIUM
CORONA AUSTRALIS
SAGITTARIUS
INDUS
NORMA
SCORPIUS
SCUTUM
MICROSCOPIUM
GRUS
LUPUS
SERPENS CAUDA
OPHIUCHUS
AQUILA
SAGITTA
CAPRICORNUS
EQUULEUS
PISCIS AUSTRINUS
LIBRA
SERPENS CAPUT
HERCULES
LYRA
VULPECULA
DELPHINUS
AQUARIUS
CORONA BOREALIS
CYGNUS
PEGASUS
CENTAURUS
VIRGO
BOÖTES
DRACO
CEPHEUS
ANDROMEDA
PISCES
SCULPTOR
PHOENIX
HYDRA
CORVUS
CANES VENATICI
CASSIOPEIA
CETUS
CRATER
COMA BERENICES
URSA MINOR
PERSEUS
TRIANGULUM
ARIES
SEXTANS
LEO
URSA MAJOR
CAMELOPARDALIS
AURIGA
TAURUS
FORNAX
HYDRA
LEO MINOR
LYNX
ERIDANUS
ANTLIA
CANCER
GEMINI
ORION
ERIDANUS
VELA
PYXIS
CANIS MINOR
MONOCEROS
LEPUS
CÆLUM
PUPPIS
CANIS MAJOR
COLUMBA
CARINA

‹ **ANDROMEDA GALAXY** ›

Just north of Beta, the second brightest star in Andromeda, there is a misty patch that is easily visible to the naked eye. It looks rather like a cloud, or nebula, but it isn't. It is actually a separate star system, or galaxy. Powerful telescopes show it to be a spiral galaxy like our own, but nearly twice as big. About 2.4 million light years away, it is the most distant object we can see with the naked eye. **132** ▶

THE CHANGING HEAVENS

THE NIGHT SKY IS ALWAYS CHANGING. The stars we see looking south at, say, 7 p.m. on a winter's evening are quite different from the ones we see looking south at 11 p.m. This happens because Earth is spinning around on its axis once a day, which makes the stars seem to wheel overhead during the night (and the Sun move across the sky during the day). Earth also circles around the Sun once a year. This makes new constellations appear each month, while others disappear. After 12 months, the skies become the same as they were originally.

This long-exposure photograph shows circular star trails around the north celestial pole.

POLE STAR

Centuries before compasses and satellite navigation systems, people navigated by the stars. In the Northern Hemisphere, they were fortunate because a reasonably bright star is located almost directly above the North Pole. Seeing this star told them that they were looking North. They called it the North Star or Pole Star – astronomers call it Polaris. Unfortunately, the Southern Hemisphere has no convenient pole star.

AD 2000   *AD 14,000*

Polaris   Polaris   Vega

EARTHLY WOBBLES

Polaris will not always be the north pole star. In about 12,000 years time, the pole star will be the bright star Vega in the constellation Lyra (the Lyre). This will happen because Earth's axis does not always point in the same direction in space. It slowly swings round, rather like a wobbling top. In 12,000 years time, Earth's axis will have swung round to point at Vega. In 26,000 years time, it will be back pointing at Polaris once again. This wobbling of Earth's axis is called precession. It is caused mainly by the gravitational attraction on Earth of the Moon and the Sun, and (very slightly) by the other planets.

Pole star of the ancients

The ancient Egyptians built their pyramids with great precision. They used the north pole star to align the bases of the pyramids accurately, north-south. But it was not the pole star we are familiar with. It was the star Thuban in the constellation Draco (the Dragon). That was the star Earth's axis pointed to about 2500 BCE when the pyramids were built. Precession has now brought the pole star into its present position – for the moment.

The pyramid of Khafre, built about 2500 BCE, is the second largest of the three pyramids at Giza, in Egypt. One theory argues that these pyramids were intentionally aligned to mirror the three main stars of Orion's belt (p.100).

SEASONAL STARS

Different constellations appear in the night sky as the months go by. Orion, for example, is found in January skies, but has vanished by June. We see different constellations as the months pass because of Earth's annual journey around the Sun. As Earth moves along its orbit, its night side faces a slightly different part of the celestial sphere night by night. After a few weeks, the changes become noticeable. After a few months, the skies look very different.

In January (above left) this sky shows: (top l-r) Canis Minor, Monoceros, Orion, Eridanus (bottom l-r) Puppis, Canis Major, Lepus. In June (above right) it shows: (top l-r) Ophiuchus, Serpens Caput, Virgo, (bottom l-r) Scorpius, Libra, Hydra.

LET'S EXPERIMENT
MAKING A PLANISPHERE

A PLANISPHERE LETS YOU "DIAL UP" the stars for any time and date. Match the time of night and the day of the month on the planisphere's scales, and a window reveals the stars on view at that time. Planispheres are based on star maps, and you can make one yourself using the maps on page 27 (for the Northern Hemisphere) or 29 (for the Southern Hemisphere). **You will need:** tracing paper; star map; pencil; ruler; glue; pair of compasses; scissors; 2 sheets of coloured card and 1 of acetate; paper fastener.

1 Making the base
Place tracing paper over the star map for your hemisphere, and copy the stars. Also draw the straight lines that split the sky into equal segments, and write the months around the edges. Divide each month into four equal parts to roughly represent weeks. Glue the tracing paper onto a sheet of card. With a pair of compasses, draw a circle around your tracing, and carefully cut it out. This is your planisphere's base.

2 Making the mask
Draw a slightly smaller circle on the other sheet of card and cut it out. This will form the mask of the planisphere. Make sure that when you place it over the base, the months scale can be seen. Now mark the 24-hour clock on the edge of the mask. Follow the examples shown in the illustration on the right – inner values for the Northern Hemisphere, outer values for the Southern.

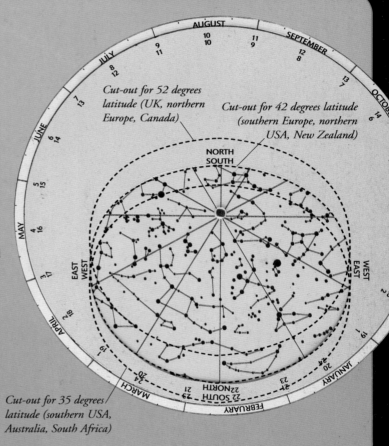

Cut-out for 52 degrees latitude (UK, northern Europe, Canada)

Cut-out for 42 degrees latitude (southern Europe, northern USA, New Zealand)

NORTH
SOUTH

Cut-out for 35 degrees latitude (southern USA, Australia, South Africa)

Paper fastener

Mask is slightly smaller than base

Acetate fixed to the back of the mask to form a window

Star map drawn on tracing paper

Base

3 Cutting the window
Now you need to cut a window in the mask. The location of the window depends on your latitude on Earth and which hemisphere you live in. Dotted lines for different latitudes are shown on the above image. Use the cut-out most suitable for where you live, copy it, and cut it out. Glue acetate to the back of the mask to cover the window. Add the compass points (inner values – Northern, outer – Southern).

4 Putting it together
Punch a hole in the centre of both the mask and the base with the paper fastener. Insert it to fasten both parts together. Your planisphere is now ready for use.

5 Dialling the stars
To use the planisphere, turn the mask until the time on the scale lines up with the date on the base scale. The stars in the window show the stars you will see in the sky. See page 23 for further planisphere information.

EXPLORING SPACE

HUMANS BEGAN TO explore space in the 1960s. Russian cosmonaut Yuri Gagarin made the first human flight into orbit on 12 April 1961. The first American in orbit was astronaut John Glenn on 20 February 1962. At that time, no one knew whether the human body could withstand the stresses of spaceflight – the punishing forces caused by the rapid acceleration at launch, followed by weightlessness in orbit. Now we know that humans can endure space travel – and for long periods. Some astronauts have spent a year or more in space, others have landed on the Moon, and plans are afoot to send them on missions to Mars.

Lift-off of space shuttle orbiter Atlantis

HIGH G-FORCES

On Earth, we are used to the force of gravity pulling downwards on our bodies. We can call this a force of 1G. But when astronauts blast off from the space shuttle launch pad, they feel a force of more than 3G tugging at their bodies. The reason they experience increased G-forces is because they accelerate rapidly as they ascend into orbit – from nothing on the ground to about 28,000 kmh (17,000 mph) in space in only about 15 minutes. As the rockets blast them upwards, their bodies are pressed downwards as though gravity has suddenly increased.

Shuttling into space

The space shuttle orbiter *Discovery* (left) gets ready to dock (link up) with the International Space Station (ISS). It is carrying new equipment and a change of crew. The winged orbiter is an amazing flying machine, which takes off like a rocket, acts like a spacecraft in orbit, then lands on a runway like a plane. Some 37 m (121 ft) long, it has a wingspan of nearly 24 m (79 ft). The orbiters launch from the Kennedy Space Center in Florida, USA, built for the Moon-landing missions of the 1960s.

MICROGRAVITY

When a spacecraft travels in orbit, it is in a state of free fall. It is falling towards Earth, but is travelling so fast that it falls only as much as Earth curves beneath it. So it always remains at the same height. Inside, the astronauts and everything else are falling too – and at the same rate. This makes them appear not to have any weight, so we popularly call this condition weightlessness or zero-G. Microgravity is another name for it. On a mission exploring microgravity, Susan Still, an American astronaut, floats effortlessly in the Spacelab laboratory (above).

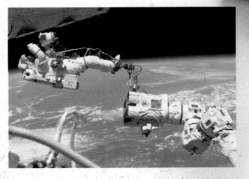

American Jerry Ross helps assemble the ISS.

On EVA

Astronauts sometimes leave their spacecraft to work in space. This extravehicular activity (EVA) is popularly called spacewalking. On EVA, astronauts wear spacesuits that supply them with oxygen to breathe and protect them from space hazards, such as dangerous radiation. Assembling the International Space Station requires lengthy spacewalks at each stage of the construction.

LET'S EXPERIMENT
HIGH AND LOW GRAVITY

ASTRONAUTS EXPERIENCE huge changes in the gravitational (G) forces acting upon them when they travel in space. At launch, when they accelerate upwards (high Gs), their bodies are pressed down and they feel heavier. But in orbit, when their bodies are free falling (zero-G), they appear to have no weight at all. In this experiment, you can see how movement upwards and downwards affects weight. **You will need:** kitchen scales, fruit.

1 Put the fruit into the scale pan. Note how heavy it is on the scale (middle picture).

2 Suddenly move the scales upwards. You will see that the fruit appears to get heavier (top picture). By accelerating the scales upwards, you have increased the G-force on the fruit.

3 Now suddenly move the scales downwards. You will notice that the fruit appears to get lighter (bottom picture). In fact it has lost nearly all of its weight. This happens because the fruit and the scales are accelerating downwards together.

The ISS orbits about 400 km (250 miles) above Earth.

SPACE MEDICS

Travelling in "weightless" space affects the human body in several ways. The study of these effects is called space medicine. Taking blood samples (left) is a regular feature of this study. One immediate effect of weightlessness is that it confuses the inner ear's balance organs. This causes a kind of motion sickness in most astronauts for a few days. Freed from gravity, the blood redistributes itself in the body, giving astronauts a fatter face and thinner legs. Muscles start to waste because they no longer have to fight against gravity. And, more worryingly, bones begin to lose mass.

Space PT

Astronauts who stay in space for long periods of time need to have regular physical training (PT) or "workouts" to keep their muscles toned up. By exercising, the astronauts in the *Skylab*, *Salyut*, and *Mir* space stations kept fit even after months in space. On the International Space Station, astronauts, such as Russian Yury Usachev (right), can exercise on a cycle ergometer in the Zvezda module. In zero-G, astronauts have to be strapped into a harness when pedalling, otherwise they would shoot upwards every time they pressed down on the pedals!

NATIONS' STATION

The International Space Station is a cooperative venture between the United States, Russia, Europe, Japan, Canada, and several other countries. The United States, through NASA, is overseeing construction and supplying much of the hardware, including laboratory and habitation modules. Europe and Japan are supplying laboratory modules, while Canada is providing a robotic handling device. The ISS is being assembled piece by piece in orbit from modules carried up by US space shuttles or Russian Proton rockets. Construction began in 1998 and should be completed in about 2006. It will then be the biggest ever orbiter measuring 100 m (330 ft) long and 75 m (250 ft) across.

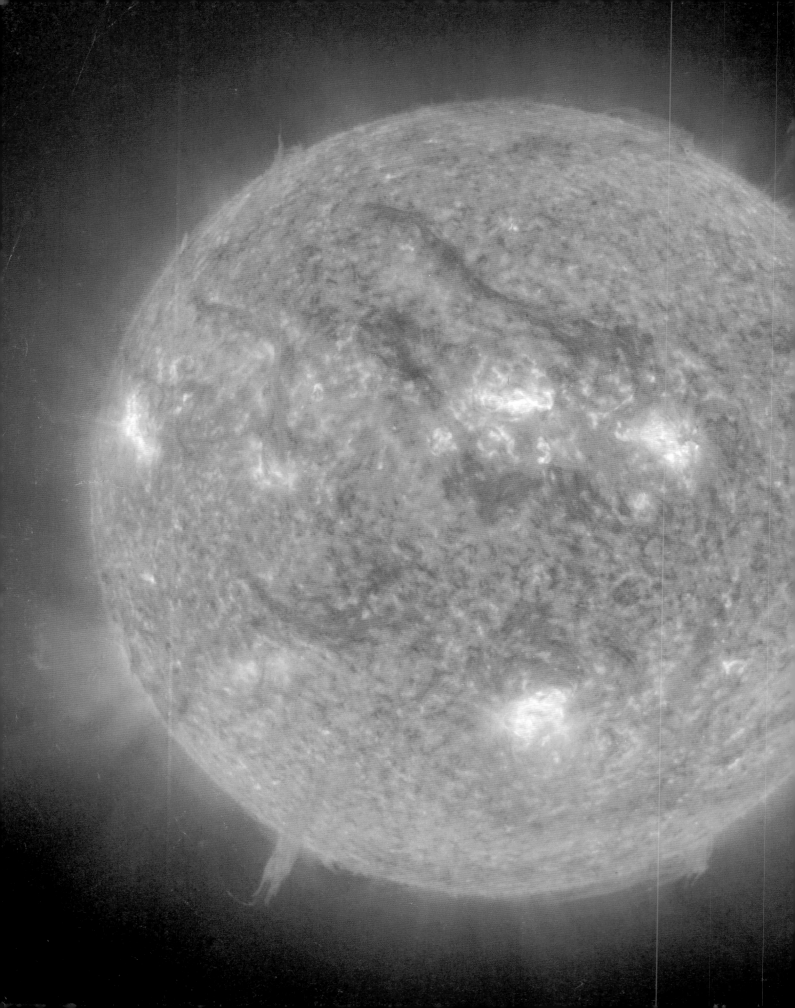

THE SOLAR SYSTEM

Picture: *A SOHO image of the Sun reveals a huge, handle-shaped body of gas (a prominence) in the atmosphere.*

EMPIRE OF THE SUN

THE SOLAR SYSTEM IS THE name for everything that comes under the influence of the Sun, our local star. With more than 99.8 per cent of the Solar System's entire mass, the Sun is the largest and most powerful body in this region of space. Its immense gravity controls an empire of nine planets that are locked in permanent orbit around it. They are attended by numerous satellites. Between and beyond the planets, swarms of rocky asteroids and icy comets also travel through the Solar System, together with dust and particles blown out by the solar wind.

ORBITING WORLDS

Everything in the Solar System is in orbit around something else – a legacy from the way the Sun and the planets collapsed from a spinning gas cloud billions of years ago. Planets, asteroids, and comets orbit the Sun, while rings and moons orbit their parent planets. An orbit is any path through space where an object's inertia – its tendency to travel in a straight line – is perfectly balanced against the pull of gravity from a more massive object. This is why objects in orbit do not simply fly off into space or fall directly towards whatever they are orbiting. Natural orbits are very rarely circular, and the closer a Solar System body comes to the Sun, the faster it must move to keep in a steady orbit. The result is that most of these objects have orbits in the form of ellipses (ovals).

Objects in the Solar System contain different materials depending on where they formed. Everything was created from an original cloud of gas and dust. However, differences in temperature and composition within the cloud mean that, in general, the bodies of the inner Solar System are made of dust and rock, while those of the outer Solar System have much more gas and ice in them.

PLANETARY FEATURES

The planets fall into two types – small, solid rocky worlds lie close to the Sun, while further out are giant balls of gas and liquid with only a small solid core. The surfaces of rocky worlds show huge variations, shaped by a variety of internal and external forces. All have craters from meteor bombardment, and signs of volcanic activity caused by heat released from beneath the surface. Venus, Earth, and Mars also have large atmospheres that have affected their evolution.

The giant planets are all fairly similar to each other. All spin rapidly, are encircled by bands of coloured clouds, and can produce huge storms in their atmospheres. All the giant planets have rings and large families of satellites. Most of these moons are heavily cratered, but some have had their surfaces reshape by other forces.

Two very different types of world, rocky Earth (far left) and giant Neptune (left), orbit the Sun in our Solar System.

---

270 BCE Astronomer Aristarchus of Samos proposes that the Earth might be orbiting the Sun.

C. AD 150 Astronomer Ptolemy supports the theory of the Earth-centred Universe.

1543 Nicolaus Copernicus suggests that the Sun might be the centre of the Solar System.

1609 Johannes Kepler shows that the planets have elliptical (oval) orbits around the Sun.

1705 Edmond Halley shows that some comets follow elliptical orbits and return at regular intervals.

1796 Pierre Simon Laplace suggests the Solar System formed from a collapsing gas cloud.

1801 The first asteroid, Ceres, is discovered by Giuseppe Piazzi.

Timeline

In this SOHO image of the Sun, the hottest areas are white.

BELTS AND CLOUDS

Between the eight largest members of the Solar System and their satellites there are billions of other swirling objects – minor members of the Solar System, ranging from the tiniest specks of dust to icy worlds the size of small planets. Most of these smaller bodies are confined to certain regions of the Solar System by the gravity of larger worlds. Between Mars and Jupiter lies an asteroid belt of rocky worlds – most just a few kilometres across, but a few much larger. These asteroids were unable to cluster together to form another rocky planet because of Jupiter's powerful gravity.

Further from the Sun, beyond Neptune, is the doughnut-shaped Edgeworth-Kuiper Belt, home of thousands of small ice dwarfs. These are similar to asteroids but instead of rock, they are made of water ice and other frozen chemicals. The largest ice dwarf, Pluto, was discovered long before others came to light, and is still classed

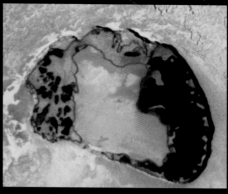

This picture of a volcanic crater on Jupiter's moon, Io, shows lava and sulphur-rich materials reacting with each other.

as a planet. Still further away is the Oort Cloud, an enormous spherical shell of icy debris that extends to at least one light year from the Sun.

SCATTERED DEBRIS

Plenty of smaller objects have orbits outside these belts with long ellipses that cross over the orbits of planets. Most familiar are the comets – dirty snowballs that plunge towards the inner Solar System from the Oort Cloud and Edgeworth-Kuiper Belt. They sometimes create spectacular sights as their icy surfaces evaporate in the strong sunlight. Behind them, they leave a trail of ice and dust particles that create beautiful but short-lived shooting stars as they plunge into Earth's atmosphere. Less visible are the Near Earth Asteroids, in orbits that come close to, and occasionally cross, our own. Some have probably been flung out of the asteroid belt, while others may be the remains of extinct comets. Countless smaller rocks move in Earth-crossing orbits and occasionally plunge to Earth as meteorites.

Comet Hale-Bopp hangs above Earth's horizon with a tail millions of kilometres long trailing behind it.

1846 Mathematicians John Couch Adams and Urbain Le Verrier predict the existence of Neptune.

1930 Clyde Tombaugh discovers Pluto, the outermost planet.

1950 Jan Oort proposes the existence of the Oort Cloud.

1951 Gerard Kuiper predicts the existence of the Kuiper Belt.

1962 *Mariner 2* becomes the first spacecraft to send back information from another planet.

1986 *Giotto* spacecraft flies past the nucleus of Halley's comet.

1992 First Edgeworth-Kuiper Belt objects are discovered by the Hubble Space Telescope.

2000 *NEAR* spacecraft goes into orbit around asteroid Eros, landing on it a year later.

ORBITING THE SUN

THE SOLAR SYSTEM IS THE REGION of space where the Sun reigns supreme. Heat, gravity, light, and particles from our local star dominate a sphere that stretches a quarter of the way to our next nearest neighbour, the star Proxima Centauri. Earth is just one of nine sizeable planets that travels, or orbits, around the Sun, locked in place by the Sun's powerful gravity. Many of these planets are themselves orbited by moons and rings. Between the planets, countless chunks of rocky or icy debris – asteroids and comets – also orbit the Sun.

View of the Solar System (not to scale)

Mercury

Sun

Asteroid belt

Mars

Pluto

Jupiter

Uranus

PLANETARY ORBITS

Although astronomers often talk of objects "circling" one another in orbit, orbits are very rarely perfect circles. In fact, most planets have orbits that are elliptical (oval-shaped). An ellipse has two focus points on its long axis to either side of its centre which help define its shape. The Sun always lies at one focus. As a result, planets get nearer and further from the Sun as they move around their orbit. The closest approach is called perihelion and the furthest distance is called aphelion. Planets move more quickly along their orbit near perihelion, and more slowly at aphelion.

◄ GRAVITY AND THE PLANETS ►

These people on a "wall of death" ride don't fall down because they are travelling around so fast that their speed gives them momentum. In the same way, the planets do not fall in towards the Sun because they are speeding around their orbits. The Sun's gravity stops them flying off into space. The nearer a planet is to the Sun the faster it must orbit.

THE SOLAR SYSTEM is shaped like a disc – the planets all orbit around the Sun's equator, near a plane that extends from the Sun to Earth's orbit and beyond. We can draw this plane as an imaginary line in the sky called the ecliptic. The Sun appears to make a circuit along the ecliptic once a year. This effect can be most obvious at sunrise or sunset.

From left to right, Venus, the Moon, and Jupiter along the ecliptic

Neptune

Saturn

Johannes Kepler (1571–1630)
German astronomer Johannes Kepler was the first person to explain that the planets moved in elliptical rather than circular orbits. At the time, astronomers thought all orbits had to be perfect circles, and this caused problems for the idea of a Sun-centred Solar System. Kepler's accurate measurements of planetary positions, made without a telescope, allowed him to form three laws of planetary motion that explained the true nature of the Solar System. This paved the way for Newton's law of gravity (p. 16).

ЛAR SYSTEM LIMITS

ere does the Solar System end? Astronomers think it ended at the orbit of the last planet, However, they are now finding hundreds l ice dwarfs (p. 50) beyond Pluto. Some mers believe that the Solar System's edge he "heliopause", somewhere beyond Pluto he solar wind mixes with the winds from n other stars. Others say it extends to the Cloud (above) – a shell of comets about two ears across, loosely held by the Sun's gravity.

Nemesis
Is there a tenth planet lurking in the outer reaches of the Solar System? Astronomers used to think that there were strange variations in Neptune's orbit that could only be explained by another planet. However, new calculations show it's unlikely that another giant planet orbits anywhere near Pluto. Another theory is that the Sun has a dark companion – a faint brown dwarf star in an orbit millions of years long. They have named this dark star Nemesis (left).

BIRTH OF THE SUN AND PLANETS

THE SUN AND ALL ITS PLANETS condensed out of a cloud of interstellar gas and dust about 5 billion years ago. First, the Sun began to shine. Then, over the next half billion years, the planets formed out of a flattened disc of dust and gas around the Sun. Astronomers have a far better idea of how the Sun formed than they do about the planets – they've already watched the birth and death of thousands of stars. However, current telescopes are not powerful enough to see any planets that may be forming around them.

THE SOLAR NEBULA

The nebula that gave birth to the Sun consisted of recycled material from an earlier generation of stars. This material was largely hydrogen and helium, but with significant amounts of heavier elements and dust. Five billion years ago, something triggered the nebula's collapse. It could have been the close approach of another star, or the shock wave from a nearby supernova (exploding star). As the nebula began to condense, it flattened into a bulging disc with a huge ball of gas, the young Sun, at its centre.

New Sun is surrounded by solar nebula.

Gas and dust mix together to form small bodies by gravitational attraction.

Planets begin to form in the thinning gas.

Ignition!

As the cloud of gas that would become the Sun collapsed inwards, it heated up and began to pull more and more material onto itself. Eventually, conditions at the centre of the cloud became so hot and dense that nuclear fusion took place, releasing enormous amounts of energy. The Sun ignited in a fierce blaze of radiation – similar to the bright stars that have just formed in this galaxy's spiral arms (above).

Thinning out

As radiation from the young Sun blasted out through the remains of the solar nebula, it started to blow away the light gases that had survived. The inner Solar System rapidly thinned out, leaving mostly dust particles called chrondules. In the outer Solar System, the radiation was weaker and so the gas survived long enough to be pulled into the massive atmospheres of the giant planets.

MANY PHENOMENA IN astronomy involve flattened discs – ranging from rings around planets to material falling onto black holes. This experiment shows why clouds of material flatten into discs. **You will need:** glass; warm water; tea leaves; sieve; spoon.

1 Soak a pinch of tea leaves in a glass of warm water and leave them to settle. Strain the water several times with the sieve until the tea leaves (fragments of nebula) are floating in clear water (space). Stir the water in a figure of eight.

2 Watch how the leaves behave as they collide and settle. Sometimes they drop at random, but often they form a circular heap (see right). When leaves moving in opposite directions collide, their movements across the glass cancel out, leaving just their movement around the glass. Eventually all the leaves are swirling around in concentric "orbits".

Dating the Solar System

The main method of dating the origins of the Solar System is to measure radioactive decay in rocks. Rocks formed in the solar nebula all would have contained the same proportions of different elements. But once locked into rocks, some elements began to change into other elements through radioactive decay. By measuring the proportions of elements in meteorites unchanged since the formation of the Solar System, scientists can estimate its age.

This meteorite, which fell in Barwell, England, is dated at 4,600 million years old.

The debris of creation

Even today, not all the material from the solar nebula is soaked up. Some large chunks form asteroids and ice dwarfs (pp. 50–51), but smaller grains of dust are scattered across the plane of the Solar System. Sunlight reflected off this material creates the zodiacal light, a faint glow along the line of the ecliptic (Earth's path around the Sun). The strongest light can be seen either side of the Sun just before dawn or after sunset.

BIRTH OF THE PLANETS

Over tens of millions of years, the chrondules in the inner Solar System began to clump together and stick to each other – a process called accretion. Eventually, a few dozen bodies – protoplanets – became big enough for their gravity to pull in more material from around them. Finally, some of these protoplanets collided to form the modern terrestrial planets. For half a billion years more, meteorites bombarded the young planets keeping their surfaces in a hot, molten state.

INSIDE THE PLANETS

MOST OF THE PLANETS in our Solar System are of two very different types. Nearest to the Sun are the rocky planets Mercury, Venus, Earth, and Mars. These are similar in size, and consist of a solid rocky sphere with a relatively shallow atmosphere. Further away, beyond the asteroid belt, lie the giant planets Jupiter, Saturn, Uranus, and Neptune – each many times the size of Earth. The giant planets also have rocky cores, but are surrounded by a vast envelope of gases and liquids. Pluto is not typical of either a rocky planet or a giant planet.

The outer atmosphere of a gas giant frequently shows bands of clouds of different colours at different heights.

Upper levels of a giant planet are gaseous. Clouds are coloured by a variety of chemicals.

Deeper inside the planet, temperatures rise, but pressure causes the gases to condense into liquids or slushy ices.

Neptune probably has a rocky core that is a little smaller than Earth.

FORMATION

How did the two types of planets form? The clue lies in their distance from the Sun and the conditions in the remains of the solar nebula after the Sun had formed. Close to the Sun, easily melted materials, such as ice, evaporated into gas and were either pulled into the Sun or blown away by the solar wind, leaving mostly rocky material behind. Further from the Sun, where gravity was weaker and temperatures lower, ice and gas survived in huge amounts to form giant planets, as shown in the picture above.

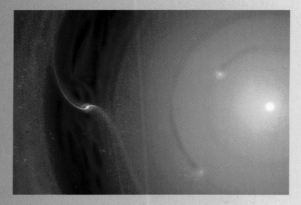

Radioactive elements in rocks heat the interiors of rocky planets.

Earth's core consists mainly of iron and nickel. It is probably solid at the centre.

Convection cells in the mantle transfer heat outwards.

Earth's crust is a solid layer a few tens of kilometres thick.

ROCK WORLDS

The collisions that form a rocky planet generate heat – the larger the planet, the hotter it gets. During formation, the rocky planets became hot enough to melt. The molten material gradually separated into layers, with the heaviest sinking to the centre to form a metal core. Inside Earth, this core is surrounded by a mantle of molten rock that carries heat upwards by convection to a solid crust. Smaller rocky planets lose heat faster. Their interior layers are not as clearly separated, and they may have cooled enough for their cores to solidify.

If you could find a tub of water big enough, Saturn would float like this tennis ball.

Mercury would sink, like this ballbearing.

Light, energetic hydrogen molecules are less affected by gravity and can escape to the outer layers of a planet's atmosphere.

GIANT PLANETS

Inside a giant planet, such as Neptune, molecules move around. Heavier molecules form layers towards the centre of the planet. A few hundred kilometres below the visible surface, pressure rises so high that it forces gases to condense into liquids. This high pressure in the interior heats the entire planet. In fact, most giant planets generate more heat inside than they receive from the Sun. Convection of heat from the centre to the outer layers of the planet may also help to form the banded weather patterns that surround most giant planets.

Differing densities

Giant planets are larger than rocky planets in both volume and mass. However, because the mass of a giant planet is spread over such a huge volume, on average its density is less than that of a smaller planet. For example, Mercury is made up of heavy materials – mostly iron – packed into a relatively small area, while Saturn has lighter-weight molecules spread over a large area. The density of Mercury is actually seven times greater than that of Saturn. If they were compared in water, Saturn would float, while Mercury would sink.

Heavier molecules are slower and more affected by gravity, causing them to fall towards the centre of a planet.

Hydrogen and gravity

Giant planets are dominated by hydrogen, the lightest element in the Universe. Hydrogen comprises more than 80 per cent of a giant planet's molecules. The strong gravity of a giant planet enables it to hold onto the light, energetic molecules. In a giant planet, hydrogen can condense into a liquid and even split into atoms. But on a small planet, like Earth, gravity is too weak to hold onto much hydrogen, which is why heavier nitrogen molecules make up a large part of Earth's atmosphere.

CRATERS AND VOLCANOES

HUGE SPACE ROCKS CAN SMASH into planets, gouging out giant craters. These impacts throw up underlying material and scatter it out in rays. Volcanic eruptions can cause lava to spurt up from beneath the surface. This molten rock oozes over the surrounding terrain, cools, and forms a new blanket of rock. It is no wonder that impacts and eruptions are the two main processes that reshape planets. On Earth, their effects can be disguised by erosion from wind, water, and movements of the planet's crust. But on other worlds, the scars of craters and volcanoes are still clear to see.

A meteorite hurtles towards the surface.

IMPACT!

Craters form when an object from space smashes into a planet. A high-pressure shock wave ripples out from the point of impact, heating and melting the surrounding rock. The wave also ripples back through the meteorite and tears it apart. As the shock wave passes, the pressure drops, and molten rocks fly out of the crater, raining down to form secondary craters. Finer material coats the area in a thin blanket of dust.

Chunks of rock spray out to form secondary craters.

A rim is pushed up around the main area of impact.

Peering into a planet
The area around a crater is scattered with rock gouged out of the surface. The first material ejected from the crater falls back to the surface first and covers the widest area. Rocks from deeper down will fall on top of this layer. Ejected material turns the surface "inside-out". It is a useful way for astronomers to look inside planets and see what materials lie below the surface.

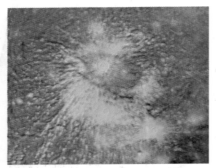

A crater on Jupiter's moon Ganymede, surrounded by rays of ejected material

Dating from craters
Any surface has to be older than the crater on top of it, and astronomers use this fact to date planetary surfaces. Lunar rock samples show that cratering was more frequent until 3.8 billion years ago, when it dwindled to the steady rate of today. The least cratered surfaces are therefore the youngest, and craters or plains that are covered by impacts must be older than the impacts themselves.

Craters on the Moon

LET'S EXPERIMENT
MAKING CRATERS

THE SURFACE OF OUR MOON shows a pattern of overlapping craters. These occur when small meteorites follow larger ones and smash into the surface, creating craters within craters. Make your own lunar surface in this experiment. **You will need:** a tray; sand; different-sized balls and marbles.

1 Fill a tray with sand and smooth the surface to make it flat.

2 Drop the largest ball to make a big crater in the sand. Remove the ball and then drop smaller ones to create overlapping patterns of craters. Larger balls completely obliterate smaller craters beneath them.

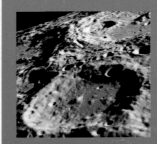

Overlapping lunar craters

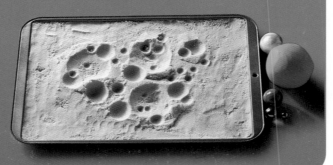

ERUPTION!

Volcanoes release hot, molten material from inside a planet. Underground pressures force the hot liquid up towards the surface, where it shoots out through a vent to cover the surrounding area. The most violent eruptions occur when a cap forms over the vent. The material can't escape and pressure builds up until the volcano finally bursts. On Earth, we are most familiar with cone-shaped volcanoes and with geysers (eruptions of escaping steam). Other planets show a wide variety of volcano types, from the huge, gently sloping shield volcanoes on Mars, to the icy geysers of Neptune's moon, Triton.

Kilauea, an active shield volcano in Hawaii

Ice geysers are believed to erupt on Saturn's moon, Enceladus.

Icy volcanoes

Volcanic activity doesn't always involve molten rock. In the outer Solar System, icy moons show signs of different types of eruptions. Geysers of slushy ice and water vapour have been discovered. Enceladus, Saturn's inner moon, has ice geysers that erupt regularly and cover the surface in snow. This gives it the brightest surface in the Solar System.

Lava landscape

Solidified lava covers about 85 per cent of the surface of Venus. This image shows the planet's tallest volcano, Maat Mons, surrounded by huge plains of lava. These lava plains form when molten rock spews up from long cracks in the surface and floods low-lying areas. On Venus, volcanic eruptions covered almost the entire planet in new rock about 500 million years ago. This rock filled most of the craters so there are very few visible today. In general, the fewer the craters, the younger the rock on a planet's surface.

LET'S EXPERIMENT
MAKING A VOLCANO

A VOLCANO ERUPTS when pressure builds up inside it and forces molten lava out of the top. In this experiment you can create a volcano by mixing vinegar with bicarbonate of soda. When they react, they produce carbon dioxide, which makes the mixture bubble up like lava. **You will need:** an adult present; old newspaper; tray; modelling clay; small bottle; funnel that fits the bottle's neck; bicarbonate of soda; beaker; pale-coloured vinegar; food colouring.

1 Place a tray on a table that is covered with old newspaper. On the tray, mould modelling clay around a small bottle to make a volcano shape, like the one below. Leave a gap at the top. Using the funnel, pour bicarbonate of soda into the bottle.

2 In a beaker, mix together some pale-coloured vinegar with some food colouring. Then pour the mixture into the neck of the volcano. When the vinegar and bicarbonate of soda react, brightly coloured "lava" will erupt from the volcano.

PLANETARY ATMOSPHERES

ATMOSPHERES ARE CRUCIAL TO the evolution of rocky planets and moons. An atmosphere helps to control the temperature, protects the surface from meteor bombardment, and even affects the geology of the solid world it surrounds. Since gas has a natural tendency to escape into space, only bodies with strong enough gravity can hold on to an atmosphere. In the Solar System, Venus, Earth, Mars, and the moon, Titan, are the only rocky worlds with enough mass to retain substantial atmospheres. For giant planets, such as Jupiter, which have no solid surface, "atmosphere" is the term to describe the outer gas envelope that surrounds the liquid mantle.

Mercury's thin air is made of atoms blasted off the surface by meteor impacts.

Titan has a thick atmosphere of nitrogen and methane.

THICK AND THIN

In general, the greater a planet's gravity, the more atmospheric gas it can hold onto. However, the nearer a planet lies to the Sun, the hotter its atmosphere will be, causing fast-moving gas molecules to escape into space. Searing hot Mercury cannot hold on to any gas and must constantly renew its thin atmosphere. In contrast, Saturn's cold, distant moon Titan, despite having half the gravity of Mercury, has a thick atmosphere. The weight of atmospheric gases is also important – light gases, such as hydrogen, escape from atmospheres far more easily than heavy gases, such as carbon dioxide.

The origin of atmospheres

Unlike the giant planets, rocky worlds such as Earth and Mars didn't get their atmospheres simply by pulling gas out of the solar nebula (pp. 40–41). Their atmospheres formed later, probably from two main sources – outgassing and bombardment. The young planets would have been far more volcanically active than they are today, and this would have spewed out a variety of gases (outgassing) as well as lava. Impacts from comets would also have brought water vapour and other important molecules to the young planets (bombardment).

Changing atmospheres

Today's planetary atmospheres bear little relation to the original primitive atmospheres. Close to the Sun, light gases such as hydrogen mostly escaped from their planets, leaving only heavier gases behind. The actions of geology, chemistry, and (on Earth) life have slowly altered the proportions of these remaining gases. For example, micro-organisms on Earth gradually converted much of our planet's carbon dioxide to oxygen, while Venus lost its water vapour through the greenhouse effect.

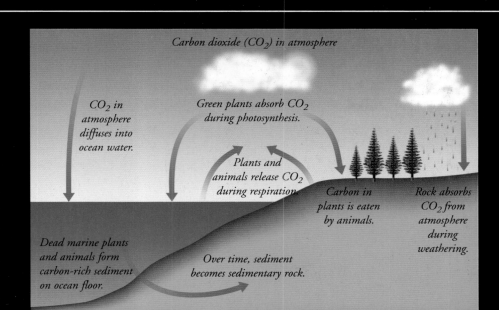

Carbon dioxide (CO₂) in atmosphere

CO₂ in atmosphere diffuses into ocean water.

Green plants absorb CO₂ during photosynthesis.

Plants and animals release CO₂ during respiration.

Carbon in plants is eaten by animals.

Rock absorbs CO₂ from atmosphere during weathering.

Dead marine plants and animals form carbon-rich sediment on ocean floor.

Over time, sediment becomes sedimentary rock.

THE CARBON CYCLE

All living things consist of, and depend upon, carbon. On Earth, carbon dioxide (CO₂) in the atmosphere sustains life through the carbon cycle. In this cycle, carbon is absorbed and released, and constantly passes from one form to another. CO₂ in Earth's atmosphere is absorbed by green plants during photosynthesis. Animals eat these plants, taking up their carbon. Both plants and animals release CO₂ back into the atmosphere when they breathe, and when they die and decay. CO₂ gas also diffuses into oceans where marine life absorbs it, before dying and falling to the ocean floor to form sedimentary rock.

The many layers of Earth's protective atmosphere are visible in this picture taken from space.

The Gaia idea

According to Professor James Lovelock's Gaia hypothesis, our planet and everything on it acts like a single giant organism, regulating its own environment to preserve the right conditions for life. The carbon cycle is just one example of Gaia at work. This cycle produces a natural "greenhouse effect" that keeps the planet warm enough for life. However, artificial interference, such as burning fossil fuels, could tip the planet out of balance with disastrous consequences for all living things.

LET'S EXPERIMENT
THE GREENHOUSE EFFECT

CARBON DIOXIDE is a small but vital component of Earth's atmosphere. It helps trap heat from the Sun and prevents it escaping into space. This experiment shows you how this "greenhouse effect" works.
You will need: 2 small glasses; water; large glass bowl; sunny area.

1 Half fill each glass with water and put them both in a sunny place. Put the clear bowl upside down over one of the glasses. Leave both glasses to stand in the sunshine for an hour.

2 Now take the bowl away and dip a finger in each glass of water to compare the temperatures of the water. The water that was under the glass will be warmer. The bowl has acted like our atmosphere – it has let heat energy in, but has prevented it from escaping.

MOONS AND RINGS

MERCURY AND VENUS ARE the only two planets in the Solar System to orbit the Sun alone. All of the other planets have moons (also known as satellites) in orbit around them. These range from bodies the size of a small planet to captured asteroids only a few kilometres across. The four giant planets – Jupiter, Saturn, Uranus and Neptune – also have ring systems. These rings are made of millions of chunks of ice and rock, each in their own separate orbit around the parent planet. Ring systems range from Saturn's magnificent bright planes to Jupiter's faint bands.

Saturn and its ring system taken by the *Voyager 1* spacecraft

F

Titania (largest moon orbiting Uranus, shown from a distance)

Oberon

Umbriel

Uranus (parent planet)

Miranda

Ariel

FAMILIES OF MOONS

A moon is a world locked in orbit around a larger parent planet. Uranus (left) has 17 known moons (only five shown here), the largest of which is Titania, at 1,578 km (980 miles) wide. Moons orbit their parent planets in ellipses (ovals), just as the planets orbit the Sun (pp. 38–39). The parent planet's gravitational pull causes tides which slow down the moon's rotation. Because of this, the moon always keeps the same face turned towards its planet. Although moons are smaller than their parent planets, and so should be cold, inactive worlds, tidal disturbances can keep them hot and active.

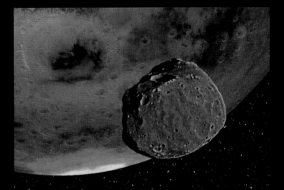

Natural satellites and captured moons
Not all satellites originated in the same way. Phobos (above) may be an asteroid captured by the gravity of Mars. Asteroids and ice dwarfs pulled into a planet's orbit are known as captured moons. Some of the satellites orbiting the giant planets formed from material left over as the planets themselves formed. These are considered natural satellites. Earth's Moon may have formed from material splashed out from the planet during an ancient collision (p. 72).

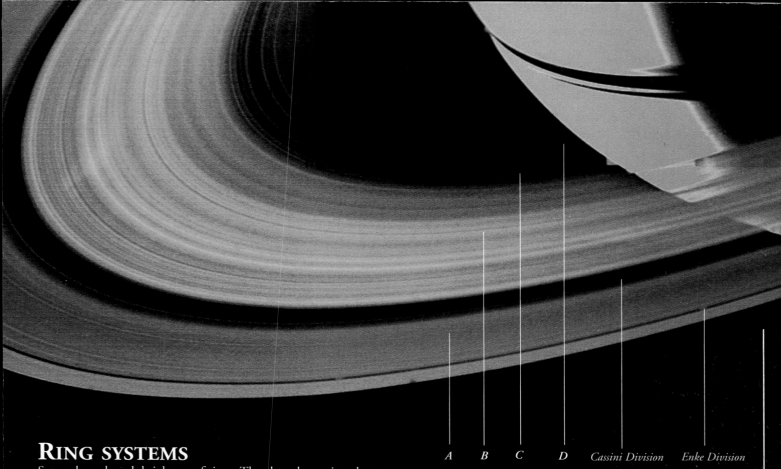

RING SYSTEMS

Saturn has a broad, bright set of rings. They have been given letters to distinguish them, and the major divisions are named. The gap between the A and B ring, for example, is known as the Cassini Division. Planetary rings are made up of millions or billions of separate chunks of ice and rock. These chunks exist in a zone in which the planet's gravity overpowers their own gravity, preventing them from coming together to form a larger satellite. Astronomers think rings may form when a small satellite strays within this zone known as the "Roche limit", and then breaks up in a collision.

A   *B*   *C*   *D*   *Cassini Division*   *Enke Division*

LET'S EXPERIMENT
BACKLIT RINGS

RINGS OF DUST or ice scatter sunlight rather than reflect it back to Earth. Spacecraft spotted the rings of Jupiter and Neptune as they were backlit by the Sun. **You will need:** an adult to help you; paper drinking straw; matches; clear bottle with cap; torch.

1 Ask an adult to set light to the straw and use it to fill a bottle with smoke. Replace the cap, darken the room, and shine the torch through the bottle from the front. You won't be able to see the smoke particles.

2 Shine the torch through the bottle from the side. The smoke scatters the light and the particles become visible.

1986U8

1986U7

Shepherd moons
Some rings have extremely fine structures, with gaps, spokes, and even kinks. These features may come and go. They seem to be linked to the gravitational effects of satellites orbiting within, or close to, the rings. Tiny "shepherd" moons often keep the narrowest rings hemmed in, such as these around Uranus (above). Fragments chipped off shepherd moons may also help replenish the rings, which are constantly being eroded.

ASTEROIDS AND ICE DWARFS

THE SPACE BETWEEN THE PLANETS is not empty – our Solar System is teeming with many millions of smaller worlds. Near the Sun are rocky asteroids, and further out are ice dwarfs. These closely related objects are tiny compared to the planets – most are less than 100 km (60 miles) across. Their gravity is too weak to pull them into spherical shapes, so they exist as jagged chunks of rock and ice. Asteroids and ice dwarfs are remnants from the early days of the Solar System – space debris that never accumulated into larger objects, and the shattered remains of worlds that might have been.

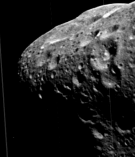

Ida is covered with a thin layer of dusty soil, known as regolith.

An artwork of the "main belt" of asteroids between Mars and Jupiter

BELTS OF ROCK AND ICE

Most of the Solar System's smaller worlds inhabit two main regions – the "main belt" between Mars and Jupiter, and the Edgeworth-Kuiper Belt (EKB) beyond Neptune. They are hemmed into these regions by the influence of the planets, but it's a common mistake to think these belts are crowded. Most of these worlds are tiny, astronomically speaking. The largest asteroid is Ceres, just 930 km (580 miles) across, while the largest EKB object may be the planet Pluto (p. 89). The composition of the belts depends on their location in the Solar System. Those close to the Sun are mostly rocky, while further out, where the temperatures are colder, they are icy.

LET'S EXPERIMENT
ASTEROID BELTS

MOST ASTEROID ORBITS ARE CONFINED by the influences of Mars and, especially, Jupiter. This experiment shows how the asteroids move together to form a belt. **You will need:** a large bowl or sink; water; coriander seeds or any small, floating objects; spoon.

1 Fill the container with water and drop in the floating objects. Using a spoon, slowly stir in large circles to separate the objects. Then move the spoon closer to the middle and stir faster.

2 When a swirling current has formed, remove the spoon. As the current settles down, the objects move from the edges of the container and begin to form a circular belt as they spin in the current. In our Solar System it is the gravity of the surrounding planets that holds the asteroids in a belt.

Collisions, though rare, can reshape the asteroids in the main belt.

Planetary pinball
Main-belt asteroids are slaves to Jupiter's gravity. It can smash them together, shattering them into tiny pieces and preventing them from becoming planets. Occasionally, Jupiter flings them out into wider orbits, leaving gaps in the belt. Some asteroids, called "Trojans", even end up in Jupiter's orbit. Most asteroids fall into circular orbits to avoid collisions, but accidents still happen. Astronomers have discovered several asteroid "families" – the remains of a single object that broke up in an impact.

Bluer patches are ejecta from young, fresh craters.

ENCOUNTERS WITH ASTEROIDS

The asteroid Ida (left) was photographed by the *Galileo* spacecraft on its way to Jupiter. Space missions such as this, as well as NEAR (the Near Earth Asteroid Rendezvous), have provided new insights into asteroids. Photographs have revealed that most are irregular lumps of rock. There are often signs that they have been blasted apart by collisions, then pulled back together by their own weak gravity. Some asteroids may be little more than orbiting rubble piles. Ida is a more substantial world, but still has deep gouges where it has suffered collisions in the past. The gravity of asteroids like these is so weak that large impacts often simply knock chips off them.

Edgeworth-Kuiper Belt

First predicted in the 1940s, the EKB was suggested as a possible origin of the short-period comets, whose orbits reach their outermost point somewhere near Neptune. Several hundred EKB objects have been found since 1992. They are so faint that they can only be discovered by looking for slow-moving "stars" in timed sequences of photos. These pictures show the first discovered EKB object – the moving "star" is actually an ice dwarf.

In 1992, a moving ice dwarf was the first EKB object to be discovered.

Near Earth Asteroids

Some asteroids, flung out of the main belt by Jupiter's gravity, fall into elongated orbits that come close to, or even cross, Earth's own. These Near Earth Asteroids (NEAs) are classed as Amor, Apollo, or Aten asteroids, depending on the shapes of their orbits. They are among the best understood asteroids because they come relatively close to Earth, and can be seen with telescopes or visited by spacecraft. In the distant future, some NEAs may even be a threat to Earth.

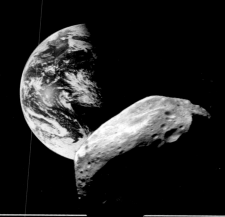

Asteroid mining

Asteroids contain huge amounts of metals and other valuable elements. Most of these elements are in their pure, easily extracted form, not locked up in chemical ores and minerals like the rocks on Earth. Already much of our nickel production comes from the site of an ancient meteorite impact in Canada. This meteorite was just a small chunk of a much larger, mineral-rich asteroid. Several private companies are now planning to send mineral prospecting satellites to NEAs, and a full-scale mining operation could one day revolutionize industry on Earth.

This sample of nickel iron contains two of the many elements found in asteroids.

COMETS

SPEEDING BALLS OF ICE AND DUST make brief visits to our skies in the form of comets. Made up of material left over from the formation of the Sun and planets, comets mostly orbit in the outer limits of the Solar System. Occasionally, they break free and hurtle through space towards the Sun. Comets are usually only visible from Earth as faint smudges of light, but sometimes they become as bright as the brightest star and develop long tails that trail impressively across the sky.

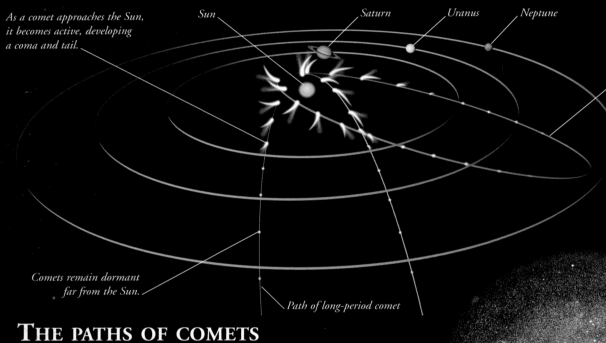

As a comet approaches the Sun, it becomes active, developing a coma and tail.

Sun   Saturn   Uranus   Neptune

Path of short-period comet

Comets remain dormant far from the Sun.

Path of long-period comet

THE PATHS OF COMETS

Comets have highly stretched elliptical (oval) orbits. Short-period comets take anything from a few decades to 200 years to orbit the Sun. Their orbits reach their outermost point in the Edgeworth-Kuiper Belt beyond Neptune. Long-period comets come from much further away in the Oort Cloud, and take thousands or millions of years to complete each orbit. Comets only become active for the brief time that they are close to the Sun, when the nucleus heats up and gives off dust and gas to form a glowing coma (head).

Dr Fred Whipple uses a 227 kg (500 lb) snowball covered with dirt to talk about the nucleus of a comet.

Dr Comet

In 1949, American astronomer Fred Whipple announced his theory on the nature of comets. He stated that a comet is like a "dirty snowball", a ball of ice, gas, and dust with a rocky nucleus. Edmond Halley (1656–1742) was the first to realize that comets returned in regular periods, but astronomers still didn't know what they were. Dr Whipple's theory was confirmed when the *Giotto* spacecraft took pictures of Halley's Comet in 1986.

The Oort Cloud

Comets originate in the Oort Cloud. This halo of icy material surrounds our Solar System and extends to about a light year away. Occasionally, collisions or the passage of nearby stars send comets plunging towards the inner Solar System. Some of these infalling comets have their orbits disrupted by the gravity of the giant planets and are pulled into shorter-period orbits. The Oort Cloud is thought to contain billions of comets.

COMET TAILS

As a comet approaches the Sun, its dark, dusty surface absorbs sunlight, warming up the ice beneath until it starts to evaporate. Jets of vapour burst out in plumes, forming a planet-sized halo of gas called the coma. The gas and dust that escape from the comet's weak gravity are blown away from the Sun to form two tails. The gas tail points directly away from the Sun and shines with the energy given off as it collides with the solar wind. The dust tail is often curved (because heavier particles lag behind the comet's orbit) and shines by reflected sunlight.

Bluish gas or ion tail

Coma hides the nucleus completely.

Whiter curving dust tail

Comet Hale-Bopp was one of the brightest comets of the 20th century.

Rocky centre

A dormant comet looks similar to a rocky asteroid, as this close-up of Comet Borrelly shows. It is usually just a few kilometres across, and irregularly shaped. Radiation from the Sun causes chemical reactions that create a thin coating of dark, carbon-based chemicals on the surface. Beneath this lie the icy "volatiles" that evaporate to form the coma and tail. Each orbit around the Sun uses up a little more of this reservoir of volatiles. Eventually, after many orbits, the comet is exhausted and its tail fades away.

LET'S EXPERIMENT
DIRTY SNOWBALLS

AS THEY APPROACH the Sun, comets heat up rapidly because of the dark soot that covers them. If they were made purely of snow and ice, comets would reflect most of the heat and light from the Sun, as this experiment shows. **You will need:** 2 ice cubes; tray or plate; black powder paint and white powder paint; lamp.

1 Take the two ice-cubes and put them on a tray or a plate. Sprinkle white powder paint on one and black powder paint on the other, until each ice cube is fully covered. Place them under a bright lamp or spotlight and leave them for a few minutes.

2 After this, you should find that the dark-coated ice cube has melted more rapidly than the light one. This is because the black powder paint absorbs heat from the lamp, while the white powder paint reflects it.

METEORS AND METEORITES

YOU MAY NOT REALIZE IT, but Earth is under constant attack from space. Some scientists estimate that we are bombarded by as much as 200 tonnes of material every day. Fortunately, most of these invaders from space are simply dust grains, left behind from the early days of the Solar System's formation. When a meteor (shooting star) reaches the ground it is known as a meteorite. The majority of meteorites found on Earth come from asteroids, but a few seem to have been blasted off the Moon and Mars. Some of the debris comes from orbiting comets, which create meteors as it burns up harmlessly in the upper atmosphere.

METEOR SHOWERS

A meteor is created by a tiny fragment of dust falling into Earth's atmosphere. As it collides with gas molecules in the upper atmosphere, the dust particle rapidly begins to vaporize and heats the air around it, making it visible. Many of the dust grains come from the tails of passing comets, which means that regular meteor showers fall when Earth crosses or comes close to a comet's orbit. Because the meteors in a shower are all travelling in the same direction, they appear to come from the same point in the sky. This point is known as the shower's radiant.

Background picture shows Leonid meteors against star trails captured in a time-lapse photograph.

Terrible Leonids
Occasionally, meteor showers can turn into spectacular storms, with hundreds of shooting stars falling every second. Storms happen when Earth crosses a comet's orbit just after the comet itself has passed by and replenished the dust trail. The most famous storm is the Leonid display which occurs every November, and which peaks every 33 years (most recently around the year 2000). This engraving shows the Leonid storm of 1833, which caused widespread panic across the USA.

Iron meteorite from the core of an asteroid

SKYWATCHING
SHOOTING STARS

TO SEE METEORS, it is best to look after midnight. At this time, our side of the Earth is meeting any incoming meteors head-on, so the meteors approach at high speed and burn up brightly. Several meteor showers repeat every year, and are named after the constellation from which they appear to radiate. The most consistent are the Perseids of early August. A full list of dates for meteor showers is provided in the Space data section (pp. 150–51).

A Perseid shower in British Columbia, Canada

ROCKS FROM THE SKY

Some 500 meteorites are thought to make it to Earth's surface every year. They rarely arrive in meteor showers, since they are larger and more solid chunks of debris, and usually follow their own orbit around the Sun. A falling meteorite may produce a brilliant, slow-moving shooting star called a bolide. Meteorites are thought to be the broken-up remains of asteroids that have destroyed each other in collisions. Because they have not been exposed to the constant changes experienced by planetary rocks, meteorites are time capsules from the early Solar System.

Stony iron from the region between the crust and the core

Chondrites consist of grains stuck together.

Stony meteorite from the crust of an asteroid

Meteorite types
There are several types of meteorite. Iron, stony-iron, and stony "achondrite" meteorites come from different parts of rocks – probably large asteroids – that had separated into layers like the planets. "Chondritic" stony meteorites seem to be unaltered samples of material from the original solar nebula.

Impact on Earth
On rare occasions, Earth takes a direct hit from a meteor or a comet. The 800-m (2,625-ft) wide Barringer Crater in Arizona was made by an object which fell to Earth some 50,000 years ago. Meteor impacts can bring valuable minerals and metals to Earth – much of the world's nickel comes from an impact site in Canada. However, the largest impacts can also have devastating effects on life, and may have been responsible for the extinction of the dinosaurs 65 million years ago.

Meteorite hunting
Unless someone actually sees a meteorite fall, lumps of rock from the sky can be very difficult to distinguish from normal stones in the landscape. To find meteorites, geologists travel to parts of the world where rocks are out of place in the landscape, such as deserts and Antarctica. Iron meteorites tend to stand out more from natural surroundings, and they can also be found using a metal detector.

Researcher David Kring uses a metal detector to search for meteorite fragments in a desert landscape.

LIFE IN THE SOLAR SYSTEM

ARE THERE ALIENS IN OUR Solar System? As far as we are aware,
Earth is the only one of the Sun's planets that supports life, and until
recently it seemed that conditions on other worlds were impossibly
hostile. However, new findings by spacecraft have shown that at
least one planet and one moon are more hospitable than they
seemed at first. New discoveries on Earth have also shown
that life is able to survive in far tougher habitats than we
once thought. These discoveries have made scientists
think again about the possibility of life on our
neighbouring planets and moons.

CONDITIONS FOR LIFE

Certain elements are vital for life to exist.
On Earth, all life is based on complex carbon
chemistry, and the same would probably be true
elsewhere. Liquid water is vital for life and until
recently, sunlight was thought to be an essential
provider of energy. However, life has now been
discovered around undersea volcanic vents in
total darkness. Creatures, such as this spider
crab (above), thrive in the heat from deep-sea
vents. Even more bizarrely, rocks deep in
the Earth's crust now seem to be packed
with bacteria that thrive far away
from both light and water.

Life on Earth
In 1953, scientists at the
University of Chicago mixed
methane, ammonia, hydrogen,
and water vapour, and passed high-
voltage sparks through it to simulate
lightning. The chemicals formed amino
acids – the building blocks of proteins upon
which all life depends. This may have been
the same reaction that sparked life on Earth.

Possible origins
Life on Earth took several billion years to develop.
For most of its history, it was no more complex than
these stromatolites – mats of fossilised algae (left) found
at Shark Bay, Australia. They are among the oldest organic
remains to have been found on Earth, ranging from
2,000–3,000 million years old. The long road to complex
life may have begun in the primordial seas, triggered by
lightning, or around deep-sea vents. According to the
"panspermia" theory, simple organisms might even have
originated in space and been carried to Earth in comets.

LIFE ELSEWHERE

The two greatest prospects for life elsewhere in the Solar System are Mars and Jupiter's moon, Europa. Mars sits just beyond the edge of the Solar System's habitable zone, and was much warmer and wetter in its past. Europa almost certainly has a deep ocean beneath its frozen crust. While Europa's mysteries are currently sealed from our view, several spacecraft have visited Mars. The *Viking* Lander (right) carried out experiments to test for life on Mars in 1976 . The results of these experiments were not conclusive.

The Mars
Viking Lander

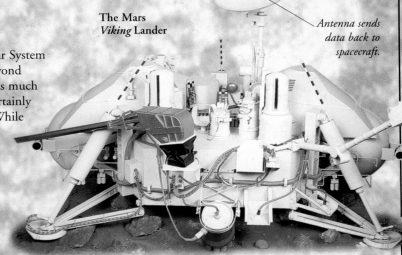

Antenna sends data back to spacecraft.

Life on Mars
In 1996, NASA scientists announced that they had found evidence for life in a meteorite from Mars. Scientists are still debating whether this rock really contains microscopic fossils and chemicals released by ancient bacteria. However, new evidence that liquid water could be present beneath the Martian surface leaves the possibility of simple life wide open (p. 77).

Moons of Jupiter
Beneath Europa's icy crust, the moon is heated by strong tides from Jupiter, probably allowing a liquid ocean to exist. NASA hopes eventually to send a probe to penetrate the ice and explore this ocean (left). Perhaps it will find life clustered around deep-sea vents like Earth's. Recent discoveries by the *Galileo* spacecraft suggest that two of Jupiter's other moons, Callisto and Ganymede, could also have subsurface oceans (p. 80).

LET'S EXPERIMENT
TESTING FOR LIFE

THE *VIKING* LANDER on Mars looked for signs of life by taking samples of frozen soil and feeding them with nutrients. This experiment shows how their tests worked, and how you can distinguish between simple chemical reactions and signs of life. You will need: 3 coloured labels; 3 glasses; clean sand; teaspoon; salt; baking powder; yeast; sugar; jug; warm water.

1 Stick a different coloured label on each glass to identify the contents, then fill the glasses one-third full of sand. Mix two teaspoons of salt into one glass, two teaspoons of baking powder into the second, and two teaspoons of yeast into the third. Put them all in the fridge overnight to cool.

2 Next day, dissolve half a cup of sugar in a jug containing two cups of warm water to make a nutrient solution. Pour equal amounts into each glass. Some minerals (salt) do not react, but others (baking powder) give short-lived chemical reactions. Biological reactions involving living cells (yeast) are less vigorous but will last longer.

Above: Electron microscope image of so-called "fossil bacteria" in the Martian meteorite ALH84001

Salt

Baking powder

Yeast

THE PLANETS

Picture: *The five naked-eye planets – Mercury, Venus, Mars, Saturn, and Jupiter – stretch out in a rare alignment, 24 April 2002.*

FAMILY OF PLANETS

THE NINE PLANETS, together with their satellites, are the largest members of the Solar System. Each is a world in itself, and while there are some similarities between them, each planet also has unique features not found anywhere else in the Solar System. Our understanding of these worlds has been transformed by the space age, with orbiting telescopes providing spectacular views, and automated spacecraft returning images and other data directly from the planets and their moons.

MERCURY AND VENUS

Mercury is the nearest planet to the Sun, followed by Venus. Both planets orbit the Sun faster than Earth. Mercury is too small to be seen clearly by Earth-based telescopes, and the difficulty in catching up with its high-speed orbit means it has only been visited by one spacecraft and only half of its surface has been mapped. Venus rotates in the opposite direction to most planets. Its hostile atmosphere causes a runaway greenhouse effect that makes the planet too hot to explore easily. The most successful missions have used space probes equipped with radar, and heavily-shielded landers.

EARTH AND MARS

Our world, Earth, is the third planet from the Sun. It has a large satellite, the Moon, that is way out of proportion to Earth's size. Some astronomers even consider Earth and its Moon a double planet. They are certainly the most intensively studied worlds in the Solar System. Hundreds of satellites have been launched to observe Earth from orbit. Dozens of robotic probes have explored the Moon, and of course, astronauts have also travelled there.

Mars, the next planet out, is most similar to Earth. Often called the Red Planet due to its colour, Mars has been explored in more depth than any other planet except Earth. It has been mapped in detail from orbit, and landers have even tested its soil for signs of life. The space age has dramatically changed our image of Mars. The possibility that there could be life on Mars was once considered science fiction. However, recent explorations reveal an active, changing world with plentiful frozen water beneath the surface, making life on Mars a realistic possibility.

JUPITER AND SATURN

Jupiter and Saturn are the two largest planets in the Solar System, and they have many similarities. Both planets have ring systems – Saturn's rings are its most visible feature – and both spin at high speeds, causing their equators to bulge. Jupiter and Saturn both have large families of moons, and both experience violent storms – the Great Red Spot on Jupiter is a storm system larger than Earth.

Because the giant planets are so far away, and separated even from each other by a vast distance, sending robotic spacecraft is particularly difficult. Much of our information about these planets comes from missions that took advantage of a unique alignment of the outer planets during the 1970s and 1980s.

The nine planets of the Solar System, in order of their distance from the Sun

Mercury

Venus

Earth

Mars

Jupiter

1957 Launch of *Sputnik*, first artificial satellite from Earth, and start of the "Space Race".

1959 *Luna* probes fly to the Moon. *Luna 3* flies past the far side of the Moon.

1962 *Mariner 2* flies past Venus.

1965 *Mariner 4* sends back first close up photos of Mars.

1969 *Apollo* spacecraft lands astronauts on the Moon.

1970 *Venera 7* probe lands on Venus.

1973 *Pioneer 10* reaches Jupiter.

1974 *Mariner 10* flies past Mercury.

1976 *Viking* probes land on Mars.

During this alignment, two "Grand Tour" spacecraft travelled between the outer planets using the planets' own gravity to change orbits and boost speed. Since the planets moved out of alignment in the late 1980s, most missions now focus on individual planets. Recently, the *Galileo* spacecraft studied Jupiter, and *Cassini* will orbit Saturn in 2004.

URANUS AND NEPTUNE

Uranus and Neptune are also giant planets, but they are further from the Sun than Jupiter and Saturn, and much smaller. Sometimes called ice giants, Uranus and Neptune both contain chemicals that give them a distinct turquoise colour. Neptune is a particularly vivid shade of blue-green, and it is also a more stormy planet than quiet Uranus. Both planets spin more slowly than the bigger giants. But like their larger cousins, Uranus and Neptune have rings and large families of moons. Neptune's largest moon, Triton, revolves around the planet in the opposite direction to Neptune's other moons, making it something of an astronomical mystery.

Much of our information about Uranus and Neptune comes from the *Voyager 2* spacecraft. This was the only mission to fulfil the complete Grand Tour, flying on from Saturn to intercept Uranus in 1986 and Neptune in 1989. Technological advances in orbiting and in Earth-based telescopes mean that we can continue to learn about these faraway planets without leaving Earth.

Earth's only natural satellite, the Moon

TINY PLUTO

Beyond Neptune orbits Pluto, in a tilted, oval-shaped path that usually makes it the furthest planet from the Sun. Pluto is also the smallest planet – even our Moon is bigger. Pluto is actually a large member of the Edgeworth-Kuiper Belt, a family of icy bodies located around and beyond this frozen world. Some astronomers believe that Pluto is too small and insignificant to be considered a planet. In the next few years, astronomers hope to send a space mission to observe Pluto, its moon Charon, and the Edgeworth-Kuiper Belt. In the meantime, using distant images from the Hubble Space Telescope, astronomers have created basic maps of Pluto's surface.

Saturn

Uranus

Neptune

Pluto

1977 *Voyager 1 and 2 begin Grand Tour of outer Solar System.*

1979 *Pioneer 11 reaches Saturn. Voyager probes find rings around Jupiter and volcanic activity on Jupiter's moon, Io.*

1980 *Voyager 1 flies past Saturn's moon, Titan.*

1986 *Voyager 2 flies past Uranus.*

1989 *Voyager 2 flies past Neptune.*

1990 *Magellan probe begins mapping Venus.*

1995 *Galileo probe goes into orbit around Jupiter.*

1997 *Pathfinder lands on Mars with Sojourner Rover, which explores surface of Mars. Cassini probe launches on 7-year flight to Saturn.*

MERCURY

AS THE PLANET NEAREST TO THE SUN, dry, rocky Mercury is roasted by solar radiation. This little world – the second smallest in the Solar System – hurtles around the Sun faster than any other planet, but spins very slowly on its axis. Mercury has a vast iron core that makes it heavy for its size, but the planet is too small to hold on to a substantial atmosphere. This exposes the surface to extreme temperature changes between day and night. Lack of atmosphere also leaves Mercury unprotected against impacts from space, and the result is a heavily scarred, cratered world.

SPEEDING ORBIT

Mercury's rapid orbit takes it around the Sun in just 88 Earth days, giving it the shortest year in the Solar System. However, the force of the Sun's gravity has slowed the planet's spin so much that one day on Mercury lasts for 58 Earth days – two-thirds of its year. As a result, most of the surface has a year of daylight followed by a year of darkness. The long day, combined with the fast, elliptical orbit has another strange effect. Some parts of the planet experience a double sunrise. The Sun appears to rise at dawn, dip below the horizon, then rise again.

Spins on its axis every 58 Earth days, 14 hours

4

8

Distance from Sun varies from 46 million km (28.6 million miles) to 69.8 million km (43.4 million miles)

1 5

7 3

Red spot marked on Mercury in this diagram acts as a point of reference

6

2

Mercury's orbit is shown here as an overhead view.

Orbit puzzle

Mercury's orbit is unusual because it turns – the outermost point slowly makes its own circular path around the Sun. This effect is mainly caused by the pull of the other planets on Mercury, but a small part cannot be accounted for by Newton's theory of gravity. It was eventually explained by the physicist Albert Einstein, who showed how space near Mercury is warped by the Sun's gravity.

LET'S EXPERIMENT
MERCURY'S DAY

THIS EXPERIMENT SHOWS how Mercury's rotation and orbit combine to give it a day that is two years long. **You will need:** an adult to help you; foamboard; scissors; elastic band; polystyrene ball; map pin; glue; light bulb and holder; 9-volt battery.

1 Cut three circles of foam board – 20 cm (8 in), 6 cm (2 in), and 3 cm (1 in) across. Create a groove around the edges of the two smaller circles with a smooth thin edge such as a pencil. These will act like the gears on a bicycle.

2 Cut a hole in the middle of the large circle so that the lightbulb and holder can fit through and rotate freely. Cut a similar hole in the smallest circle, but make this one a tight fit. Now push the holder through the larger circle and glue the smaller circle onto it.

3 Push a pin up through the large circle 6 cm (2 in) from the centre, and then push the 6-cm (2 in) circle down on the centre of it. Push the polystyrene ball onto the pin and glue it in place – this represents Mercury.

4 Stretch the elastic band around the two gears, connect the light to a battery (this represents the Sun), and darken the room to give Mercury a night and day side. By turning the large circle you should find that Mercury rotates as it orbits. Stick a map pin into the planet to mark a single point, and watch how long it takes for this point to move from one "sunrise" to the next.

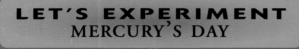

Sun

Mercury

SURFACE FEATURES

Most of Mercury's craters were formed by comet impacts. Near the planet's poles, some of the craters' basins are kept permanently in shadow. Astronomers think that these might shelter reserves of ice. The planet's most unique features are its towering cliffs, called scarps. The scarps wind their way across the landscape, often cutting craters in half. It seems that Mercury expanded and shrank again after most of its craters had formed. This would have caused areas of the crust to split apart and drop down below, or pop up above their neighbours.

Caloris Basin

The largest feature on Mercury is the enormous Caloris Basin. This is the result of an impact so big that it formed a crater measuring a monstrous 1,340 km (840 miles) across. Many of Mercury's hills and mountain ranges are arranged in rings and rays related to the centre of the basin. The shock from the impact even rippled all the way around the planet, churning up the landscape on the other side to form so-called "weird terrain".

Crust

Rocky mantle

Heavy iron core

Inside Mercury

The shapes of Mercury's craters suggest that the planet has strong gravity for its size. Material flung out during meteorite impacts did not travel as far as material flung out on a world such as the Moon. In fact, Mercury is denser than any other world in the Solar System. Astronomers think it has an unusually large iron core, and that an impact early in its history knocked away much of the planet's outer mantle and crust.

SKYWATCHING
GLIMPSING MERCURY

OF THE FIVE planets visible to the naked eye, Mercury can be most difficult to spot because it is always close to the Sun. Even at maximum distance from the Sun ("elongation"), it only rises an hour before or sets an hour after the Sun, so it is often lost in twilight. During maximum elongation, Mercury can be glimpsed before dawn or after sunset in a near-dark sky.

Mercury (ringed) is the lowest of the three bright star-like objects seen at sunset.

VENUS

A PLANET ALMOST THE same size as Earth, Venus lies just a little closer to the Sun. This world is the nearest thing to hell in the Solar System. Thick, poisonous clouds cover the surface, where the temperature is high enough to melt lead. The planet's atmospheric pressure is 92 times greater than Earth's – a visiting human would be crushed in seconds. Venus also rotates in the opposite direction to most planets, and at a much slower rate. It takes 243 Earth days to rotate just once, but 225 Earth days to orbit the Sun. This means a day on Venus lasts longer than its year.

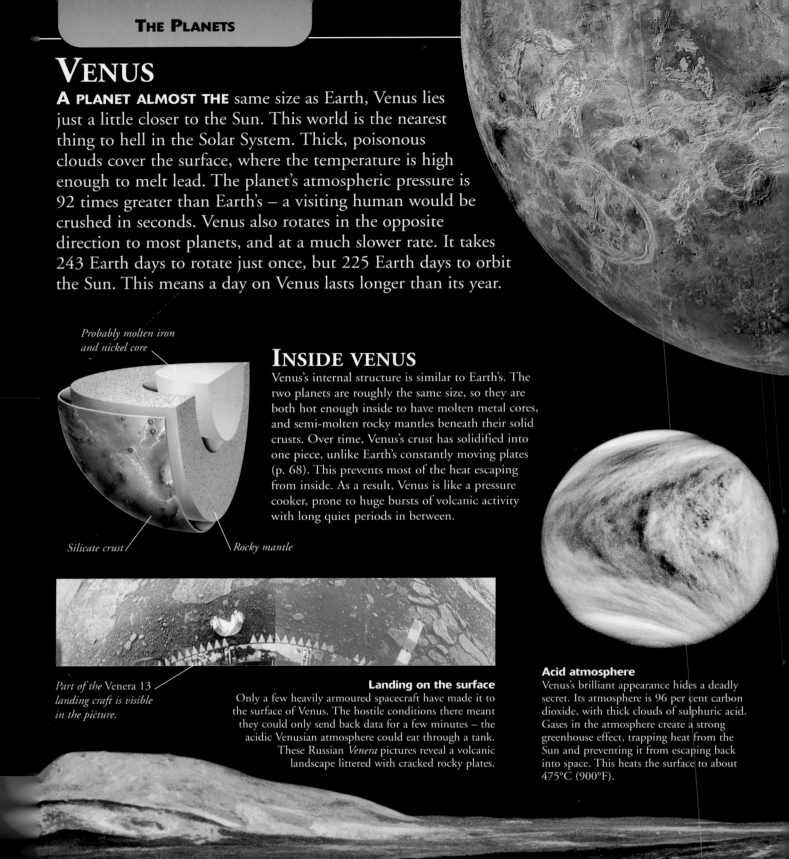

Probably molten iron and nickel core

INSIDE VENUS

Venus's internal structure is similar to Earth's. The two planets are roughly the same size, so they are both hot enough inside to have molten metal cores, and semi-molten rocky mantles beneath their solid crusts. Over time, Venus's crust has solidified into one piece, unlike Earth's constantly moving plates (p. 68). This prevents most of the heat escaping from inside. As a result, Venus is like a pressure cooker, prone to huge bursts of volcanic activity with long quiet periods in between.

Silicate crust

Rocky mantle

Part of the Venera 13 *landing craft is visible in the picture.*

Landing on the surface
Only a few heavily armoured spacecraft have made it to the surface of Venus. The hostile conditions there meant they could only send back data for a few minutes – the acidic Venusian atmosphere could eat through a tank. These Russian *Venera* pictures reveal a volcanic landscape littered with cracked rocky plates.

Acid atmosphere
Venus's brilliant appearance hides a deadly secret. Its atmosphere is 96 per cent carbon dioxide, with thick clouds of sulphuric acid. Gases in the atmosphere create a strong greenhouse effect, trapping heat from the Sun and preventing it from escaping back into space. This heats the surface to about 475°C (900°F).

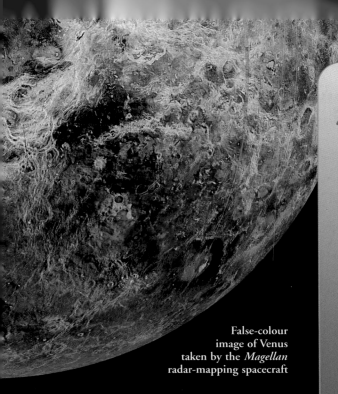

False-colour image of Venus taken by the *Magellan* radar-mapping spacecraft

BENEATH THE VEIL

Scientists can only peer through Venus's clouds using radar. Radio waves bounce back from the planet to an orbiting space probe and reveal information about the surface, such as its height and texture. Radar maps of Venus show that it is a world of deep canyons and high volcanic mountains. Venus has very few craters, but is covered in solidified lava flows. It seems that most of the planet was resurfaced during violent volcanic eruptions about 500 million years ago.

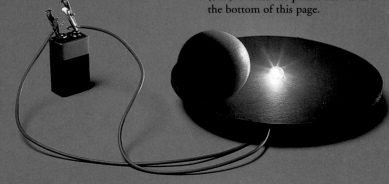
Venusian volcanoes

Venus is scattered with mountainous volcanoes such as Gula Mons (right). Some, like Maxwell Montes, are higher than Earth's Mount Everest. No-one knows whether these volcanoes are active today. However, space probes falling through the atmosphere have detected fierce lightning storms above the summits, similar to those that occur above Earth's active volcanoes. As many as 25 lightning bolts strike every second.

False-colour image of the volcanic mountain Gula Mons

EARTH

OUR HOME WORLD – the third "rock" from the Sun – is unique in the Solar System. Earth is the only planet known to support life, and there are good reasons for this. Its location is just near enough to the Sun to give it a stable, temperate climate – neither too hot nor too cold. Also, strong gravity means that the planet can hold on to a protective atmosphere. Crucially, Earth is the only planet with plentiful liquid surface water and an atmosphere rich in oxygen and nitrogen. This combination allows about 30 million different species of life to thrive.

Earth spins on its axis once every 23 hours, 56 minutes. We round this off to a 24-hour day.

Sun

Earth orbits the Sun once every 365.25 days, a length of time known as a year.

Earth's axis is tilted at 23.5 degrees.

EARTH IN ORBIT

Our planet Earth rotates on its axis once a day, and orbits the Sun once a year at a distance of about 150 million km (93 million miles). From the surface of the planet, the sky appears to spin around the Earth once every day, while the Sun seems to move around the sky against the background stars once a year. Although close to a perfect circle, Earth's orbit is in fact elliptical (oval). This means it is 5 million km (3 million miles) closer to the Sun in January than in July.

Midday in northern midwinter: The Sun is low in the sky and has little heating effect.

Midday in northern midsummer: The Sun is high in the sky and creates hot weather.

Sun

Seasons in the Northern Hemisphere

The seasons

Earth tilts on its axis at 23.5 degrees as it orbits the Sun. This means that each pole is sometimes tilted more towards the Sun, and at other times tilted away. This affects the length of time the Sun spends above the horizon at any location, the height it reaches in the sky at midday, and the amount of heat and light that location receives. It is these factors that create the seasons.

The habitable zone

Earth's orbit puts it right in the middle of the Solar System's "habitable zone", where liquid water can exist on the surface of a suitable planet. The presence of large amounts of water on the surface makes life on Earth possible, and shapes many of its surface features. Temperature is also an important factor. Whereas Mercury is far too hot and Neptune is far too cold, our planet Earth has the perfect temperature for life to thrive.

‹ EARTH'S SATELLITE ›

The Moon has been orbiting Earth for some 4.5 billion years. Its large size and proximity to Earth mean that it has some important effects on its parent planet. The Moon causes strong tides in Earth's oceans, and may even protect us from impacts from space.

The Moon, seen from space

70 ▶

CLIMATE CONTROL

Although Earth lies in the habitable zone, life here would still be impossible if it weren't for the atmosphere and oceans. These hold on to heat, keeping the planet cool in daytime and warm at night. They also circulate heat from the warm Equator, which receives the most sunlight, to the poles, which receive the least. These warm and cool areas are marked red and blue on the map above. Earth's atmosphere and oceans ensure that temperatures vary by no more than about 100°C (180°F) anywhere on the planet. Compare this with the airless Moon, where temperatures can vary by an extreme 300°C (540°F).

Atmosphere for life

Earth's atmosphere is made up of nitrogen and oxygen, with a small but vital amount of carbon dioxide. Oxygen allows humans and animals to breathe. It also forms an ozone layer that protects us against radiation from space. Carbon dioxide allows plants to survive and generate oxygen. Water from the oceans evaporates into the atmosphere, where the vapour forms clouds. It falls back to Earth as rain and snow. The balance between all these gases is incredibly delicate.

INVENTED BY FRENCH physicist Jean Foucault in 1851, Foucault's pendulum is a clever way of proving that Earth is spinning. It is simply a pendulum with a very long, slow swing, which stays in the same place while Earth rotates beneath it. **The demonstrator will need:** large plastic bottle with cap; hand drill; 2 hookeye screws; sand; funnel; string; plank of wood; modelling clay; short pencil; card.

1 Drill a small hole in the bottle cap, and screw a hookeye into it. Give it a tug to make sure it is secure. Pour sand through the funnel into the bottle until it is two-thirds full. Screw the cap on tightly and check the hookeye can bear the bottle's weight.

2 Fix a plank with another hookeye in place at the top of a drop of more than 5 m (15 ft) – for example, at the top of a stairwell. Thread the string securely through the hookeye at the top then tie it to the bottle at the bottom of the drop. Fix the short pencil to the bottom of the bottle with modelling clay to make a pointer.

3 Set your pendulum moving in a wide swing. Watch the pencil mark the direction of the swing on a large piece of card placed under the bottle. Keep checking the marks on the card every 20 minutes. The pendulum's direction should gradually change as Earth rotates beneath it.

INSIDE EARTH

EARTH IS ONE OF THE MOST geologically active planets in the Solar System. Ours is a restless world – intense heat generated in Earth's core is carried upwards where it disturbs the rocky surface continents, causing them to shift around. This movement, known as continental drift, is constantly shaping Earth's features. The segments that make up the continents, called tectonic plates, are crunching together, to form mountain ranges, or splitting apart, to cause great rifts in the crust. Weather and water are also major movers and shakers – they carve out coastlines and erode rocks to form sediment, which helps carbonate minerals to form.

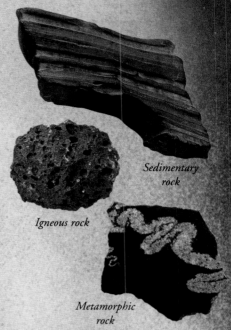

Sedimentary rock

Igneous rock

Metamorphic rock

EARTH'S STRUCTURE

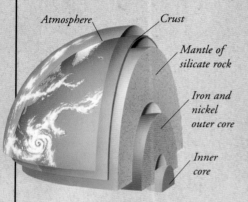

Atmosphere
Crust
Mantle of silicate rock
Iron and nickel outer core
Inner core

Beneath a solid crust, Earth's interior is kept mostly molten by heat trapped during its creation, and energy given off by radioactive elements deep inside the planet. Just under the crust lies a layer of molten rock called the mantle. This surrounds the planet's core, which is mostly made of iron and nickel. The outer layers of the core are molten metal, and spin to generate Earth's magnetic field. The inner core has probably solidified under the immense pressure.

Rock cycle
Earth's crust consists of three types of rock – igneous, sedimentary, and metamorphic. Igneous rocks are spewed out as molten lava by volcanoes, and then set solid. When eroded by water or air, they turn into particles that settle in layers. These layers are then compressed into sedimentary rocks. If sedimentary rocks are heated and compressed enough, they can melt again, forming metamorphic rock.

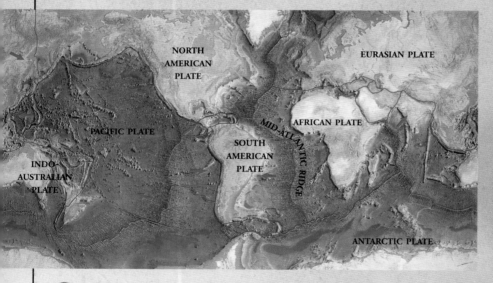

NORTH AMERICAN PLATE

EURASIAN PLATE

MID-ATLANTIC RIDGE

AFRICAN PLATE

PACIFIC PLATE

SOUTH AMERICAN PLATE

INDO-AUSTRALIAN PLATE

ANTARCTIC PLATE

Alfred Wegener
The idea of continental drift was first described in 1915 by German geophysicist Alfred Wegener (1880–1930). He had noticed how the coastlines of widely separated continents – such as Africa and South America – seemed to match up with each other. Wegener suggested that some 200 million years ago, the continents were all joined together in one giant landmass called Pangaea. In 1915, his ideas were ridiculed, but today geologists have found firm evidence to prove that the continents did indeed drift apart.

CONTINENTS ON THE MOVE

Unlike Venus, Earth's crust is not a single solid shell – it is split into some large tectonic plates and many smaller ones. Some of the lower, thinner, and younger plates consist entirely of ocean floor. Others are larger and thicker, and include continents, seen in the map above. The plates float on Earth's molten, semi-liquid mantle. As they move, the continents are carried with them and the seas change shape. The plate boundaries are often areas of intense volcanic and seismic activity, marked by deep rifts, strings of volcanoes, and long, winding ridges. Fortunately for us, continental drift is very slow – plates move at a rate of about 1 cm (0.5 in) each year.

RESTLESS EARTH

Earth has more than 1,000 active land volcanoes, and many more under the sea. Volcanoes are fissures (vents or holes) in Earth's crust that allow molten rock to rise from the hot interior and spill onto the surface. Where Earth's plates pull apart, new crust is created as lava emerges to fill the gaps. Where plates collide, long belts of volcanoes form as one plate sinks and melts. Places where plates grind past each other are earthquake zones. Volcanoes and earthquakes are violent reminders that the plates never stop moving.

Separating plates

Most of the areas where plates are separating lie beneath the sea, but in a few areas they cross over land. A good example of this is the Mid-Atlantic ridge at Thingvellir, Iceland (above). Here, you can clearly see the dramatic split between the North American plate on the left and the Eurasian plate on the right. Where the plates have moved apart, the crust between them has collapsed, forming a steep-sided rift valley. The region is very active volcanically.

Making mountains

Where plates collide, they push up mountains or create volcanoes. The Himalayas (left, seen from space), are still crumpling upwards from a collision that began 50 million years ago, when the Indian plate slammed into Asia. In other areas, plates are pushed (subducted) beneath higher continents. As the subducted plate melts, the lava escapes through volcanoes along the rim of the overlying plate.

LET'S EXPERIMENT
CONVECTION CURRENTS

PLATE TECTONICS HAPPEN because Earth's mantle is in constant motion, carrying heat from around the molten core out towards the cooler crust. The upward motion of fluids carrying heat is called convection. This experiment shows convection in action. **You will need:** an adult to help you; 2 wooden blocks; tealight candle; heatproof glass bowl; cooking oil; dropper; food colouring.

1 Place a tealight candle between two wooden blocks, leaving a little space on either side of the candle. Ask an adult to light the candle. Half fill the bowl with cooking oil and stand it firmly over the blocks. With the dropper, squeeze a few drops of food colouring into the bowl.

2 As the oil at the bottom heats up, it becomes less dense, rising through the heavier, cooler oil and carrying food colouring with it. As it loses heat at the surface, the coloured oil is pushed aside by new oil from below, and sinks back down. In a similar way, convection keeps the tectonic plates in constant motion.

THE MOON

IN OUR ORBIT AROUND THE SUN, we are accompanied by the Moon, Earth's lone satellite. The Moon is unusual among the Solar System's satellites because it is so large in proportion to its planet. At 3,475 km (2,159 miles) in diameter, it is more than a quarter the size of Earth, making it the dominant object in our night sky. Over billions of years, Earth's gravitational pull has slowed the Moon's rotation so that now one side is permanently locked facing Earth. Because the Moon is so large and relatively close, it has some powerful effects on our planet.

ORBIT AND PHASES

The Moon orbits Earth once every 27.3 days, and always has the same face turned towards us. Its average distance from Earth is about 384,000 km (239,000 miles). The Moon has no light of its own, but shines through reflected light from the Sun. During its orbit around Earth, the Moon's disc seems to assume different shapes. These are known as phases, and a complete cycle takes 29.5 days. A New Moon is between us and the Sun – sunlight falls on the Moon's far side, so we cannot see it. A Full Moon is when the Moon is exactly opposite the Sun, and all the sunlight falls on its Earth-turned side.

The Sun's corona is visible during a total eclipse.

8. Crescent
A thin sliver is visible. The Moon has nearly waned.

7. Last Quarter
Half the Moon is visible. A quarter of the cycle remains.

6. Gibbous
The Moon is said to be waning, or shrinking.

5. Full Moon
The Moon faces directly towards the Sun.

Orbital path of the Moon

View of the Moon from Earth

Earth

1. New Moon
The Moon's face points towards the Sun and cannot be seen from Earth.

2. Crescent
The Moon is said to be waxing, or growing.

3. First Quarter
The Moon has completed a quarter of its orbit.

4. Gibbous
The Moon is said to be waxing gibbous.

High tide

Tidal pull of the Moon
As the Moon's gravity pulls upon Earth, it causes the water in the oceans to bulge out on the side facing the Moon. This leaves an equal bulge on the opposite side of the planet, where the pull of the Moon's gravity is weaker. As the Earth rotates each day, these bulges stay in the same place, causing the sea level to rise as we pass under each bulge (high tide), and fall when we are between bulges (low tide). The Bay of Fundy, Newfoundland (left and right), experiences dramatic high and low tides.

Low tide

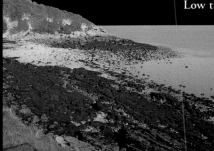

ECLIPSES

By a strange coincidence, the Sun and Moon appear to be the same size in the sky. The Moon is roughly 400 times smaller than the Sun, but also 400 times closer to Earth. When the Moon occasionally passes across the Sun, in a solar eclipse, it can cover the brilliant disc completely, revealing the Sun's faint outer layers. Similarly, the Earth can sometimes cast its shadow over the Moon, causing a lunar eclipse. Eclipses do not happen every month because the Moon's orbit is tilted at an angle to the Sun's path around the sky, and so it normally passes above or below the Sun.

The Sun's light travels towards Earth.

The Moon moves between the Earth and the Sun.

The centre of the Moon's shadow causes a total solar eclipse.

Solar eclipse

Solar eclipses can be total or partial. In a total eclipse, the Moon blocks out the Sun perfectly. But its shadow covers only a tiny area of Earth's surface (diagram, right). The surrounding regions, where the Sun and Moon are not quite aligned, see a partial eclipse, as the Moon appears to take a bite out of the Sun.

The Sun's light travels towards Earth.

Half of Earth is in daylight. The night side is in shadow.

The Moon moves into Earth's shadow. A lunar eclipse occurs.

Lunar eclipse

In a lunar eclipse, Earth casts its shadow on the Moon. Lunar eclipses can be seen from anywhere on Earth where the Full Moon appears above the horizon. Often, the Moon does not disappear completely, because Earth's atmosphere acts like a lens and bends some reddish-coloured sunlight towards it.

The Moon has a reddish glow during a lunar eclipse.

LET'S EXPERIMENT
LUNAR ECLIPSE

Only red light illuminates the Moon during a lunar eclipse. This is because Earth's atmosphere scatters light, splitting it into separate colours. Blue light scatters sideways, making the sky blue. Red scatters the least, and reaches the Moon to give it a pink glow. **You will need:** Two different-sized globes or balls; desk lamp; clear plastic bottle; water; teaspoon of milk.

1 Line up the two globes and the lamp at equal distances from each other, so that the larger globe (representing Earth) is between the smaller globe (the Moon) and the lamp (the Sun). Darken the room, turn on the lamp and shine the "Sun's" light on "Earth". The "Moon" will be hidden in "Earth's" shadow.

2 Now mix an "atmosphere" of 1 teaspoon of milk in a clear plastic bottle full of water. The milk suspended in water will affect light in the same way as the gases in Earth's atmosphere. The atmosphere causes sunlight to bend and scatter.

3 Put the "atmosphere" in place by holding the bottle above "Earth". What happens to the Moon? You'll find that it has a dim, pinkish glow, as in a lunar eclipse.

THE LUNAR WORLD

OUR MOON IS A WORLD in its own right – larger than Pluto and almost the same size as Mercury. It is close enough to Earth for us to see its dark- and light-coloured features, even with the naked eye, and remains the only celestial body to have been visited by astronauts. The world they landed on is barren and cratered, lacking any atmosphere or liquid water. Heavily scarred mountain ranges surround wide "seas" covered in rock and grey dust. But even the variations in the Moon's greyness, and the craters themselves, have revealed a great deal about the Moon's history.

Rocky mantle *Partly molten outer core* *Possibly solid inner core*

INSIDE THE MOON

Like Earth, the Moon is a solid, rocky world. Because it is much smaller and has less mass than Earth, it has cooled down more rapidly. The Moon, therefore, has a thicker crust and mantle, and a smaller, probably solidified core – if one exists at all. Earth's gravity pulled the core and mantle closer to the surface on the lunar near side, which made it more volcanically active than the far side.

Crust of granite-like rock

Ejected material clumped together to form the Moon.

Origin of the Moon

The usual theories for how satellites are formed don't apply to our Moon. It is too large a world to have been born from the debris left over after Earth was formed, and also too large simply to have been a passing body captured by Earth's gravity. Moon rocks provide the clue to our satellite's origins. They seem to contain pieces of our own planet and of another world. According to the "big splash" theory, an object about the size of Mars travelling at high speed must have collided with the young Earth, as in the artist's impression above. Molten material from the two bodies splashed out into space. This then clumped together in orbit to form the Moon.

SKYWATCHING
LUNAR FEATURES

THE BEST WAY to study the Moon's surface is with a pair of binoculars or an ordinary telescope. These will reveal individual craters and mountain ranges. Because the Moon's features are most visible when they are casting shadows, it is best to look at them at an early or late phase in the lunar cycle – when the Moon is waxing or waning (p. 70). At these times, the line dividing the dark side from the lit side, known as the terminator, gives the best definition to the Moon's landscape.

REGOLITH

Because the Moon has no atmosphere to protect it, there is nothing to stop even the tiniest particle from space hitting the surface and making an impact crater. Billions of years of bombardment by meteorites have pounded the entire lunar surface into a loose collection of rocks and dust called the regolith. This extends down to a depth of about 100 m (330 ft), and is underlaid with a deeper layer of fractured rock formed by earlier, larger impacts. Despite this, the lunar surface is quite stable to walk on, as the *Apollo* astronauts, who took this picture, discovered.

HIGHLANDS AND MARIA

The Moon has two main types of terrain – the bright highlands and the dark grey plains, or maria (from the Latin for "seas"). Maria lie in the lowest basins on the near side of the Moon. They are made of basalt, an iron-rich volcanic rock, and are usually surrounded by mountains. The highlands are the oldest surviving parts of the Moon's crust, and are covered in craters from meteor impacts in the early days of the Solar System. The maria, which are quite smooth, must have formed after these bombardments had ended. In places maria cover the more ancient craters, which shows that they are younger than the highlands.

Dark maria

Bright highlands

Lava erupts through fractures in the crust to form maria.

Lava seas
The maria formed when huge volcanic fissures opened up across the surface of the Moon more than 3 billion years ago. The lava flooded the basins left by meteor impacts, eventually solidifying to form dark, flat surfaces. In some places the maria are "wrinkled" where lava piled up as it washed across the surface.

Precious deposits
This false-colour map made by the *Galileo* spacecraft shows the various chemical and mineral deposits on the Moon. Deposits of precious metals, such as titanium, may one day make Moon-mining a commercial reality. Water ice (thought to lie hidden in shadowy craters near the lunar poles) would make a permanent lunar base much easier to sustain.

Instruments were left behind on the Moon to measure moonquakes.

Moonquakes
Today, the Moon is not quite a dead world, because Earth's tidal pull continues to cause quakes below the surface. A few astronomers have reported seeing orange and yellow smudges on the Moon – possibly underground gases escaping during moonquakes. Experiments carried out by astronauts included measuring the Moon's seismic activity (above).

MARS – THE RED PLANET

MARS, OUR SMALL NEIGHBOURING planet, has long fascinated astronomers. The fourth "rock" from the Sun is a distinctive red object in our night sky, with landscape features that can be seen from Earth. For centuries, observers have been intrigued by its shifting red sands and white, frozen poles. Although dry and cold, it is still the planet that most resembles Earth, and we may yet find simple, microbial life forms there. Mars has a 25-hour day, a tilt of 25 degrees, ice caps, and seasons.

The gash across the centre of the planet is a vast canyon called the Valles Marineris.

MARTIAN MOTION

Mars orbits beyond Earth in an elliptical orbit, its distance from the Sun varying greatly during each Martian year. Because Earth is closer to the Sun, it orbits faster than Mars. When the two planets line up on the same side of the Sun at "opposition", Mars's motion appears very odd for a few weeks. First it seems to drift backwards in the sky as Earth overtakes it, like the runner in the picture below. This is known as retrograde motion. Then it appears to move forwards again as Earth continues along its orbit (diagram, right).

These dark circles are massive volcanoes.

Apparent path of Mars

Outer runner moves backwards from viewpoint of faster runner on inside.

Inner runner overtakes outer runner.

Orbit of Mars

Sun

Orbit of Earth

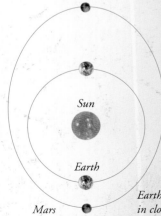

Earth and Mars are in distant opposition.

SKYWATCHING
MARS

MARS IS EASY to spot because of its colour. Seen from Earth, its brightness changes more than any other planet. When it is on the far side of the Sun from Earth, it is quite faint. However, Mars is one of the brightest objects in the sky when Earth and Mars pass near each other every two years. Because Mars's orbit is so elliptical, the distance between the two planets at "opposition" varies greatly (diagram, left). The closest opposition of 56 million km (35 million miles) occurs only rarely.

Sun

Earth

Mars

Earth and Mars are in close opposition.

At its brightest, Mars outshines Jupiter. Seen here at dusk, Mars is on the left, Jupiter is on the right.

RED TERRAIN

Through a telescope, Mars looks like a red disc marked with dark and light patches, some permanent, and some shifting. Until the space age, astronomers thought these might be signs of water or vegetation. Orbital photographs reveal that the northern hemisphere is covered by low flat plains, while in the south there are cratered highlands similar to those on our Moon. A huge bump, called the Tharsis Bulge, rises out of the northern hemisphere. It is capped with gigantic, extinct volcanoes, and bordered by a vast canyon system, many times larger than anything similar on Earth.

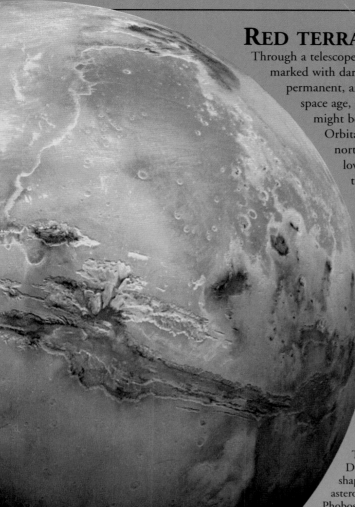

Deimos

Phobos

Martian moons

Two tiny moons, Phobos and Deimos, orbit Mars. These oddly shaped satellites are probably captured asteroids, just a few kilometres across. Phobos orbits at just 6,000 km (3,700 miles) above Mars, and is slowly spiralling in closer. Eventually it will break up and hit the planet.

Ice caps

Mars's most easily seen features are its polar caps, which grow and shrink with the seasons. The northern polar cap is mostly water ice, while the southern cap is largely frozen carbon dioxide. This image exaggerates the layered appearance of the poles.

Schiaparelli's map shows channels joining the dark plains.

Canals on Mars

In the late 1800s, many astronomers saw dark lines on the surface of Mars. An Italian astronomer called Giovanni Schiaparelli named them *canali*, which simply means channels, but a mistranslation meant that people thought of them as artificial canals built by Martians. We now know that the lines are an optical illusion, caused by the eye "joining up" the dark dots.

LET'S EXPERIMENT
MARTIAN DUST

MARS'S STRIKING colour is produced by the same chemical that makes rust red – iron oxide. Long ago, the planet may have had plentiful liquid water, which caused the iron to rust. In this experiment, you can turn sand into Martian dust. **You will need:** baking tray; sand; dishwashing gloves; scissors; wire wool; jug of water.

The wire wool has turned to red dust.

1 Fill half the baking tray with sand. Wearing gloves, cut the wire wool into 2.5-cm (1-in) pieces and mix them into the sand. Now pour in just enough water to cover the wire wool and the sand. Leave the dish in a safe place.

2 In order to rust, iron must be exposed to moisture and oxygen. The water will evaporate in a couple of days, so go on adding water to keep the mixture moist. After three days, see how red the sand has become.

THE MARTIAN SURFACE

SPACECRAFT MISSIONS TO MARS have revealed a freezing, barren place, without liquid water or vegetation. Earlier in its history, the planet may have been warm and wet, perhaps even with primitive life. Scientists are still unsure why it became the cold desert it is today. Mars is nevertheless an amazingly complex world, with some of the most spectacular "tourist attractions" in the Solar System – the largest volcanoes and canyons known to science, and polar ice caps that "smoke" when the frozen carbon dioxide melts in springtime.

Flow channels along the canyon walls are evidence of past liquid water.

INSIDE MARS

Mantle of silicate rock

Rock crust

Iron core

Mars has a simple internal structure, with a mantle of silicate rock surrounding a small iron core. Because Mars is smaller than Earth, it has cooled down more rapidly. Lava no longer erupts onto the surface, and its core has probably solidified. When Mars was still active, its volcanoes and volcanic flood plains grew to an enormous size because the planet has no moving crust. This meant that lava poured from the same areas over millions of years.

Martian sand dunes

The grandest canyon

A fault system of canyons known as Valles Marineris cuts a deep slash across the middle of Mars. This system is so long that it would stretch all the way across the United States. Its walls plunge to an average depth of 6 km (4 miles). The picture above shows a part of the canyon called the Ophir Chasm, which formed by a rifting (pulling apart) of the Martian crust.

MARTIAN PANORAMA

The Martian surface was formed in the distant past by meteorite bombardments, quakes, volcanic eruptions, and floods. Today, only wind and sand shape the terrain through weathering and erosion. This panorama, taken by NASA's *Mars Pathfinder,* shows a typical Martian landscape. Shattered rocks, perhaps dumped by a massive flood millions of years ago, are surrounded by a shifting sea of fine, red sand.

Mighty Olympus
Olympus Mons is the largest volcano in the Solar System. It is wider than England and rises 27 km (16 miles) above average ground level. The volcano is long extinct, but may have been less than impressive when active. The lava oozed out gently over time, slowly building up to the mountain's record-breaking height.

Olympus Mons compared to scale with Earth's Mount Everest

8,850 m
(29,035 ft)

27,000 m
(88,500 ft)

Primitive life may have begin in warm lakes.

The dusty air forms an orange haze.

RED SKIES
Mars has a thin atmosphere, mostly made of carbon dioxide. There is no breathable oxygen and no ozone layer, which means that the planet is exposed to dangerous ultraviolet radiation. However, clouds of carbon dioxide and water vapour regularly form, and high winds whip up dust devils similar to Earth's tornadoes. Martian skies have a pinkish tinge because of the fine red dust suspended in the atmosphere.

The oceans of Mars
Dried-up floodplains show that Mars must have had plentiful liquid water sometime in its past. Today, vast amounts of water lie frozen beneath the surface. It is intriguing to think that Mars may once have been covered by oceans. This image shows how Mars may have looked as it started to dry out and grow colder.

Perfect storm
Martian weather can become very active as the planet nears the Sun. Great storms whip the tiny dust particles into the air, and envelop the entire planet in a red shroud. Because Martian dust is so fine, it can stay in the atmosphere for weeks.

Mars before storm

Storm envelops entire planet.

Sand is very fine and powder-like.

Two low-lying hills named Twin Peaks

Solar panels

Aerial

Rock analyzer

Spiked wheels

The Pathfinder mission
Following the success of its 1976 *Viking* landings, NASA went on to exceed expectations with its 1997 *Mars Pathfinder* mission. *Mars Pathfinder* deployed a 60-cm (24-in) long robot buggy called *Sojourner* (left), which explored the nearby landscape, powered by solar panels on its back. *Sojourner* was fitted with an X-ray spectrometer – a "nose" that allowed it to "sniff" the rocks it came across and identify the chemicals within them. This was the first NASA mission to relay its results straight onto the world wide web.

JUPITER

WRACKED BY COLOURFUL STORMS wide enough to swallow Earth, Jupiter is the largest planet in the Solar System. It is separated from the inner planets by the asteroid belt, and has an orbit three times wider than that of Mars. Jupiter is also the fastest spinning planet – it completes a full rotation on its axis in less than ten hours. This causes its equator to bulge outwards and its clouds to wrap into swirling bands, giving the planet its distinctive patterned appearance.

Liquid hydrogen and helium

Atmosphere

INSIDE JUPITER

Although Jupiter is sometimes called a gas giant, only the outer 1,000 km (620 miles) or so is gas. Deeper inside the planet, enormous pressure from above turns the gases into liquid. Jupiter is mostly made up of the light element hydrogen. If you could travel into the planet, you would encounter seas of liquid hydrogen and helium, and a strange form of the element that behaves like liquid metal. At the centre there is a rocky core about the same size as Earth.

Metallic hydrogen

Possible solid core at centre

Jupiter's moon, Europa, casts a shadow on the planet.

SKYWATCHING
JUPITER AND ITS MOONS

BECAUSE JUPITER IS so huge and bright, it is quite easy to spot. With binoculars, it appears as a small disc. You may also be able see the planet's four brightest moons. In the picture above we can see Europa (nearest to Jupiter), Io (above Europa), and Ganymede (lower left). A small telescope can show the bands in its atmosphere and maybe even the Great Red Spot.

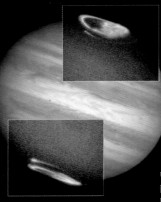

Auroras on Jupiter's north and south magnetic poles.

Jupiter's magnetism
The metallic hydrogen swirling deep inside Jupiter gives the planet a powerful magnetic field. The field streams away from the Sun just like Earth's magnetosphere (pp. 98–99), and can be detected as far away as Saturn. Jupiter's field sweeps up particles from the solar wind and pulls them down onto the planet's poles. This produces rings of auroral storms (left) where the particles collide with atmospheric gas.

STORM WORLD

Jupiter's upper atmosphere is a swirl of colossal storms. Varying colours of cloud appear at different levels in the atmosphere. These are created by chemicals condensing and forming ice crystals at different temperatures. Blue clouds lie deepest in the atmosphere, with dark brownish "belts" of ammonium hydrogen sulphide above them. The cream cloud bands, or "zones", are higher than the belts, and composed of ammonia crystals. Red features, such as the Great Red Spot, are highest of all and may get their colour from phosphor compounds.

Fireball created by the comet's impact

Deep impact

Jupiter's gravity is so great that it often draws in passing objects. This may play an important role in keeping the inner Solar System safe and protecting us from impacts. In 1994, Comet Shoemaker-Levy 9 smashed into Jupiter. The impact stirred up chemicals from deep within the planet and allowed astronomers to look at what lies beneath the clouds.

The Great Red Spot

Jupiter's most impressive feature is the Great Red Spot – a huge storm that has been raging for 200 years or more. Its red colouring comes from chemicals that only form high in the atmosphere. As on Earth, Jupiter's storms are low-pressure areas where the atmosphere bulges slightly outward. The Great Red Spot is 8 km (5 miles) higher than the surrounding clouds.

LET'S EXPERIMENT
CREATING A STORM

JUPITER'S STORMS, LIKE ANY weather system, are hard to understand and are constantly changing, affected by the turbulence of the planet's atmosphere. Sometimes the storms dwindle to nothing, sometimes they grow to enormous sizes by pulling in other storms from around them. This experiment shows you how to mimic Jupiter's storms.
You will need: bowl; full-fat milk; yellow and red food colouring; washing-up liquid.

1 Pour one cup of milk into a large bowl, then add one drop of each of the food colourings. Very gently swirl the bowl around to mimic the movement of Jupiter's atmosphere.

2 Now put one drop of washing-up liquid onto each of the drops of food colouring. Give the bowl another gentle spin and watch the storm brewing.

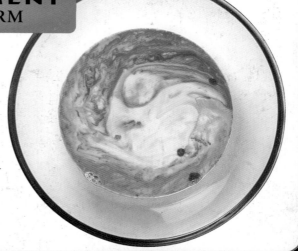

JUPITER'S MOONS

AT LEAST 39 MOONS orbit the planet Jupiter. Most of
the outer moons are tiny, dark, and have wildly irregular
orbits – a sure sign that they are captured asteroids. Only
the eight innermost moons were formed at the same time
as Jupiter. From Jupiter outwards, these are the tiny moons
Metis, Adrastea, Amalthea, and Thebe, followed by the
larger Europa, Io, Ganymede, and Callisto. The last four
were discovered by Galileo, and are the same size or bigger
than our own Moon. Each of these four "Galilean" moons
is a unique world in its own right.

*Io is the most
volcanically
active world in
the Solar System.*

CALLISTO AND GANYMEDE

The outer Galilean moons, Callisto and Ganymede,
are the largest – in fact Ganymede is the largest
moon in the Solar System. Both of them seem
to be made from a mixture of rock and ice,
separated into layers. Callisto is strewn
with craters, which reveal the brilliant
ice hidden beneath its dark surface.
Ganymede's lighter patches show where
an earlier bright surface melted, refroze,
and set into darker material. Intriguingly,
strong magnetic fields around these moons
indicate that both of them may have liquid
oceans of salty water beneath their surfaces.

*Callisto's dark
surface is covered
in bright, icy craters.*

LET'S EXPERIMENT
CALLISTO'S CRATERS

CALLISTO'S SURFACE IS FULL OF bright, rayed craters. These form when
meteorites strike the dark surface and throw out bright ice from the
layers below. The following experiment shows this process. **You will
need:** old newspaper; sieve; flour; cocoa
powder; stones or marbles.

1 Lay out a large area of old
newspaper on the floor. Sieve
flour onto the newspaper to form a
round, heaped mound. Sieve a thin
layer of cocoa powder over the top
so that all the flour is covered.

2 Stand at the edge of the mound
and drop a stone or marble
into the centre. The impact of your
"meteorite" forms a crater and shoots
out flour over the cocoa powder in rays.
Drop more "meteorites" to make your
own Callisto surface, full of rayed craters.

*Ganymede,
Jupiter's largest
moon, is almost the
size of Mercury.*

Io and Europa

The inner Galilean moons, Io and Europa, take the full force of Jupiter's gravitational pull. This tugs at different regions of the moons, pulls them out of shape, and heats them up. The result is two very different worlds. Io, the inner satellite, is a world of fierce volcanoes. Europa is almost its opposite. Its entire surface is a vast plain of brilliant ice, criss-crossed by cracks where the ice has melted and refrozen. Despite this, Europa may have much in common with Io. Astronomers have measured their masses and found that both moons are mostly rocky, unlike Ganymede and Callisto, which have far more ice.

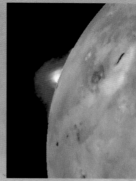
Loki is an active volcano on the surface of Io.

Volcano world

Io is so volcanically active that its entire surface can be reshaped in just decades. This activity was first discovered by the *Voyager 1* spacecraft that flew past Jupiter in 1979. *Voyager* revealed that Io had no impact craters, so its surface must be very young. The spacecraft also photographed geysers of molten sulphur spitting high into the sky. This sulphur, present in different chemical forms or "allotropes", gives Io its vibrant colours.

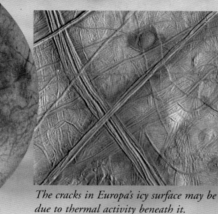
The cracks in Europa's icy surface may be due to thermal activity beneath it.

Europa may have a liquid ocean beneath its smooth surface.

Ocean world?

Europa is a smooth planet covered in pinkish ice. But the lines that cross its surface show that the planet is very active. The best explanation for these cracks is that a liquid water ocean lies beneath the icy crust, kept warm by tidal heating from Jupiter. As the tides cause Europa's crust to flex and crack, water gushes upwards, freezing when it is exposed to space, and healing the opening with fresh ice. Some astronomers think that Europa may have undersea volcanoes, similar to those on Earth.

LET'S EXPERIMENT
GANYMEDE'S FROZEN PLATES

GANYMEDE'S SURFACE CONSISTS OF OLDER terrain surrounded by younger icy regions. Astronomers think that large asteroid impacts may have punched through the ancient surface and allowed slushy ice to seep up through the cracks before the surface refroze completely. This experiment shows what the surface looks like now. **You will need:** water; shallow baking tray; freezer; food colouring; heat-resistant glass dish; wooden spoon.

1 Pour water into a baking tray and freeze it overnight. The following day, half-fill a dish with water, tinted with food colouring. Cool this dish in the freezer for about 10 minutes, then remove it.

2 Remove the baking tray from the freezer. Use a wooden spoon to smash the ice into jagged chunks. Tip the chunks into the coloured water and refreeze for about an hour. The jumbled plates surrounded by freshly formed ice resemble Ganymede's surface.

Galileo Galilei (1564–1642)

The four brightest moons of Jupiter were all discovered by Galileo Galilei, an Italian scientist. He was one of the first people to observe the skies with a telescope. His many discoveries, including these moons, led Galileo to realize that the planets orbited the Sun. This finding brought him into conflict with the Catholic Church, which taught that the heavenly bodies revolved around Earth.

SATURN

A SPECTACULAR GASSY WORLD, Saturn is the second largest planet in the Solar System. Its most famous feature is its ring system, which is more than twice the size of the planet itself. The main rings are very thin and bright and can be seen from Earth with a small telescope. Saturn is the most distant planet that can be seen with the naked eye and was known to ancient astronomers long before the invention of the telescope. The planet orbits the Sun with a family of at least 30 known satellites.

Saturn's rings are 100,000 km (62,000 miles) across, but less than 1 km (0.6 miles) thick.

RINGED PLANET

Saturn's rings change their appearance throughout the planet's 30-year orbit. Like Earth, Saturn is tilted on its axis, and our view of the rings depends on how they are tilted towards us. On opposite sides of the orbit, the rings are wide open, and we see them from high above or from below. At other times, the rings are edge-on to us, and almost seem to disappear. Saturn's 27-degree tilt causes seasons on the planet, just as Earth's tilt does (p. 66).

Hubble Space Telescope images of Saturn, captured between 1996 and 2000

Saturn has a bulging waistline due to its rapid rotation period of less than 11 hours.

Atmospheric planet
Saturn's high proportion of lightweight gases means that it has the lowest density of any planet in the Solar System. Although it contains almost the same chemicals as Jupiter, Saturn is far less colourful. Cream bands of cloud in various shades loop around the planet, driven by high-speed winds. In fact, Saturn's brighter colours are muted by a haze of white ammonia clouds. Such clouds only form on Saturn because its upper atmosphere is much colder than Jupiter's. This enables the ammonia to freeze into ice crystals.

Amazing rings
Saturn's brightest rings, shown in this false-colour picture, are made from ice boulders, ranging from 1 cm (0.4 in) to 10 m (33 ft) in size. They are broadly divided into the fainter C ring or Crepe ring (closest to the planet), and the brighter A and B rings, separated by the Cassini Division (p. 49). There are other rings both inside and outside this bright trio, but these are made of far smaller particles, and are much harder to see.

Viewed from Earth, Saturn's rings are seen at different angles depending on the time of year.

LET'S EXPERIMENT
SATURN'S BULGING EQUATOR

SATURN'S EQUATOR BULGES more than any other planet because of its rapid rotation and low gravity. This experiment shows why the equator tends to bulge.
You will need: scissors; ruler; coloured paper; drinking straws; tape; wooden stick; modelling clay; elastic band; pencil.

1 Cut 20 strips of coloured paper, each measuring 5 x 300 mm (1/4 x 12 in), plus two lengths of drinking straw 25 mm (1 in) long. Slide the lengths of straw onto each end of the stick, and tape each end of the paper strips to both straw sections.

2 Cover the tape on each straw with an additional strip of paper and check that the straws can move freely up and down the stick. Now put a large blob of modelling clay on the bottom of the stick. Tie an elastic band to the top of the stick, and attach a pencil to the free end of the band to make a handle.

3 Holding the model by the handle, twist the stick around a dozen or more times to wind up the elastic band. Let the stick go, and watch how your model planet spins and its waistline bulges. This is because the paper strips are trying to escape from the "planet" where they are most weakly held.

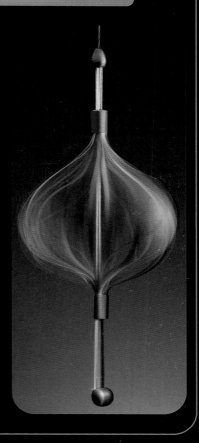

TITAN

Saturn's largest moon is Titan, one of the most mysterious worlds in the Solar System. It seems to be different from Saturn's other moons. It is the size of a small planet and shrouded beneath an orange chemical haze, with an atmosphere of nitrogen and methane gases. Below the haze, Titan is probably an icy world covered in slicks of oily hydrocarbon chemicals. During formation, its interior grew hot enough to melt, and volcanoes and geysers would have belched gases from the moon's interior. This has formed a primitive atmosphere that may resemble Earth's own early atmosphere. Our first proper look at the surface will come when the _Huygens_ probe (above) parachutes into Titan's atmosphere in 2005.

Christiaan Huygens (1629–95)
Dutch astronomer Christiaan Huygens discovered Saturn's giant moon, Titan, in 1655. He was also the first person to recognize the nature of Saturn's rings. Until Huygen's studies, the rings had been seen as mysterious bulges or "handles" attached to the planet. Huygens built the best telescopes of his age, and was also interested in other areas of science. His inventions included the pendulum clock.

Cosmic bullseye
Saturn has a total of at least 30 moons. Many of these are captured asteroids, but 17 are natural and formed with the planet itself. In general, they are icy worlds, sometimes with traces of ancient activity caused by tides from their giant parent planet. The innermost moon, named Mimas, suffered an enormous impact early in its history. It still bears the scar – an enormous crater covering one third of the planet's diameter (seen above).

URANUS

URANUS IS THE SEVENTH PLANET from the Sun. It lies roughly twice as far away as Saturn, circling the Sun once every 84 Earth years. Because of its distance from the Sun, the planet gets extremely cold. It was only discovered in 1781 by the German-born astronomer William Herschel, using one of the best telescopes of the time. Uranus is one of two small outer giants with a distinctive blue-green colour caused by the scattering of methane gas in its atmosphere. Compared to other giants, Uranus is a quiet world with few storms.

WORLD ON ITS SIDE

As Uranus orbits the Sun, it is tilted at a 98-degree angle – and literally rolls around its orbit. This odd tilt, probably caused by a collision with another world early in the history of the Solar System, seems to have had a strange effect on the planet's weather. Although some parts of Uranus have nights that last about 40 years, the temperature across it's surface is remarkably even. Movement of heat around the planet may prevent normal weather systems from developing.

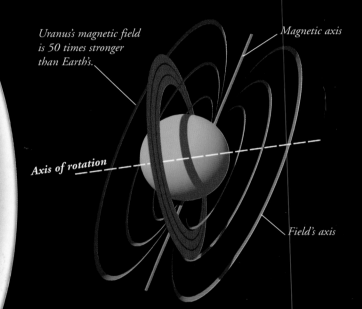

Uranus's magnetic field is 50 times stronger than Earth's.

Magnetic axis

Axis of rotation

Field's axis

Uranian magnetic field

While Uranus's tilt may seem strange, its magnetic field is even more bizarre. It is tilted back at an extreme angle from its rotation, and the field line doesn't pass through the centre of the planet. Beneath the outer atmosphere of hydrogen, helium, and a little methane, Uranus has a slushy mantle of liquids and frozen heavier chemicals that surround a rocky core. It seems that the planet's magnetic field is produced in this mantle, rather than in the core.

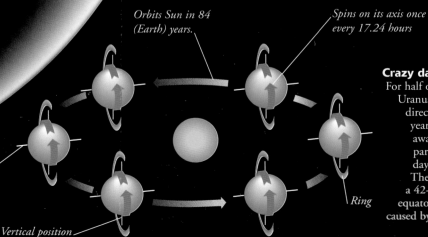

Orbits Sun in 84 (Earth) years.

Spins on its axis once every 17.24 hours

Crazy days

For half of its 84-year orbit, Uranus's north pole points directly at the Sun, while 42 years later, it points directly away. As a result, different parts of Uranus experience days of different length. The polar regions have a 42-year day, while the equator has a 17-hour day caused by the planet's rotation.

Axis tilts from the vertical by 98 degrees.

Vertical position

Ring

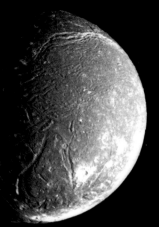

Mysterious Miranda

Uranus's moon Miranda is 480 km (300 miles) across, and is probably the weirdest looking world in the Solar System. Its surface is a crazy patchwork of different types of terrain. Astronomers used to think that it had once shattered apart and reassembled itself. Most now think that Miranda has been partially melted and reshaped by the gravitational pulls of Uranus and larger, more distant moons.

A view of Ariel, taken in 1999 by *Voyager 2*.

RINGS AND MOONS

Uranus is surrounded by a family of 21 moons and numerous dark rings, all with orbits tipped over like the planet itself. The five largest moons are Miranda, Ariel, Umbriel, Titania, and Oberon. All these worlds show signs of geological activity in their distant past. The activity probably continued for longest on the small moons closest to the planet, Miranda and Ariel. The smaller satellites include distant captured asteroids and tiny shepherd moons (p. 49).

A *Voyager 2* false-colour image (below) clearly shows nine of Uranus's 11 known rings.

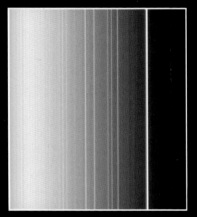

Thin rings of Uranus

The rings of Uranus are very different from those around Saturn – they are narrow and made from some of the darkest material in the Solar System. They were only discovered in 1977 when they passed in front of a distant star and caused its light to flicker. The fine structure of Uranus's rings probably means that each is hemmed in by a pair of tiny shepherd moons, and the dark colour may mean they are covered with methane or other carbon-based chemicals.

LET'S EXPERIMENT
DISCOVERING RINGS

When one object in space blocks our view of another, it is called an "occultation".

URANUS'S UNUSUAL TILT allowed astronomers to discover its series of narrow rings. When the planet passed in front of a distant star, the rings blocked out some of the star's light, causing its brightness to flicker slightly. You can observe this effect using some homemade rings and a torch.

You will need: an adult to help; black foamboard (from art-supply shops); 11 black pencils; torch.

1 Stick the sharp end of 11 pencils into the foamboard, so that they stand upright in a line (left). The pencils represent Uranus's rings. Place a torch about 1 m (3 ft) away from the pencils. The torch represents a distant star.

2 With the room darkened, switch on the torch and look through the rings towards the torch. Move the rings from side to side, and observe how they block the starlight.

NEPTUNE

THE EIGHTH PLANET FROM THE SUN is a bitterly cold
and dark world. Neptune is almost a twin to Uranus in
size and colour. However, it is much more active, with
the most violent weather of any planet in the Solar
System. Its internal structure is similar to that of Uranus,
but it is tilted at a more normal angle (28.3 degrees,
compared to Uranus's 98-degree tilt). Neptune was the
first planet to be discovered by calculation rather than
luck. Astronomers knew it existed because its gravity
affected the orbit of Uranus. In 1846, they
found Neptune exactly where predicted.

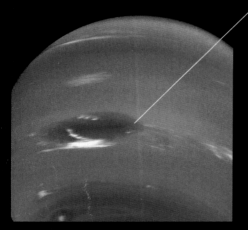

*The Great Dark Spot, as
seen in 1989, with white
scooters to its south*

STORMY WEATHER

Neptune has some of the strongest
winds in the Solar System, reaching
speeds of up to 2,000 kmh (1,250 mph).
Despite being much further from the Sun,
the planet's clouds are roughly the same
temperature as Uranus's, at –214°C
(–350°F). This is because Neptune, unlike
Uranus, generates more energy inside than it
receives from the Sun. Heat escaping from inside
drives the weather and generates the storms. Neptune
rotates once every 16 hours, and the speed of rotation
stretches its clouds around it in swirling bands.

Dark spots and scooters
Neptune's clouds move at different speeds and
in different directions depending on their depth
in the atmosphere. Dark spots are lower in the
atmosphere and circle relatively slowly, blown
backwards by winds in the opposite direction
to the planet's rotation. High white "scooters",
which cast shadows on the bluer clouds below,
are blown around the planet by following winds.

STRANGE RINGS

For years, astronomers were uncertain whether Neptune
had a ring system. Sometimes, when the planet passed in
front of distant stars, its rings seemed to dim the star's
light, but at other times they did not. Some astronomers
thought the planet might just have ring arcs – small
segments of rings in independent orbits. The spacecraft
Voyager 2 solved the mystery in 1989, when it turned its
camera back to photograph Neptune and its rings in
silhouette. This image shows that Neptune does
indeed have rings, but they are thicker on one
side of the planet than on the other.

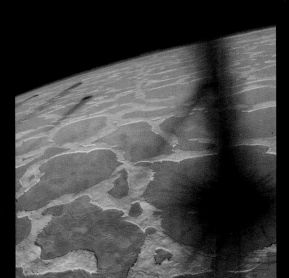

TRITON

Neptune has at least eight satellites, but seven of them are dwarfed by Triton, which is the size of Earth's moon. Triton follows a perfectly circular orbit, but moves the "wrong" way around the planet. Astronomers think that it may be a world very similar to Pluto, and that it strayed into Neptune's gravitational grasp. The planet pulled Triton into reverse orbit, flinging most of Neptune's original satellites out of the Solar System.

Discovery of Triton

William Lassell was an amateur astronomer who discovered Neptune's satellite Triton within weeks of the planet's own discovery in 1846. Lassell was an English brewer with a keen interest in astronomy. He devised his own machinery for making reflecting telescopes at a time when most telescopes used lenses. Lassell's superior mirrors also allowed him to discover Hyperion, a satellite of Saturn, and several hundred new nebulas.

William Lassell (1799–1880)

The dimpled surface of Triton may show where its interior melted and bubbled up through the surface.

LET'S EXPERIMENT
CONDENSING ATMOSPHERE

TRITON IS SO COLD that most of its thin nitrogen atmosphere froze onto the surface as solid ice. In this experiment, you can copy the freezer effect with steam. **You will need:** an adult to help you; modelling clay; string; stick; bowl of hot water.

1 Form a round ball of modelling clay to represent Triton. Tie the string around the middle of the ball and attach the other end of the string to a stick. Put "Triton" in the freezer for a few hours.

2 Ask an adult to boil some water. Take your model moon out of the freezer and hold it by the stick over the rising steam for a few seconds. Remove it, and you should see that the steam has condensed onto the surface of the model moon as a thin layer of ice.

Ice geysers on Triton

Triton is an icy world unlike any other moon, with a variety of landscapes. The dark, sooty streaks visible on its surface come from ice geysers (above). Despite being one of the coldest places in the Solar System, Triton has active volcanoes. It seems that the tidal forces created by Triton's reverse orbit keep its surface active.

PLUTO AND CHARON

THE TINY WORLD OF PLUTO is just two-thirds
the size of our Moon, and some astronomers
doubt that it's really a planet at all. Because
of its eccentric 248-Earth-year orbit, Pluto
is not always the furthest planet from the
Sun. For 20 years of each orbit, it comes
closer to the Sun than Neptune. Unlike
the other outer planets that are made
of gas and liquid, Pluto is a solid ball
of rock and ice. It is also unique
among the Solar System worlds
because it is a "double planet",
locked in an endless waltz
with its large moon Charon.

Charon

A DOUBLE PLANET

At nearly half Pluto's size, Charon is much larger,
relative to its planet, than any other moon in the
Solar System. It also orbits extremely close to Pluto,
just 18,500 km (11,500 miles) above the surface. Like all
natural satellites, Charon has one face permanently locked
towards its planet. However, its effect on Pluto is very strong.
Its gravitational pull has slowed Pluto's rotation to the same
speed as Charon's orbit – one spin every 6.4 days. This
means that from one side of Pluto, Charon is always
visible, while it is never seen
at all from the other side.

*Pluto and
Charon are
held together
like the weights
on a dumbbell.
They are locked in
orbit facing each other.*

*Tombaugh found Pluto by comparing photos
taken on 23rd and 29th January, 1930.*

DISCOVERY

Pluto was discovered in 1930 as the
result of a deliberate search. At the time,
astronomers thought that apparent wobbles
in the orbit of Neptune suggested there might be another
world beyond it, and Clyde Tombaugh (1906–97), an American
astronomer, began to survey the heavens. Because the planet was
so faint, he could only find it by photographing the same area of
sky a few nights apart, then looking for objects that had moved.
Tombaugh was lucky – he found Pluto within a few months.
Astronomers now know that Neptune has no unexplained
wobbles, so his search was inspired by a miscalculation.

**Clyde Tombaugh,
the discoverer of
Pluto, studies
images in a blink
comparator.**

Pluto

*Pluto's orbit is remarkably
different from the rest of
the Solar System.*

Pluto's orbit
Pluto's path around the Sun is the most
elongated of any planet's. It ranges from
4.5 to 7.4 billion km (2.8 to 4.6 billion
miles) from the Sun. Occasionally, Pluto
actually comes within Neptune's orbit, but
this always happens when Neptune is far
away so there is no danger of collision.
Pluto's orbit is also tilted wildly compared
to the other planets – at an angle of
17 degrees from the ecliptic (the plane
around which the other planets orbit).

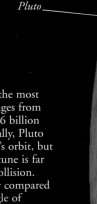

Frozen atmosphere

Pluto is currently in its 50-year warm season. It is orbiting close enough for the Sun's heat to evaporate its surface ices – mostly nitrogen, methane, and carbon monoxide. This gives the planet a thin atmosphere. Soon Pluto's orbit will take it away from the Sun. It will cool down and the atmosphere will refreeze and remain solid for the next 200 years. NASA scientists hope to send a high-speed mission to Pluto before its atmosphere freezes and disappears.

Mist rises from this frozen lake on Earth in a similar way to gases evaporating from Pluto's surface ice.

LET'S EXPERIMENT
DOUBLE PLANET

THIS EXPERIMENT SHOWS that Pluto and Charon orbit around an invisible point between them, known as the barycentre. They are locked in position facing one another, so some areas of Pluto will never see Charon. **You will need:** modelling clay (two different colours); a piece of wooden dowelling; scissors; string.

1 Roll two different coloured balls of modelling clay to make "Pluto" 50 mm (2 in) and "Charon" 25 mm (1 in) in diameter. Push them onto the ends of a piece of wooden dowelling. Cut string to size and tie it around the dowelling. Hang the string from a fixed point.

2 Find the barycentre by sliding the string along the dowelling until the apparatus balances (like a see-saw). Push the smaller planet to make the apparatus spin. Notice the different paths Pluto and Charon take as they orbit around their barycentre.

Varuna, the largest known EKB object, is almost half Pluto's size.

Pluto is the smallest planet in the Solar System.

Mercury is the second smallest planet, but has more than twice the diameter of Pluto.

Is Pluto a planet?

For decades, astronomers worried that Pluto was strangely out of place at the edge of the Solar System. They now know that it is just one of many similar objects in the Edgeworth-Kuiper Belt (EKB). Some astronomers now think Pluto should be downgraded from a planet to an EKB object, but at present it is officially classed in both groups. The picture above shows Pluto to scale with Mercury and with the large EKB object, Varuna.

The first maps

Because Pluto is so far away, it has not yet been visited by a spacecraft. Nevertheless, astronomers have mapped its surface. They used the fact that twice in Pluto's year (equivalent to about 248 Earth years), Charon passes in front of or behind Pluto. In the 1980s, they measured the changes in Pluto and Charon's overall light during one of these eclipses, and were able to build up the first maps. Since then, maps of Pluto have been refined by observations from the Hubble Space Telescope.

A two-colour map of Pluto's surface

THE STARS

Picture: *Young, white-hot stars shine brilliantly in the Pleiades cluster.*

STARS NEAR AND FAR

EVERY NIGHT WHEN THE SKY grows dark, we see stars come out in their thousands. How tiny they seem, and how far away. However, if we were to travel for millions and millions of kilometres to see the stars close up, we would find that they look much like our Sun. For our Sun is also a star, but it is very much closer to us. By studying the light and other radiation that stars give out, astronomers have discovered a great deal about them. They know how big and how hot they are, how fast they travel, how they are born, and how they die.

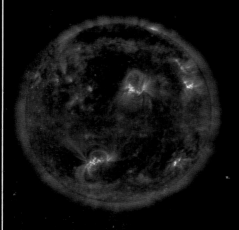

The Sun's very hot atmosphere is visible in this false-colour, ultraviolet image.

WHAT IS A STAR?

Like the Sun, stars are huge globes of searing hot gases. Some are smaller than the Sun, while others are very much bigger. Inside stars, temperatures reach tens of millions of degrees Celsius.

Stars are mostly made of hydrogen, the lightest of all gases. They use the hydrogen as fuel in nuclear reactions (processes) that produce huge amounts of energy. This is what keeps stars shining. Stars give off most of their energy as light and heat, just like the Sun. But they also give off energy in the form of other kinds of radiation, such as ultraviolet rays and X-rays.

STARS IN THE SKY

The stars look as if they are all a similar distance away from us – as if they are stuck on the inside of a dark sphere surrounding Earth. (This is what ancient astronomers believed.) In fact the stars all lie different distances away – distances so enormous that they are almost impossible to imagine. If we could travel at the speed of a light beam, it would take us more than four years to reach even the nearest stars! Astronomers therefore say that these stars lie more than four light years away. The most distant stars in the sky are many thousands of times further away still.

Like the Sun, the stars are hurtling through space at enormous speeds. We can't see them move because they lie too far away. They appear to be fixed in their place in space, always forming the same patterns, which we can learn to recognize. It is these star patterns, the constellations, that help us find our way around the night sky.

THE LIVES OF STARS

The stars in the night sky never seem to change. We see the same stars today that ancient astronomers saw thousands of years ago, and the same stars will still grace our skies in thousands of years' time. But stars do change. Like living things, they are born, grow up, and finally die. Unlike people, however, stars live for hundreds of millions or even tens of billions of years. That is why, over a few thousand years, they appear not to change at all.

Stars are born inside nebulas (clouds of gas and dust). Nebulas are found scattered among stars in many parts of the sky. A star forms where a dense part of a nebula collapses under the weight of its own gravity. As the ball of gas shrinks, it heats up. When it gets hot enough, nuclear reactions start inside it, producing enough energy to make it shine – as a new star.

The dark clouds of gas and dust in the Eagle Nebula give birth to stars.

Timeline

c. 150 BCE Hipparchus draws up a catalogue of stars and devises the magnitude system of brightness.

1054 Chinese astronomers record a supernova, which becomes the Crab Nebula.

1610 Galileo becomes the first to observe and record sunspots, using the telescope he built.

1815 Joseph von Fraunhofer discovers and maps the dark lines in the Sun's spectrum, thereafter known as Fraunhofer lines.

1838 Friedrich Bessel works out the first accurate distance to a star (61 Cygni) using the principle of parallax.

1906 Einar Hertzsprung discovers the relationship between the colour of a star and its true brightness.

CLUSTERS

The nebulas in which stars form are vast, and often many stars are born in the same region at the same time. Some stars are born close together, and become companions linked by gravity. Two-star sytems are common – we call them binary stars.

Sometimes several hundred stars may be born at the same time and scatter over quite a wide area. We can see many such groupings, called open clusters, of young stars in the heavens. The individual stars do not attract each other very strongly, so they slowly drift apart.

An open cluster of young stars in Canis Major

STAR DEATH

Most stars live for a very long time. They keep shining until they use up all their hydrogen fuel. Then they start to die.

First they swell up to 20, 30, or more times their original size, and turn redder in colour, becoming red giants. However,

This huge ring of expanding gases around this planetary nebula has been puffed out by the smaller of the two stars in the middle, which is dying.

a red giant does not stay giant-sized for long. It begins puffing out clouds of gas and dust from its outer layers. Soon all that remains is the star's tiny hot core. The star has then become a white dwarf, and its radiation lights up the clouds of matter it puffed out. We call such clouds planetary nebulas.

OUT WITH A BANG

Stars that are much bigger than the Sun have a very different ending. Instead of fading away quietly as a white dwarf, they go out with a bang. They also swell up to become red giants, but keep on swelling many times bigger still to become supergiants.

However, supergiants are so unstable that they soon blast themselves apart in a supernova explosion. The star's core collapses in on itself, and, depending on its

mass, forms a tiny neutron star or a black hole. A neutron star is a dense mass made up of atomic particles called neutrons. A black hole is a region of space with enormous gravity that will gobble up anything that comes too close, even light.

RESURRECTION

The death of a star is not quite the end of the story. In fact, it can signal a new beginning. This is because the matter that dying stars puff or blast out introduces new material into the clouds of matter already present in space. And this new material will find its way into the heart of any new stars that the clouds produce.

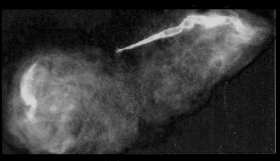

A jet of particles forms near a massive black hole.

OUR LOCAL STAR

THE SUN IS THE NEAREST STAR to Earth. At a distance of about 150 million km (93 million miles), it is hundreds of thousands of times closer to us than the next nearest star. Like other stars, the Sun is a great globe of intensely hot gases. Measuring about 1.4 million km (870,000 miles) in diameter, it is 109 times larger than Earth and contains 750 times more matter than all the other bodies in the Solar System put together. The Sun is made of two main elements – hydrogen and helium. It also contains small quantities of 70 other elements.

THE NUCLEAR FURNACE

Inside the Sun's core, temperatures reach up to 15 million °C (27 million °F) and pressures rise to millions of atmospheres. Under these intense conditions, the nuclei (centres) of hydrogen atoms fuse together and change into helium. These nuclear reactions produce the enormous amounts of energy the Sun needs to keep shining. The energy travels outwards until it reaches the Sun's photosphere (surface). From there it escapes into space, mostly as light and infrared and ultraviolet radiation.

The core is the region which produces the Sun's energy.

In the convective zone, rising convection currents carry energy to the surface.

Nuclear fusion of hydrogen

A cross-section has been added to this image of the solar surface taken by SOHO, the Solar and Heliospheric Observatory.

Neutrino released

Positron released

Protons (hydrogen nuclei)

A prominence is a mass of gas hanging in the Sun's atmosphere.

Neutron

Gamma rays given off

Two proton-proton-neutron groups fuse to form a helium nucleus, and two protons are ejected.

Neutron

> **WARNING!**
> Never look directly at the Sun, especially through binoculars or telescopes. Its glare may blind you.

When two protons collide, one changes into a neutron, releasing a positron and a neutrino.

Another proton fuses with a proton-neutron pair.

Nuclear fusion

The nuclear reactions taking place in the Sun's core are known as fusion reactions because hydrogen nuclei fuse (join together) to form helium. The main fusion process is outlined in this diagram (left). It shows how hydrogen nuclei, or protons, combine in stages to form helium. Some change into neutrons, and other particles or rays are given off as fusion takes place.

In the radiative zone, energy travels out from the core as radiation.

‹ LIFE ON EARTH ›

Nearly all life on Earth depends ultimately on the Sun. The Sun's light allows plants to make their food by the process of photosynthesis. Animals must eat plants – or eat other animals that eat plants – to live. The Sun's energy supplies Earth with enough warmth to allow a comfortable environment in which living things can thrive. **66 ▶**

CORONA

Like Earth, the Sun is surrounded by an atmosphere of thin gases. We usually can't see this layer because of the glare from the Sun's surface, or photosphere. During a total eclipse of the Sun, however, when the photosphere is masked by the Moon, we can glimpse the Sun's atmosphere. It appears as a pearly white halo called the corona ("crown") and extends millions of kilometres out into space. Its temperature can reach 3 million °C (5.4 million °F).

The corona is visible during a total eclipse of the Sun.

The photosphere is the Sun's visible surface, where light is emitted.

The colour sphere

The lowest and densest part of the Sun's atmosphere has a pinkish tinge, which is why it is called the chromosphere ("colour sphere"). It is about 5,000 km (3,100 miles) thick. Again, we can see it only during a total eclipse. Little jets of gas called spicules project from the chromosphere into the thinner corona.

Chromosphere

Loop prominence

An arc of bright points known as Baily's beads

LET'S EXPERIMENT
SOLAR COOKER

2 The curved aluminium surface acts like a concave mirror. It concentrates the Sun's energy at a focal point above the lid and toasts the bread.

ON DAYS WHEN the skies are clear and dry, infrared radiation from the Sun can be strong. You can capture some of this solar energy to toast bread in a simple experiment. **You will need:** an adult present; dustbin lid; aluminium foil; toasting fork; bread.

Concentrated solar energy toasts bread.

1 Cover the inside of the lid with foil, keeping it smooth. Gently press it into the curve of the lid to make a dish shape. Point the lid at the Sun, and use the fork to hold a slice of bread above the centre of the lid at the point where the Sun's light and heat are concentrated.

THE STORMY SUN

FROM EARTH, THE SUN appears bland and unchanging. But nothing could be further from the truth. The Sun is in constant turmoil, with its surface and atmosphere seething violently like a stormy sea. Bubbles of searing hot gas 1,000 km (600 miles) wide are erupting everywhere, huge explosions make the surface quake and generate enormous waves, and brilliant streamers of fiery gas arch out and punch their way high into the solar atmosphere. One of the causes of the Sun's turbulent nature is its powerful magnetism, which can be thousands of times stronger than Earth's magnetism.

FLARING UP

When examined closely, the surface of the Sun is not uniformly bright. Particularly bright patches appear on it from time to time. The brightest patches are caused by immense explosions known as solar flares, which occur in the lower atmosphere. They are triggered by the sudden release of pent-up magnetic energy. Solar flares eject streams of electrically charged particles into space at speeds of millions of kilometres an hour.

Solar flare

Grainy surface
In close-up pictures, the surface of the Sun looks grainy – as if it's covered with grains of wheat. This effect, called granulation, is caused by little pockets of hot gas rising up from below. These pockets are known as convection cells.

The Sun's seething surface is clearly visible in this ultraviolet image taken by the SOHO observatory.

Photosphere

Granulation effect on Sun's surface

SUNSPOTS

Dark patches called sunspots sometimes appear on the Sun's surface. Small ones, called pores, can be less than 1,000 km (600 miles) across. But the biggest ones can reach 100,000 km (60,000 miles) across. Sunspots are about 1,500°C (2,700°F) cooler than the rest of the surface and erupt in regions of intense magnetic activity.

Sunspot

Penumbra (light region)

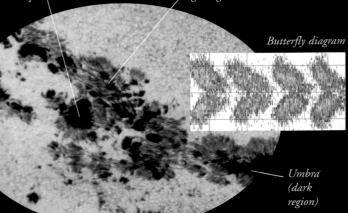

Butterfly diagram

Umbra (dark region)

Solar butterflies
Sunspots come and go over a period of 11 years, known as the sunspot cycle. At the beginning of a cycle, sunspots appear furthest away from the Sun's equator both in the north and the south. They creep nearer the equator as the cycle proceeds. When the position of sunspots is plotted on a graph against time, the result is a characteristic pattern that looks rather like a series of butterflies with open wings. That is why the graph is called a butterfly diagram.

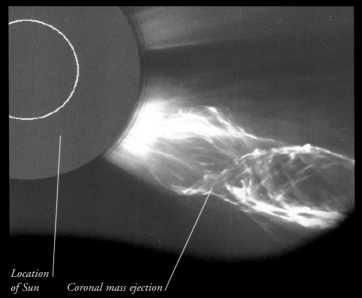

Location
of Sun

Coronal mass ejection

ERUPTIONS AND EJECTIONS

Some of the most spectacular features of the stormy Sun are
the huge fountains of fiery gas that leap high above its surface.
These are called prominences (p. 94). They can be hundreds
of thousands of kilometres high and often hang in the Sun's
atmosphere for weeks at a time. Sometimes, the Sun also ejects
great blasts of charged particles, or plasma, from the corona into
space. These blasts are called coronal mass ejections, or CMEs for
short, and their occurrence can intensify the solar wind (p.98).

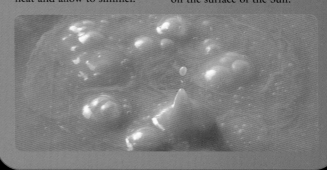
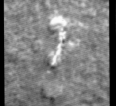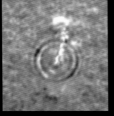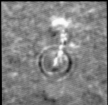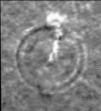

*A sunquake spreads rapidly
across the Sun's surface.*

Sunquakes

Violent solar flares can trigger enormous
waves on the Sun's surface, similar to the
way earthquakes send waves across the
ground. We call such disturbances sunquakes.
The waves they cause spread across the
surface of the Sun in ever-widening ripples,
just like the ripples you see on water when
you throw a stone into a pond.

*Arching fountains of hot
gas in the Sun's corona,
spotted by NASA's
TRACE spacecraft.*

Loops in the corona

In ordinary photographs, very little
structure can be seen in the Sun's pearly
white corona (its outer atmosphere). But,
seen in ultraviolet light, the corona is filled
with millions of arching fountains of hot
gas. Known as coronal loops, these
fountains follow the invisible looping lines
of the Sun's magnetic field. Some loops
reach 500,000 km (300,000 miles) high,
and they may leap over a distance
equivalent to the width of 30 Earths.

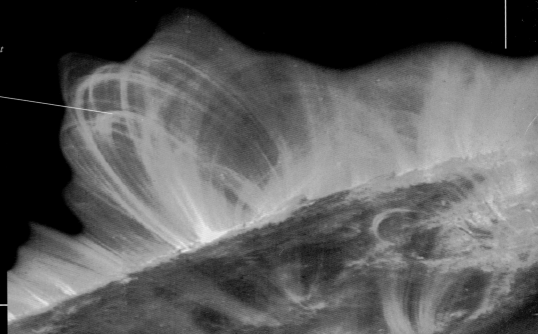

SPACE WEATHER

THE CONDITIONS IN SPACE around Earth are constantly changing. Astronomers talk about the changing "space weather". The main factor that affects space weather is the solar wind. This is a stream of particles that constantly flows out of the Sun's corona, at an average speed of about 500 km (300 miles) per second. These particles – mainly protons and electrons – are electrically charged and form what is called a plasma. Because the Sun is rotating, the solar wind spirals away from the corona. It takes about four to five days to reach Earth, where it comes up against, and interacts with, the planet's magnetic field.

MAGNETIC COCOON

Earth's magnetic field extends far out into space, forming a kind of magnetic bubble, which we call the magnetosphere. The pressure of the solar wind squeezes the magnetosphere on the upstream side, but extends it downstream into a long tail (the magnetotail). The lines of force in the magnetosphere deflect most of the solar wind particles around Earth. However, some get trapped in ring-shaped regions known as the Van Allen radiation belts.

Solar wind interacts with magnetosphere

Magnetotail

Magnetosphere

Auroras reach an altitude of about 120 km (75 miles).

Earth

Solar wind squeezes Earth's magnetosphere.

Van Allen radiation belts trap some particles from the solar wind.

NORTHERN LIGHTS

Spectacular colour light displays called the *aurora borealis*, or Northern Lights, occur in the skies around the North Pole. There are similar displays around the South Pole. Auroras occur when magnetic surges associated with the solar wind disturb the electrons trapped in Earth's magnetosphere. The electrons are funnelled down towards the poles, where they collide with air molecules, ionize them, and give them extra energy. This energy is emitted as beautiful coloured light.

Main image: a brilliant green *aurora borealis* seen from Alaska, USA.

The Southern Lights
Displays of the aurora that occur in the skies around the South Pole are called the *aurora australis*, or Southern Lights. Astronauts in the space shuttle photographed this unusual view of the Southern Lights (above).

Spiralling solar wind

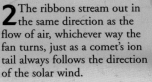

MAGNETIC STORMS

Cities such as Toronto, Canada (above), which lie near auroral regions, are prone to the effects of solar wind. This blows strongest when the Sun is most active, particularly with flares. Solar flares hurl vast streams of particles into space, which squeeze the magnetosphere and cause sudden increases in Earth's magnetic field at ground level. These magnetic storms affect compasses, disrupt radio, and in extreme cases knock out power supplies, causing blackouts.

Comet Hyakutake (1996) with its long ion tail

TELLING TAILS

Comets often develop two long tails as they journey towards the Sun (p. 53). The tails are made of particles leaving the comet's body, or nucleus. A slightly curved, yellowish dust tail forms when pressure from solar radiation pushes away the comet's dust particles. A straight, bluish ion tail can be seen when the magnetism of the solar wind acts against charged particles (ions) coming from the comet. Both tails always point away from the Sun.

Van Allen's belts
The Van Allen radiation belts are named after American physicist James Van Allen (born 1914). He devised the instruments on the first US satellite, *Explorer 1* (1959), which detected the band of electrified particles high above Earth.

LET'S EXPERIMENT
COMET TAILS

YOU CAN USE ribbons and a fan to imitate the way comet tails always point away from the Sun. **You will need:** an adult to help you; fan with guard; transparent sticky tape; thin ribbons or strips of tissue paper.

1 Make sure the fan isn't plugged into an electrical socket. Tape one end of several lengths of ribbon to the fan guard. Ask an adult to plug the fan into a socket and switch on.

2 The ribbons stream out in the same direction as the flow of air, whichever way the fan turns, just as a comet's ion tail always follows the direction of the solar wind.

DISTANT STARS

THE BRIGHTEST STAR in the southern constellation of Centaurus (the Centaur) is called Alpha Centauri. Apart from the Sun, it is the nearest bright star to Earth. To reach it, we would have to travel more than 40 million million kilometres (25 million million miles). That's more than 250,000 times further away from Earth than the Sun. Other stars lie thousands of times further away still. Distances like these are impossible to imagine. The kilometre or mile is much too small a unit to measure distances to the stars. That's why astronomers use other units, such as the light year.

THE LIGHT YEAR

Alpha Centauri is so far away that its light, travelling at about 300,000 km (186,000 miles) per second, takes more than four years to reach us. We say that it lies more than four light years away. Astronomers use the light year – the distance light travels in a year – as a unit to measure the vast distances in space. The light year is a much more convenient unit than the kilometre or the mile. Astronomers also use a unit called the parsec (which equals 3.26 light years).

Alpha Centauri

Crux, the Southern Cross

Lifetimes away
To get an idea of Alpha Centauri's distance, let's imagine we're trying to reach it in the space shuttle, which travels at 28,000 kmh (17,000 mph). That's about 10 times faster than a rifle bullet. Yet even at this speed it would still take us 39,000 years! This just shows how impossible it will be to travel to the stars unless we invent quite different kinds of propulsion.

FOOLING THE EYE

The constellation of Orion (main picture) is one of the best-known star patterns in the sky. But its stars are not really grouped together in space in this pattern. They actually lie very far from each other. We see them together only because they happen to lie in the same direction in space from our viewpoint. The same is true for the other constellations. The scale below shows how far apart the main stars in Orion (see inset key) really are. The most distant star, Alnilam, is more than 1,000 light years further away from us than the closest one, Bellatrix.

0 LIGHT YEARS`

243 Bellatrix

427 Betelgeuse

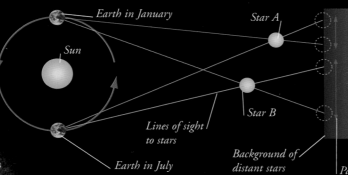

Earth in January

Sun

Star A

Lines of sight
to stars

Star B

Earth in July

Background of
distant stars

Parallax shifts

PARALLAX SHIFT

Astronomers use the principle of parallax to measure the distance to nearby stars. They note how a star shifts position against the background of distant stars when viewed from opposite ends of Earth's orbit round the Sun. Star B is nearest because it has a larger shift than distant star A. The amount of the shift allows astronomers to calculate the star's distance using simple geometry

LET'S EXPERIMENT
HOW PARALLAX WORKS

WHEN YOU LOOK at a nearby object, first with one eye and then the other, the object appears to move from side to side against a distant background. Astronomers use this effect, called parallax, to measure the distance of stars. In this experiment you'll see how parallax works. **You will need:** a sheet of dark paper, stick-on stars, and a pencil. Stick some stars onto the paper, then fix the sheet to a wall. Stick another star to the end of the pencil.

Note where the pencil star appears among the background stars on the sheet.

Your pencil star has shifted to the right among the background stars.

1 Stand about 2 m (6 ft) from the wall, and hold up the pencil at arm's length so that you can see it in front of the sheet. Cover your left eye, and look at the pencil star with your right eye.

2 Now cover your right eye, and look at the pencil star with your left eye. The star will shift its position among the background stars on the sheet. Repeat the experiment holding the pencil star closer towards you.

Heka
(Meissa)

Betelgeuse

Bellatrix

Alnitak   Mintaka
       Alnilam

Orion Nebula

Saiph   Rigel

Key to stars of Orion

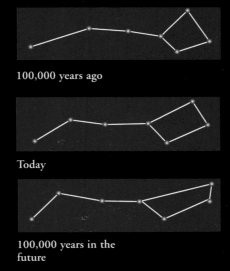

100,000 years ago

Today

100,000 years in the future

Changing shapes
All stars travel through space at high speed – some at hundreds of kilometres/miles per second. Most stars are so far away that we can't see them move. But over hundreds of thousands of years star movements will gradually change the shape of the constellations. This diagram (left) shows how significantly the shape of the Plough will have changed over 200,000 years.

722 Saiph

773 Rigel

817 Alnitak

916 Mintaka

1,055 Heka (Meissa)

1,300 Orion Nebula

1,342 Alnilam

STARLIGHT

AT FIRST SIGHT, all the stars in the sky look much the same – little pinpricks of light shining out in the blackness of space. But astronomers have found that there are many types of stars – big and small, hot and cool, blue and red. Some stars move towards us, while others are speeding away. Some shine steadily, while others vary in brightness. Astronomers know this by studying the rays of light that stars give out, and by splitting up this light into a spread of colour, or spectrum.

COLOURED LIGHTS

On a clear night, the stars seem to sparkle like white diamonds, blue sapphires, and red rubies. Even with the naked eye, we can see that stars have different colours. The giant star Aldebaran in the constellation Taurus (the Bull) looks distinctly red (p. 110). So does Betelgeuse in nearby Orion. Red stars stand out in this image (right). The fuzzy object is a neighbouring galaxy, NGC 6822.

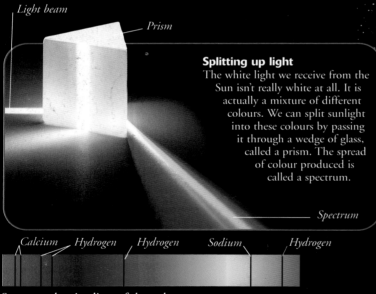

Light beam

Prism

Splitting up light
The white light we receive from the Sun isn't really white at all. It is actually a mixture of different colours. We can split sunlight into these colours by passing it through a wedge of glass, called a prism. The spread of colour produced is called a spectrum.

Spectrum

Calcium *Hydrogen* *Hydrogen* *Sodium* *Hydrogen*

Spectrum showing lines of three elements

SPECTRAL LINES

Like sunlight, the light from stars can also be split up into a coloured spectrum. When a star's spectrum is examined, patterns of lines are found running across it. These are produced by chemical elements in the star's atmosphere, which absorb or give out radiation of different wavelengths. The wavelengths are different for every chemical element, so by looking at the lines, astronomers can tell what the star is made of. Dark lines caused by atoms absorbing radiation are called absorption lines. Bright lines caused by atoms giving out radiation are called emission lines.

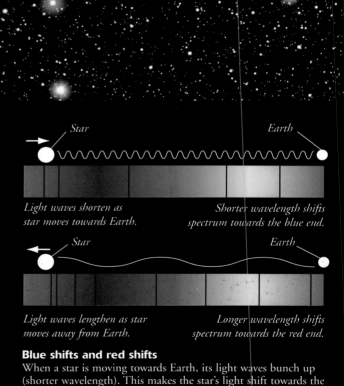

Star   *Earth*

Light waves shorten as star moves towards Earth.   *Shorter wavelength shifts spectrum towards the blue end.*

Star   *Earth*

Light waves lengthen as star moves away from Earth.   *Longer wavelength shifts spectrum towards the red end.*

Blue shifts and red shifts
When a star is moving towards Earth, its light waves bunch up (shorter wavelength). This makes the star's light shift towards the blue end of the spectrum. When a star moves away from us, the light waves stretch out (longer wavelength), and shift towards the red end of the spectrum. This is called the Doppler effect.

Class M
2,100–3,200°C
(3,800–5,800°F)
e.g. Betelgeuse in Orion

Class K
3,300–4,600°C
(5,900–8,300°F)
e.g. Arcturus
in Boötes

Class G
4,700–5,700°C
(8,500–10,300°F)
e.g. the Sun

Class F
5,800–7,100°C
(10,500–12,800°F)
e.g. Canopus in
Carina

Class A
7,200–9,600°C
(13,000–17,300°F)
e.g. Vega in Lyra

Class B
9,700–28,000°C
(17,500–50,400°F)
e.g. Rigel in Orion

Class O
29,000–40,000°C
(52,200–72,000°F)
e.g. Mintaka in Orion

DEMONSTRATING
THE COLOURS OF HEAT

When a substance is heated, it changes colour. You can see this if you have an electric light fitted with a dimmer switch. If the switch is only just turned on, only a little electric current flows through the light bulb. The filament warms up and glows a dull red. As you turn up the switch, more and more current flows through the filament in the bulb, which glows first orange, then yellow, then white as it gets hotter. The same thing happens when an iron bar is heated. It changes colour from red to white as its temperature rises.

Star colours
In the same way as a heated iron bar, the colour of a star is an indication of the temperature of its surface. Stars are grouped into different classes according to their temperature. The seven main classes are O, B, A, F, G, K, and M, with O the hottest and M the coolest.

1 Red-hot
When the end of the iron bar is heated, it gradually changes colour from grey to dull red. The heat gives the atoms in the iron more energy, which they give off as dull red light.

2 Orange-hot
As the iron bar gets hotter, its colour changes from dull red to orange. The extra heat makes the iron atoms vibrate more vigorously, and they now give off a brighter, orange light.

3 Yellow-hot
As the iron bar is heated still more, the tip gives off an even brighter, yellow light.

4 White-hot
Here the tip of the iron bar has been heated up nearly to its melting point, about 1,500°C (2,730°F). It is giving off white light.

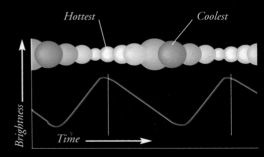

Venus

Sirius (brightest star in the whole sky)

Polaris

Faintest star visible to the naked eye

Faintest star visible with binoculars

Faintest star visible in sky survey photographs

-4 -3 -2 -1 0 +1 +2 +3 +4 +5 +6 +7 +8 +9 +10 +11 +12 +13 +14 +15 +16 +17 +18 +19 +20 +21 +22

STAR MAGNITUDES
Astronomers measure the brightness of stars on a magnitude scale – the brighter the star, the lower the magnitude. The stars we can see with the naked eye are generally between first and sixth magnitudes, although a few very bright stars, such as Sirius, have negative magnitudes. Fainter stars that we can only see using telescopes are given magnitudes greater than six.

Hottest

Coolest

Brightness

Time

Pulsating variables
A type of variable star called a Cepheid varies in brightness because it pulsates, or regularly expands and contracts, as it nears the end of its life. As it gets bigger, it cools and emits less light. As it gets smaller, it becomes hotter and emits more light. This graph shows how the star's light output varies.

A STAR IS BORN

STARS ARE BEING BORN – and are dying – all the time in the heavens. They are born inside nebulas, the clouds of gas and dust that exist in the space between the stars. In particular, they are born within dense, dark regions known as giant molecular clouds, made up mainly of hydrogen gas. Gravity makes a dense part of a cloud collapse into an ever smaller, ever hotter ball, which begins to glow as a protostar. Later, hotter still, nuclear processes begin inside it, and the protostar is transformed into a shining beacon in the Universe – another brilliant star.

MOLECULAR CLOUDS

The dark molecular clouds that are the birthplace of stars are very cold, typically about -260°C (-440°F). At such temperatures, their gas and dust particles move very slowly indeed. Gravity pulls the gas molecules together to make clumps that are denser than the rest of the cloud. Within these clumps, gas collects in even denser cores which will become individual stars or double stars. The denser these cores become, the greater their gravity, the more gas they attract, and the faster they collapse.

The Orion Nebula is a vast star-forming region. Behind its bright clouds of gas is a huge, dark molecular cloud.

PROTOSTARS

In the centre of a collapsing core, in a molecular cloud, the matter is being squeezed, or compressed, by the material raining down on it. As the central region becomes compressed, its temperature rises. It gives off energy and starts to glow. At this point, we call it a protostar. Its shape becomes spherical and it starts to rotate rapidly. When temperatures inside the protostar reach about 10 million °C (18 million °F), atoms of hydrogen gas start fusing together. Enough energy is released in this nuclear fusion process to make the protostar shine as a true star.

A dense core inside a molecular cloud collapses inwards to form a protostar.

Planets in the making

When the Sun was born, a disc of matter formed around it too. It was from this disc that Earth and the other planets eventually formed. Astronomers believe that discs of gas and dust form around most stars when they are born, and that planets may eventually form inside them. That is why they are called protoplanetary discs, or proplyds. The picture above shows a proplyd (dark ring) around a newborn star in the Orion Nebula.

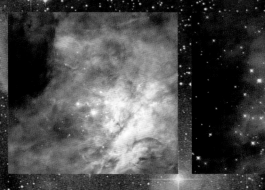

Failed star
Not all stars that start to form in collapsing clouds achieve stardom. Some don't have enough mass to become stars. They shrink under gravity but don't heat up enough to trigger off nuclear reactions. Without these reactions, they can't shine like proper stars. Instead they glow feebly, as brown dwarfs. In infrared images of the Orion Nebula (far right), astronomers have picked out many dim brown dwarfs, which are not visible in ordinary light (right).

Ultraviolet light from a small cluster of stars called the Trapezium provides the energy to make the whole nebula glow.

‹ CLUSTERING TOGETHER ›

The dark clouds of gas and dust in which stars are born measure many light years across. Within these vast stellar nurseries, tens or even hundreds of stars may be born at the same time. These clusters of young stars can be seen throughout the heavens. Their intense ultraviolet light often makes the gas cloud that surrounds them glow as a bright nebula. 110 ▶

A cluster of new stars lights up gas in the Cone Nebula in Monoceros (the Unicorn).

LET'S EXPERIMENT
GENERATING HEAT

STARS FORM WHEN clouds of gas and dust collapse under their own weight. As a cloud shrinks, its matter gets more and more compressed, which makes it heat up. In this experiment you can see how compression can generate heat. **You will need:** a bicycle and a bicycle pump.

1 Let some air out of one of the bicycle's tyres through the valve, then attach the pump to it. Pump up the tyre as fast as you can. Your pump compresses air and forces it into the tyre, compressing the air that's there.

2 Touch the pump's connector. It feels hot because compressing air raises its temperature. In stars, gravity compresses gases more and more until their temperature reaches millions of degrees.

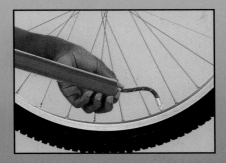

LIFE CYCLE OF STARS

Just like living things, stars are born, live out their lives, then die. Starbirth is a relatively quick process, taking just hundreds of thousands of years. Afterwards, stars may shine steadily for several billion years. As they die, again relatively quickly, they shed much of their matter into space. This finds its way into the molecular clouds that will, in time, spawn a clutch of new stars.

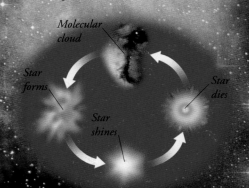

Molecular cloud

Star forms

Star dies

Star shines

VARIETIES OF STARS

BY CAREFULLY EXAMINING STARLIGHT, astronomers have found that stars come in many different sizes and masses, as well as colours, temperatures, and brightnesses. Many stars are a lot like our Sun, because the Sun is an average type of star. Two defining features of stars are their true brightness (absolute magnitude) and their spectral type, which indicates their colour and temperature. When these two features are plotted on a graph, similar stars appear together. This graph is called the Hertzsprung-Russell (HR) diagram after the astronomers who devised it.

Hot, blue-white star, 7 times the size of the Sun

Sun, about 1,400,000 km (900,000 miles) in diameter

Red giant, 30 times the size of the Sun

White dwarf, typically about the size of Earth

SIZE MATTERS

The Sun seems big to us, but it is dwarfed by the stars we call red giants and supergiants. These gigantic orbs are tens and hundreds of times larger in diameter than the Sun. On the other hand, the Sun is typically up to a hundred times bigger across than the stars we call red and white dwarfs. In general, stars do not vary this widely in mass. The heaviest stars have perhaps up to 50 times the Sun's mass, while the lightest ones have only about one-tenth its mass.

Supergiant, 10 times the size of a red giant

TRUE BRIGHTNESS

The brightness, or magnitude (p. 103), of a star as we see it in the sky doesn't tell us how bright it really is. Deneb (above), only appears bright because it's close to Earth. We see its "apparent magnitude", which depends on how far away it is. The true brightness, or "absolute magnitude", of stars can only be compared if we view them from the same distance. Astronomers define absolute magnitude as the brightness of a star as it would appear to us if we were about 33 light years (10 parsecs) away.

LET'S EXPERIMENT
COMPARING MASSES

A HUGE RED GIANT that is 30 times bigger in diameter than the Sun is not 30 times heavier. Indeed, on average, a red giant has about the same mass as the Sun. This experiment helps you understand the difference between mass and size. **You will need:** an adult present; weighing scales; large bowl; popcorn kernels; vegetable oil; saucepan with lid; cooking hob.

1 Stand the empty bowl on the scales and adjust the pointer to read zero. Pour some kernels and a little oil into the bowl and weigh them. Tip the bowl's contents into a pan, stir well, and cover. With adult supervision, heat on a hob until the popcorn pops.

2 Tip the popcorn back into the bowl and weigh it again. You'll find it weighs the same as before. The popcorn has expanded in size, but its mass has stayed the same. Similarly, a star like the Sun expands to become a red giant, without changing its mass.

Spectrum of hot
B-type star

Spectrum of cool
M-type star

SPECTRAL TYPES

Just like sunlight, starlight can be
split up into a rainbow of colours,
or spectrum (p. 102). Different stars
have different spectra, which allows
astronomers to classify them into
different spectral types – O, B, A, F,
G, K, and M. (These types are best
remembered by the unforgettable
mnemonic: Oh, Be a Fine Guy, Kiss
Me!) The pictures above show typical
spectra of a hot, blue-white B-type
star, and a much cooler, red M-type
star. Note that the cooler star has
many more dark lines in its spectrum.

‹ CITY-SIZED STARS ›

The smallest stars of all are much smaller than
white dwarfs – and are typically only about
20 km (12 miles) across. They are neutron
stars, so-called because they are made up of
atomic particles called neutrons. Neutron
stars form when massive stars collapse and
die. Ordinary atomic matter in their core
is crushed and converted into neutrons. We
can detect neutron stars when the pulses of
energy they give out sweep past Earth.  118 ▶

*A neutron star (blue) is about the
size of a big city such as London.*

THE HR DIAGRAM

Astronomers Ejnar Hertzsprung in Denmark and Henry Norris Russell in
the USA devised the HR diagram in the early 1900s. A simplified version
is shown below. When absolute magnitudes are plotted against spectral
types, most stars lie on a broad diagonal line, called the main sequence.
Their position on this line is determined by their mass – the most massive
are top left, the least massive are bottom right. Giant and supergiant stars
are found above the line, and white dwarfs below it. Sometimes the
diagram is plotted with luminosity instead of absolute magnitude.
Luminosity is the star's true brightness compared with that of the Sun.

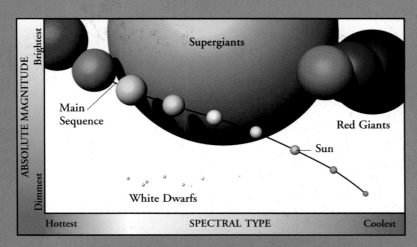

On the main sequence
Stars spend most of their lives on the main
sequence. During this time, they shine steadily,
with little change in brightness or temperature,
as they convert the hydrogen in their cores into
helium. The Sun has been on the main sequence
for about 5 billion years and will remain there
for about another 5 billion years. It will then
swell in size and join the group of cooler,
brighter red giants above the main sequence.

STARS WITH PLANETS

THE SUN IS AT THE CENTRE of our Solar System, with planets and other bodies circling around it. Not so long ago, no one knew for certain if other stars had planets. Now we know that they do. In 1991, astronomers discovered tiny planets circling around a pulsar, and four years later around an ordinary star, 51 Pegasi. By 2002, more than 90 planets had been discovered outside our Solar System. We call them extrasolar planets. These planets are much too small to be visible using ordinary telescopes. They can only be detected indirectly by the effect they have on their parent stars.

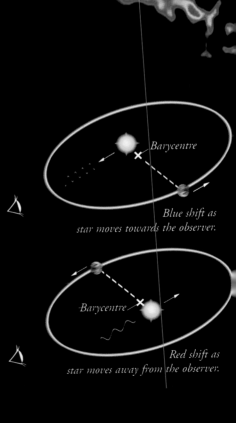

Parent star

The star wobbles as the planet orbits around it.

Planets may be forming in this disc around Beta Pictoris.

IN THE INFRARED

Early evidence of planetary systems around other stars came when spacecraft began using instruments that were sensitive to infrared light. Objects that were invisible in normal light were detectable in infrared. IRAS (infrared astronomy satellite) pioneered this technique in 1983 when it spotted discs of matter around a number of stars. They included Beta Pictoris (right) and Vega, one of the brightest stars. These discs contain the necessary chemical elements to create planets, so it's possible that planets are forming around these stars.

Blocking out the star's light in this image allows the disc of matter around it to be detected.

Dusty discs
With its greater eye for detail, the Hubble Space Telescope has spied hundreds of dusty discs around other stars. Because the material in these discs may one day turn into planets, the discs are called protoplanetary discs, or proplyds (p. 104). The proplyd in the above picture was spotted in the Orion Nebula. It shows up as a bright arc, which reflects light from nearby stars. The star being orbited by the disc appears here as a red blob.

TELL-TALE WOBBLES

Astronomers detect extrasolar planets indirectly by looking for stars that wobble. A star and its planet orbit around a common centre of gravity, the barycentre. This makes the star move alternately towards us and away from us (right). With very sensitive instruments, astronomers can detect these movements by observing the shift of dark lines in the star's spectrum (p. 102). When the star travels towards us, its light waves seem to shorten. The dark lines shift towards the blue end of the spectrum. When the star travels away from us, its light waves seem to lengthen. The lines then shift towards the red end of the spectrum.

Barycentre

Blue shift as star moves towards the observer.

Barycentre

Red shift as star moves away from the observer.

*The large
planet's gravity
tugs at the star.*

*Planets have been detected
around stars as far away as
90 light years from Earth.*

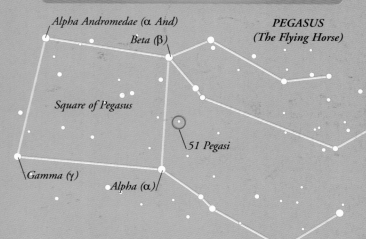

Alpha Andromedae (α And)

Beta (β)

*PEGASUS
(The Flying Horse)*

Square of Pegasus

51 Pegasi

Gamma (γ)

Alpha (α)

Terrestrial Planet Finder (TPF)

Searching for planets like Earth

A new generation of astronomy spacecraft
is being designed to search for, and examine,
planets orbiting nearby stars. NASA's Terrestrial
Planet Finder will use a multiple telescope array
to provide high-resolution images of other solar
systems. It should be sensitive enough to detect
planets as small as Earth. It will also carry
instruments to find out what the planets are
made of and even if they might support life.

IN THE CONSTELLATION PEGASUS (the Flying Horse), there is a faint
star named 51 Pegasi. It lies close to one side of the famous Square of
Pegasus (see diagram). As it is so faint, measuring only about the fifth
magnitude in stellar brightness, it's best to view it through binoculars.
No one bothered much about 51 Pegasi until 1995, when a planet
was discovered around it. This was the first planet to be found around
an ordinary star, similar to the Sun. But don't expect to see the planet
using binoculars! It's so tiny that not even the most powerful telescopes
can spot it. This planet appears to have about half the mass of Jupiter,
but orbits less than 10 million km (6 million miles) from its star.

CLUSTERS AND BINARIES

MOST STARS DO NOT TRAVEL ALONE through space, like the Sun. Instead, they travel with one or more other stars as their companions. This is because a number of stars are usually born at the same time, within the same cloud of gas and dust. Star systems with two stars, called binaries, are common. There are also many loose groupings of 100 or more young, hot stars, which we call open clusters. The best-known open cluster is the Pleiades, or Seven Sisters, in the constellation Taurus (pp. 90–1), which contains more than 3,000 stars. Over time, these stars will drift apart.

GLOBES OF STARS

Sometimes stars cluster together in their hundreds of thousands to form great globe shapes. We call them globular clusters. This magnificent globular cluster (right) is Omega Centauri, found about 16,500 light years away from Earth, in the constellation Centaurus. We know of about 150 globulars in our Galaxy. They are made up mainly of ancient stars, typically about 10 billion years old. Open clusters are always found in the disc of our Galaxy, but globulars can be found far above and far below this disc. They follow independent orbits around the bulge at the centre of the Galaxy. Globular clusters of old stars are often found in other galaxies too.

SKYWATCHING
SPOTTING CLUSTERS

TAURUS BOASTS TWO of the most brilliant open clusters in the heavens, the Hyades and the Pleiades. Look for the reddish first-magnitude star Aldebaran that marks the eye of the Bull. Scattered around it are the fainter stars of the Hyades. Aldebaran itself is not part of the cluster. The Pleiades (M45), further out, is unmistakable. Its other name, the Seven Sisters, suggests that we can see its seven brightest stars, but most people have difficulty spotting six. Both clusters can be seen with the naked eye, but using binoculars will give you better results.

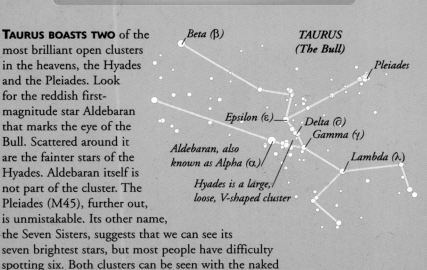

Beta (β)

TAURUS
(The Bull)

Pleiades

Epsilon (ε)

Delta (δ)
Gamma (γ)

Aldebaran, also
known as Alpha (α)

Lambda (λ)

Hyades is a large,
loose, V-shaped cluster

Messier numbers
The French astronomer Charles Joseph Messier was an avid hunter of comets. But like other astronomers, he often confused them with other fuzzy objects – star clusters and nebulas. So he compiled a list of these objects. We now identify clusters and nebulas by the number he gave them. The Crab Nebula is M1 (Messier number 1), the Pleiades cluster is M45.

Charles Joseph Messier (1730–1817)

SEEING DOUBLE

In many parts of the sky we see stars that appear close together. We call them double stars. Sometimes these stars aren't actually near each other. They only look close because they lie in the same line of sight – we call them optical doubles. Other pairs of stars are genuinely close to each other in space, and are bound together by gravity. These are called binaries. The two stars, or components, in a binary system circle around a common centre of gravity, called the barycentre. The location of this centre depends on the respective masses of the two stars. In some apparent binary systems, each star is made up of two components (see right).

Barycentre

Binary system of equal mass stars

Binary system of unequal mass stars

Multiple star system with four components

‹ SUPER SUPERNOVA ›

Some binaries are interacting – the stars are so close together that matter can pass between them. When one star is a white dwarf, it can attract so much matter from its companion that it ends up too heavy to support itself. It collapses and blasts apart as a supernova. This is the most powerful type of supernova (Type I). 117 ▶

A large star with a white dwarf companion

LET'S EXPERIMENT
ECLIPSING BINARY STARS

THE CONSTELLATION PERSEUS contains a binary star called Algol, which varies in brightness. Algol is known as an eclipsing binary. It has a small, bright star and a large, dull star, which periodically pass in front of (eclipse) each other. When this happens, Algol's overall brightness decreases. You can make a model of the Algol system.
You will need: an adult's help; old newspaper; table-tennis ball; orange paint; craft knife; 2 pen torches; modelling clay.

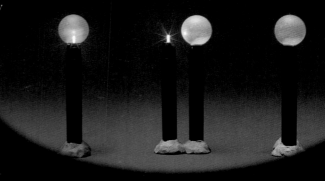

Algol contains a big, dull star and a small, bright one.

1 Cover a table with old newspaper to make a working surface. Paint the table-tennis ball orange and let it dry. Ask an adult to cut a hole in it with the craft knife. The hole must be big enough to fit over one of the pen-torch bulbs.

2 Switch on the torches and twist off the heads to expose the bulbs. Fit the orange ball over one bulb to represent Algol's big, dull star. The other bare bulb represents the small, bright star. Using the clay, stand your bright star (torch) upright.

3 Place your dull star next to the bright one. In the dark, note how bright the two stars are when they are side by side. Now move the dull star around the bright one as if it were in orbit. When the dull star is behind the bright one, notice that the overall brightness dips slightly because the bright star covers some of the dull one. The overall brightness dips most when the dull star eclipses the bright one. The same thing happens with Algol, as its stars periodically eclipse each other.

BETWEEN THE STARS

WE USUALLY THINK OF the Universe as a dark, empty space, speckled with bright stars. But this isn't quite true. The space between the stars is not completely empty. Here and there it contains faint wisps of gas and tiny solid particles of dust. We call these materials interstellar matter. In certain regions, this matter builds up into denser clouds that we can detect. These clouds are known as nebulas, and often appear as shining, misty patches. Some shine because they contain stars that give extra energy to their molecules and make them glow.

ORION SPECTACULAR

The most outstanding nebula in the heavens is found in Orion (M42). It is easy to see with the naked eye, appearing as a misty patch among the stars. In this picture (right), M42 is the largest feature. It is an emission nebula, made to glow by the radiation from the Trapezium, a multiple star system embedded within the brightest part of the nebula. Overall, the nebula measures about 16 light years across and lies about 1,500 light years away. The smaller nebula above M42 is a reflection nebula. It shines because it reflects the light from nearby stars.

SKYWATCHING
THE ORION NEBULA

THE MAGNIFICENT Orion Nebula can be appreciated equally well by astronomers in both hemispheres, because it straddles the celestial equator. The Nebula is easy to find since it lies just beneath the three bright stars that outline Orion's Belt. It makes up part of the Hunter's sword.

ORION
(The Mighty Hunter)

Lambda (λ)

Betelgeuse, also known as Alpha (α)

Gamma (γ)

Delta (δ)

Epsilon (ε)

Orion's Belt

Zeta (ζ)

Orion Nebula (M42)

Rigel, also known as Beta (ß)

Kappa (κ)

The horse's head
There is another shining nebula in Orion, near the star Zeta in Orion's Belt. When you look through a telescope, you can see within Orion what looks like a dark horse's head. This is the Horsehead Nebula. It is a dark cloud of gas and dust with nothing to make it shine. It blocks out the light from the bright nebula behind it. Within dark clouds like this, called molecular clouds (p. 104), stars are born.

PILLARS OF CREATION

This Hubble Space Telescope picture has been called the "pillars of creation". It shows columns of dark gas in which stars are forming. The columns are located at the edge of a dark molecular cloud in the Eagle Nebula (M16), in Serpens. Gradually the columns will disappear because the intense ultraviolet light of nearby stars will make them evaporate. Dense globules of gas will then be left, which will, in turn, eventually evaporate. These structures have been called EGGs (evaporating gaseous globules).

Streamers of gas that are boiling away.

Columns are silhouetted against bright ultraviolet light from hot stars.

Eerie dark columns in the Eagle Nebula, pictured by the Hubble Space Telescope.

Carbon (C)

Nitrogen (N)

Formic acid (CH_2O_2)

Oxygen (O)

Ammonia (NH_3)

Hydrogen (H)

Hydrogen sulphide (H_2S)

Sulphur (S)

INTERSTELLAR MATTER

Interstellar matter is made up mostly of hydrogen, the most common element in the Universe. But more than 80 other different substances have also been detected in nebulas. We call them interstellar molecules. Models of three are shown above – ammonia, hydrogen sulphide, and formic acid. Others include water, alcohol, and glycine. Glycine is particularly interesting because it is a simple amino acid, and amino acids are among the building blocks of life.

DEATH OF SUNLIKE STARS

A STAR SPENDS MOST OF ITS LIFE shining steadily, producing energy by fusing the hydrogen in its core. But eventually, after millions or billions of years, it uses up all the hydrogen and starts to die. The way a star dies depends on its mass. Stars similar in mass to the Sun die relatively quietly. They gradually swell up and grow redder, becoming red giants. These giant stars then puff off matter into space and shrink to become white dwarfs. As time passes, these hot, tiny stars cool and fade. More massive stars, however, go out with a bang.

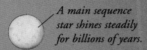

A main sequence star shines steadily for billions of years.

The dying Sun

The Sun is now about 5 billion years old, and should not start to die for another 5 billion years. When it does, it will swell up into a red giant, probably about 30 times bigger in diameter than it is now, maybe more. It might even expand enough to swallow up the planet Mercury. As a red giant, the Sun should shine a thousand times brighter than it does now, for about 2 billion years before shrinking into a white dwarf.

RED GIANTS

When all the hydrogen in the core of a star is used up, only helium remains. This means that nuclear fusion reactions are no longer possible, so the core begins to collapse under gravity, releasing energy. This heats up the outer atmosphere of the star, which greatly expands in size. The star becomes giant-sized and its surface becomes cooler and redder. The shrinking core soon gets hot enough to trigger new nuclear reactions, fusing the helium into carbon and oxygen.

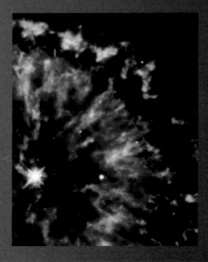

SKYWATCHING
RED GIANTS

ARCTURUS, the lead star in Boötes, is a red giant. Its name means "bear's guard", and it is found at the tail end of this kite-like constellation. With a visual magnitude of –0.1, Arcturus is the fourth brightest star in the heavens and has a noticeable orange tinge.

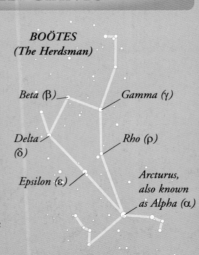

*BOÖTES
(The Herdsman)*

Beta (β)

Gamma (γ)

Delta (δ)

Rho (ρ)

Epsilon (ε)

Arcturus, also known as Alpha (α)

When the wi...
Over time, red g...
a lot of their ma...
layers flow out in...
type of stellar wi...
process is often a...
by the pulsation...
expansions and c...
that many red gi...
The hot, white d...
picture (left) has...
clouds and st...
for thousands...

PLANETARY NEBULAS

When a red giant star has used up all the helium in its core, all nuclear reactions cease. The core collapses rapidly, releasing energy that heats up the star's outer layers. This energy release is so sudden that the outer layers are blown away into space. The expelled gas and dust form a swirling, ever-expanding shell around the white-hot remains of the star. It becomes one of the most beautiful sights in the heavens, a planetary nebula. Such objects were given this name because through smaller telescopes they look like the disc of a planet.

The Eskimo planetary nebula is so called because it looks like a face inside a fur parka.

Hot, newly formed white dwarf star

Star changes colour as it slowly cools and fades.

DENSE DWARFS

The core of matter at the centre of a planetary nebula is only a fraction of the size of the original star. We call it a white dwarf. Typically, it is about the same size as Earth, but it is very much denser – as much as a million times denser than water. White dwarfs are not made up of ordinary matter, which consists of electrons circling around a central mass, the nucleus. Gravity has squashed the electrons and nuclei together, forming what is called degenerate matter. Newly formed white dwarfs are very hot, with a surface temperature reaching tens of thousands of degrees.

A matchbox full of white dwarf matter is so dense that it would weigh as much as an elephant.

MATCHES
40

LET'S EXPERIMENT
STARDUST

IN ITS CORE, a red giant makes carbon, which it later puffs out into space. The carbon then cools to form solid specks of stardust. In this experiment you can imitate this process. **You will need:** an adult's help; candle and holder; matches; small plate; oven gloves.

1 Place the candle in the holder and ask an adult to light it. Using an oven glove, the adult should hold the plate so that it touches the flame.

2 As the flame touches the plate, you'll see black soot begin to form. Moving the plate around creates a swirling pattern.

3 The flame contains tiny, invisible particles of carbon. When the flame touches the cold plate, the particles condense and build up to form soot. In space, sooty material from a red giant floats slowly away from the star.

DEATH OF MASSIVE STARS

STARS MORE MASSIVE THAN the Sun end their lives spectacularly. As they die, they swell up into enormous supergiants, but do not stay that way for long. Soon they blast themselves apart as supernovas. These are among the greatest explosions in the Universe. On average, supernovas are visible in our Galaxy about once every 300 years. In 1987, a supernova in a neighbouring galaxy, the Large Magellanic Cloud, was visible to the naked eye. We see its remains today as an expanding cloud of gas and dust.

Massive blue-white giant star burns hydrogen.

The star swells as its hydrogen runs out, turning first yellow, then red, as its surface cools.

SUPERGIANTS

A typical supergiant star is hundreds of times bigger in diameter than the Sun and about ten times the size of a red giant. It forms when a massive star, much bigger than the Sun, swells in size when the hydrogen in its core runs out. New nuclear processes then start to fuse helium into carbon. But, unlike the smaller, sunlike stars, carbon builds up so much that the core collapses under the weight. The energy released by this collapse produces high enough temperatures to trigger off further fusion reactions. They convert the carbon into other elements, such as magnesium, sulphur, silicon, and finally iron. Nuclear reactions cease with iron because it cannot fuse into anything else. Iron builds up in the core, setting the stage for the superstar's violent end.

Chandrasekhar's limit
Indian-born astrophysicist Subrahmanyan Chandrasekhar (1910–95) was noted for his study of dying stars. He worked out the Chandrasekhar limit for core mass. This decides whether a star becomes a white dwarf or explodes as a supernova. For his work, Chandrasekhar was awarded the 1983 Nobel Prize for Physics.

Supergiant can be up to 1,000 times bigger in diameter than the Sun.

SUPER EXPLOSIONS

When a supergiant's iron core becomes more than 1.4 times more massive than the Sun (the Chandrasekhar limit), it collapses in on itself. Its matter is crushed into a smaller and smaller space. The core's collapse makes the star's outer layers collapse too. This process releases a huge amount of energy, causing a fantastic explosion that rips the star apart. It becomes a supernova. The collapsed core may become either a neutron star or a black hole.

This gold was created during a supernova.

Gold producer
The nuclear processes inside massive stars produce iron by fusing together lighter elements. But they cannot create heavier elements, such as gold. Only supernovas can produce enough energy to trigger new fusion reactions. All the heavier elements in the Universe were made during these explosions.

A neutron star is a tiny city-sized star, made up of neutrons.

The aftermath
The matter blasted out in a supernova explosion forms a vast and ever-expanding cloud around the remains of the original star. We call this cloud a supernova remnant. This picture (left) shows the remnant of a supernova that exploded in the constellation Cassiopeia about 300 years ago. The image was taken by the Chandra Observatory using X-ray wavelengths. The remnant, named Cassiopeia A, is a powerful source of X-ray and radio waves, but cannot be seen in visible light.

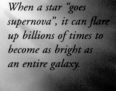

When a star "goes supernova", it can flare up billions of times to become as bright as an entire galaxy.

A black hole's gravity is so strong, even light cannot escape from it.

LET'S EXPERIMENT
BOUNCING BLAST

WHEN A MASSIVE star "goes supernova", its core collapses and shrinks. The star's outer layers collapse too. They rebound from the core so violently that the star is blasted apart. In this experiment, you can imitate the collision of the outer layers (small ball) and the core (larger ball). **You will need:** tennis ball; larger bouncy ball.

1 In a large open space, hold up the tennis ball and drop it. Notice how high it bounces. Repeat with the larger ball. On its own, each ball bounces to roughly three-quarters the height from which it was dropped.

2 Now hold the tennis ball on top of the other ball, as shown in the picture (left). Drop them together. The large ball hits the ground and bounces. The tennis ball bounces on top of the large ball.

3 The tennis ball gains extra energy from the large ball's bounce and shoots high into the air. This is just like the collapsing gas and dust in a supernova that rebounds off the star's core and blasts off into space.

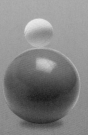

PULSARS AND BLACK HOLES

WHEN A MASSIVE STAR DIES, its core collapses. As the core shrinks, gravity crushes its matter. The atoms are squashed and the electrons are forced inside the nucleus (atomic centre), where they combine with protons to create neutrons. The whole mass transforms into neutrons and a neutron star is born. Some neutron stars are known as pulsars because they rotate rapidly, giving off pulses of radiation. Sometimes, if the collapsing core has more than three times the Sun's mass, the neutron star continues to shrink. Its gravity becomes so strong that even light rays cannot escape – it forms a black hole in space.

THE CRAB'S PULSE

Within the constellation Taurus there is an expanding cloud of gas, known as the Crab Nebula (M1). It is the remains of a star that went supernova in the year 1054. In the heart of this nebula is an object that flashes pulses of light towards Earth 30 times a second. Astronomers call this object a pulsar and believe it to be a spinning neutron star. Cambridge radio astronomer Jocelyn Bell discovered the first pulsar in 1967 by detecting regular pulses of radio waves from space (p. 19).

LET'S EXPERIMENT
MAKING A PULSAR

PULSARS ARE RAPIDLY spinning neutron stars, which flash twin beams of radiation into space. This radiation is usually radio waves, but some pulsars, like the Crab pulsar, give off beams of visible light. We can only see pulsars flashing when their beams sweep across our line of sight. You can make your own pulsar in this experiment. **You will need:** 2 pen torches; adhesive putty; thin card; tape; scissors; string.

The torch beams seem to pulse on and off as they whizz past your eyes.

1 Using adhesive putty, join the back ends of the pen torches together so that they shine in opposite directions. Wrap card around the join and tape it tightly to hold the torches firmly together in a straight line. Cut a length of string and tie it around the taped join.

2 Hang the string from a fixed point, and balance the torches. Switch them on and spin them round. View the torches at eye level in a dark room. The beams whizz past your eyes, and the light seems to flash on and off. View the beams from different angles – the pulse isn't always seen.

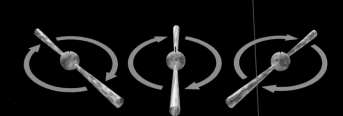

Pulsar off   *Pulsar on*   *Pulsar off*

A COSMIC LIGHTHOUSE

When a neutron star spins, the highly concentrated magnetic field around it rotates too. This rotating field causes electrically charged particles (protons and electrons) to gyrate. As they move, they give off energy as electromagnetic radiation (pp. 18–19). The star beams out this radiation from its two magnetic poles. These beams sweep around the star like beams from a great celestial lighthouse (as the above diagrams show). If the beams sweep past Earth, we can detect the radiation pulsing on and off. However, if the pulsar spins at a different angle, the beams miss Earth, and the pulsar remains undetected.

THE ULTIMATE ABYSS

The biggest stars have cores with more than three times the Sun's mass. In these cases, when a core collapses, it goes beyond the neutron star stage. As it shrinks smaller, its gravity becomes enormous. Not even a mass of neutrons can withstand it, and they get squashed. Eventually, the gravity becomes so great that light cannot escape. The core becomes invisible, leaving a black hole in space. This hole has such intense gravity that it swallows anything that comes near it. Astronomers believe that, inside the black hole, the core has been crushed into a tiny point, called a singularity.

Blue-giant companion star

Gravity from black hole pulls gas from companion star.

Accretion disc rotates rapidly.

Gas temperatures rise up to 100 million °C (180 million °F) near the black hole.

Black hole

Detecting black holes

Seeing a black hole in the blackness of space is not possible. But we can detect one indirectly when it has a close companion in a binary system (p. 111). The hole's powerful gravity pulls matter from the companion star, and this forms a whirling "accretion disc". Friction within this disc makes the gas very hot and causes it to emit continuous, detectable X-rays.

Powerful X-rays are emitted by the superhot, whirling gas.

The astronaut strays near the black hole, but looks normal.

The astronaut's body begins to stretch and his image begins to redden as light rays lengthen.

Spaghettification

If an astronaut were unfortunate enough to fall into a black hole, he would be stretched out long and thin like spaghetti. He would suffer this fate because gravity inside a black hole builds up very quickly. As soon as his legs entered the hole, they would experience much stronger gravity than his head and be stretched out to incredible lengths. This process would continue until his whole body was spaghettified.

The stretching increases and the image gets even redder.

Hawking's minis

Tiny black holes the size of atoms but with a mass of billions of tonnes may have been created when the Universe was born. British physicist Stephen Hawking (born 1942) has suggested that the intense gravity around a mini black hole might cause it to release radiation. This "Hawking radiation" drains away the energy and mass until eventually the black hole disappears in an explosive blast of gamma rays.

GALAXIES

Picture: *Spectacular spiral galaxy ESO 269-57 lies 155 million light years away. Hundreds more galaxies can be seen in the background.*

STAR ISLANDS

WHEREVER WE LOOK IN THE NIGHT SKY, there are countless numbers of stars scattered about in space. Every star that we see with the naked eye belongs to a group called a galaxy – our home galaxy in fact, which we call the Milky Way. The Milky Way may contain as many as 200 billion stars, and is just one of perhaps 100 billion galaxies in the Universe. Almost all the stars in the Universe live inside these gigantic "star islands". The galaxies themselves are found in clusters, and these in turn form larger groups called superclusters, separated from each other by vast expanses of space.

THE MILKY WAY

To night-sky observers, the Milky Way is a hazy band of light that arches across the heavens. When viewed through binoculars or a telescope, it appears as a mass of faint stars, seemingly packed close together. This is the view we have of our Galaxy from inside it.

The Milky Way Galaxy is shaped like a disc with a bulge at the centre. When we look towards its middle, there is a greater "depth" of stars, which makes them appear crowded together.

In the Northern Hemisphere, the Milky Way is brightest in the constellations Cygnus and Aquila, and in the Southern Hemisphere, in Sagittarius and Scorpius.

MAPPING THE GALAXY

It was only in the 1700s that astronomers began thinking about what our Galaxy was really like. The astronomer William Herschel in England realized that the band of the

This part of the Milky Way is seen in the constellation Cygnus. Colourful nebulas stand out among dense star "fields".

Milky Way appears as it does because Earth lies inside a layer of stars.

By counting the stars in selected regions of the sky, Herschel worked out roughly how stars are distributed within the Milky Way. With this information, he came up with the first ever map of the Galaxy. He reckoned that it was shaped rather like a disc or lens – thickest in the middle and thinning towards the edges.

Herschel also searched the sky for

This satellite view of the Milky Way, seen in infrared light, clearly shows the lens shape that Herschel described. The dense dust clouds that exist between the stars are also visible.

nebulas, discovering more than 2,000 of them. In doing this, he was continuing the work of Charles Messier. The objects Messier numbered are still known today by the prefix "M" for Messier object (p. 110). Herschel even wondered whether some of these fuzzy objects might be separate "island universes", or galaxies.

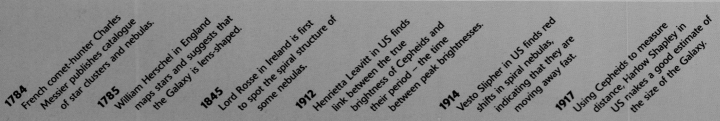

1784 French comet-hunter Charles Messier publishes catalogue of star clusters and nebulas.

1785 William Herschel in England maps stars and suggests that the Galaxy is lens-shaped.

1845 Lord Rosse in Ireland is first to spot the spiral structure of some nebulas.

1912 Henrietta Leavitt in US finds link between the true brightness of Cepheids and their period – the time between peak brightnesses.

1914 Vesto Slipher in US finds red shifts in spiral nebulas, indicating that they are moving away fast.

1917 Using Cepheids to measure distance, Harlow Shapley in US makes a good estimate of the size of the Galaxy.

Timeline

SPECTACULAR SPIRALS

In the 1840s, an Irish nobleman named William Parsons, Lord Rosse, built a huge telescope called the *Leviathan*. He used it to look at Messier object number 51 and saw that it had a spiral structure. Later studies showed that many nebulas had a similar spiral shape.

The Whirlpool Galaxy (M51) is a spectacular face-on spiral galaxy. Stars are forming along the red-coloured regions of the arms.

But were they part of our Galaxy or were they outside it? No one knew the answer, because no one even knew how big our Galaxy was or how far away the nebulas were.

NEAR AND FAR

It was not until 1917 that US astronomer Harlow Shapley provided an estimate for the size of the Milky Way, using variable stars called Cepheids as a guide to distance. Shapley believed that our Galaxy was about 300,000 light years across (about three times larger than it really is). So did the spiral nebulas lie outside the Galaxy?

In 1923, the great US astronomer Edwin Hubble found one that did – the famous Andromeda. He spotted a Cepheid in one of its spiral arms, and worked out that it was 900,000 light years away. This put it far beyond the Milky Way. Hubble went on to study many other galaxies and found evidence that they were all rushing away from us. This meant that the Universe must be expanding.

HYPERACTIVITY

Hubble classified galaxies into four main types – spirals, barred spirals, ellipticals, and irregulars. All galaxies are one or the

The Large Magellanic Cloud (detail, below) lies 160,000 light years beyond our Galaxy.

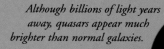

Although billions of light years away, quasars appear much brighter than normal galaxies.

other. However, a few are noted for their amazingly high-energy output, and we call these active galaxies.

Quasars are one type of active galaxy. They are no larger than our Solar System, but they have the energy output of hundreds of ordinary galaxies. Their energy may be emitted as light, X-rays, and radio waves. Astronomers believe the "engine" that powers a quasar and all other active galaxies is a black hole.

Quasars are also extraordinary for their remoteness. Many appear to lie near the very edge of the observable Universe – more than 10 billion light years away.

DEEP SPACE

Large ground-based telescopes can spot quasars at such distances because quasars are so bright. But ground telescopes can't spot ordinary galaxies that far away. Up in space, however, the Hubble Space Telescope can. In 1995, it spent 10 days looking at a small region of sky in Ursa

The Hubble Deep Field image shows galaxies as they were in the early Universe.

Major. The image it produced is known as the Hubble Deep Field. Some galaxies in it are more than 10 billion light years away. It's taken their light that long to reach us, so we're seeing them as they were 10 billion years ago – only a few billion years after the Universe was born. By studying this image, we can look back in time.

1923 Edwin Hubble in US proves that spiral nebulas lie beyond the Galaxy. He calls them extragalactic nebulas.

1929 Hubble discovers that galaxies move faster the further away they are, leading to the idea of an expanding Universe.

1943 Carl Seyfert in US discovers galaxies with ultrabright centres, now known to be active galaxies.

1950s Radio astronomers discover radio galaxies, now also known to be active galaxies.

1963 Maarten Schmidt in the Netherlands identifies radio source 3C273 with visible object, the first known quasar.

1995 Hubble Space Telescope pictures very remote galaxies in Hubble Deep Field image.

OUR HOME GALAXY

The Milky Way, as it would look from far out in space

THE SUN IS JUST ONE of about 200 billion stars that form the Milky Way Galaxy – our home in the Universe. The Milky Way was born from a huge ball of hot gas that collapsed under the weight of its own gravity and flattened out to become a typical spiral galaxy. It is a rotating disc with a huge bulge in the middle. Long arms spiral out from the bulge, full of bright new stars and dense clouds of gas and dust. The Galaxy is vast, measuring some 100,000 light years in diameter, although the disc is only about 2,000 light years thick.

THE BULGE

The bulge, or nucleus, of the Galaxy has the shape of a flattened sphere, and is about 6,000 light years thick. It contains masses of old, red and yellow stars, which give it a yellowish glow. They are packed closer together than the stars in the spiral arms, which are generally much younger. Radio astronomy has revealed that the middle of the bulge is a complex place. There are vast molecular clouds, fast-moving jets of gas, and a tilted, rotating gas disc. Right at the very heart of the galaxy lies a massive black hole (p. 126).

SKY WATCHING
THE MILKY WAY

YOU NEED A clear night to observe the Milky Way, away from the light pollution of urban areas. It appears at its brightest between June and September, when Earth's night-time side is turned towards the galactic centre.

The Milky Way in the constellations Cassiopeia and Perseus

In the halo
The bulge and disc of the Galaxy contain the most stars. The disc stars travel in the plane of the disc, orbiting the Galaxy's centre. The bulge stars stay within the bulge. But some stars form groups known as globular clusters. These travel in independent orbits outside the bulge in a region known as the halo – a huge sphere that surrounds the whole Galaxy. The halo is about 150,000 light years across and contains mysterious dark matter that we can't see or detect (p. 144).

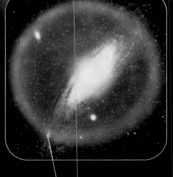

Artist's impression of the halo of dark matter around a spiral galaxy

Glorious globulars
The globular clusters that travel outside the bulge are quite different from the young open clusters found in the spiral arms. Stars in globular clusters are old and are packed into huge, globe-shaped masses (p. 110). They can measure about 100 light years across and contain hundreds of thousands of stars. They may stray as far as 300,000 light years from the plane of the Galaxy. Globular clusters were formed from the Galaxy's original material and are typically 10 billion years old.

The dense globular cluster, M80

THE MILKY CIRCLE

In the night sky, the Milky Way is the pale band of light that arches across the heavens. It was named the Milky Circle by the ancient Greeks, who believed it was a stream of milk from the goddess Hera's breast. The Milky Way is our cross-section view of the Galaxy. It is brightest in the constellation Sagittarius (the Archer), which lies in the direction of the Galaxy's centre. What seem to be dark rifts, or holes, in the Milky Way are actually huge dark clouds of dust that block the light from stars behind.

Radio image of Milky Way

Mapping the galaxy
Ordinary photographs can't show what's behind the Milky Way's dark dust clouds, so astronomers use radio telescopes (right) to take radio pictures. Radio waves from interstellar hydrogen gas pass through the dust and reveal what's behind. In this radio picture of the Galaxy (above), red shows the most intense radio emission.

INSIDE THE MILKY WAY

BY PROBING THE MILKY WAY with radio telescopes, astronomers have discovered the Galaxy's shape and composition. Radio images show that objects such as stars and gas clouds are concentrated in long, curved regions we call spiral arms. These curl out from the oval-shaped bulge at the Galaxy's centre. The heart of the Galaxy is a highly disturbed and energetic region containing dense clusters of stars and a black hole, which is marked by an intense radio source called Sagittarius A.

THE SPIRAL ARMS

The Galaxy's two major arms are called Sagittarius and Perseus. The Sagittarius Arm sweeps all the way around the Galaxy. It contains some of the most spectacular sights in the heavens, such as the Eagle, Omega, Trifid, Lagoon, and Carina nebulas. The Perseus Arm, which lies further out, is more disjointed. Between the two lies the Orion Arm, also called the Local Arm. This is where our Sun and Solar System are located, about 28,000 light years from the galactic centre. Orion was once thought to be a bridge between the Sagittarius and Perseus Arms, but is now known to be a spiral arm in its own right.

Sagittarius A
The powerful radio source Sagittarius A marks the exact centre of the Galaxy. It lies in a region of intense magnetism. Radio images of the centre (left) show a curved feature called the Arc, which is part of the Radio Lobe, a ring-shaped area of magnetized gas.

The Arc

Sagittarius Dwarf Galaxy

OUTER ARM

SAGITTARIUS ARM

NORMA ARM

GALACTIC CENTRE

3 KILOPARSEC ARM

SCUTUM-CRUX

SAGITTARIUS ARM

Cygnus X-1
Crab Nebula
Cassiopeia A

ORION ARM

PERSEUS ARM

The Sun

Carina Ne

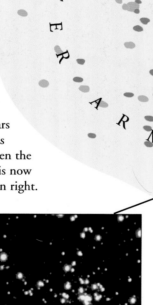

Double Cluster in Perseus
The Double Cluster is a close pair of open star clusters, also known as chi (left) and h Persei (right). They are notable for their large number of very hot, bright O and B stars (p. 103). The two clusters are about 50 light years apart and 7,000 light years from Earth. The pair each contains several thousand stars, and lies at the centre of a much larger, looser group (association) of young stars.

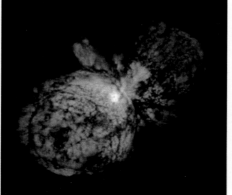

Eta Carinae
The Carina nebula is home to Eta Carinae, a star 100 times more massive and millions of times brighter than the Sun. This Hubble picture shows the star cocooned in the cloud of dust it ejected when it flared up in 1843 to become one of the brightest stars visible in the southern sky. Eta Carinae is very unstable and could explode as a supernova at any time.

IN THE NEIGHBOURHOOD

The map on this page shows a more detailed view of the Orion Arm in the neighbourhood of the Sun. It covers a region about 5,000 light years in diameter and shows the approximate locations of familiar stars such as Rigel, clusters such as the Pleiades, and nebulas such as the Horsehead. Vast hydrogen gas clouds pervade this part of the Galaxy, making it a region rich in star formation. "Stellar nurseries" are plentiful, for example, in the Orion, North American, and Rho Ophiuchi nebulas.

Rho Ophiuchi
The star Rho Ophiuchi (centre right) and the red giant star Antares (top left) lie within one of the most colourful regions of the sky. The red colours in the picture show where radiation from Antares and Sigma Scorpii (lower left) are exciting gas atoms and making them glow. Blue colours show where fine dust is reflecting starlight.

COLOUR KEY TO MAPS

- Hydrogen gas clouds
- Nebula concentrations
- Molecular clouds
- Star associations
- Supernova remnants
- Interstellar bubbles
- Star clusters and giant stars

Loop II and III are the remains of massive stars that exploded as supernovas.

North American and Pelican nebulas

Deneb

Dumbbell nebula

Antares

LOOP I

Loop I is a huge bubble blown up by violent winds boiling off massive young stars.

LOOP III

Hyades

The Coalsack, a giant molecular cloud

Acrux

Gum nebula

The Sun

Canopus

Pleiades cluster

Betelgeuse

Polaris

LOOP II

Taurus Dark Cloud

Rigel

Barnard's loop is a supernova remnant about 300 light years across.

Orion Nebula

Horsehead Nebula

Epsilon Aurigae

Cone Nebula

Great Rift in Cygnus
A dark lane runs through the Milky Way in the constellation Cygnus, cutting through the glowing nebulas and dense star fields. This is the Great Rift, a huge molecular cloud of gas and dust so dense that it blocks out the light from the starfields behind. Intense star formation is going on inside the cloud, and radiation from young, hot stars near the cloud's edges is producing the luminous billows of hydrogen gas, visible in the picture above.

Helix nebula
At a distance of only 500 light years, the Helix nebula is the nearest planetary nebula to Earth. The star at the centre is dying. In its death throes, it has twice puffed off its outer layers in clouds of gas, giving the nebula its double-ring shape. As it shrinks into a white dwarf, intense radiation from the hot little star makes the gas glow.

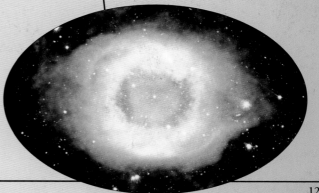

GALAXIES GALORE

BILLIONS OF GALAXIES exist beyond the Milky Way, each packed with stars in their millions of millions. Many are great spiral structures like our Galaxy, but others have different shapes. Some of the biggest are vast oval masses, which we call ellipticals. Others have no particular shape at all, so we call them irregulars. Every galaxy is held together by gravity, but astronomers still have no real idea of what makes them the shape they are.

Galaxy pioneer

US astronomer Edwin Hubble first began studying what appeared to be nebulas in 1919. In 1923, he proved that many lay beyond our Galaxy and were in fact separate galaxies. By analyzing light from these distant objects, Hubble found that the further the galaxy, the faster it was speeding away from us. This major discovery, known as Hubble's law, established that the Universe is expanding.

Edwin Hubble (1889–1953)

Galaxy M104:
Type Sa

Galaxy M81:
Type Sb

Galaxy M83:
Type Sc

Galaxy M87:
Type E0

Galaxy M32:
Type E2

Galaxy M59:
Type E5

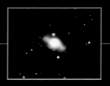

Galaxy NGC 4650:
Type SBa

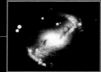

Galaxy NGC 5383:
Type SBb

Galaxy NGC
6744: Type SBc

HUBBLE'S TUNING FORK

Edwin Hubble devised the method still used today to classify galaxies. He divided them into different types according to their shape and arranged them into a type of tuning fork pattern, as shown above. The main types are ellipticals, spirals, and barred spirals. The ellipticals (E) are subdivided into different types 0–7 according to how round or oval they are. The spirals (S) and barred spirals (SB) are subdivided a, b, and c, according to how open their spiral arms are, c being the most open type.

Galaxy NGC 4414

Galaxy NGC 1365

SPIRALS

Spiral galaxies such as the Milky Way are among the most spectacular objects in the Universe. A dense ball of old stars in the centre, or nucleus, is orbited by a thinner disc of young stars, gas, and dust. The stars congregate in spiral arms that curve out from the nucleus. From Earth, we see spirals at different angles – from side views to full face, when they appear at their most beautiful. Galaxy NGC 4414 (left) is a dusty spiral, with intense star formation taking place in its arms.

Barred spirals

As many as half of all spiral galaxies have a bar of stars through the nucleus. Known as barred spirals, their arms curve out from the ends of the bar. Galaxy NGC 1365 (above) is a beautiful example found in the Fornax cluster of galaxies.

Galaxy NGC 4881

ELLIPTICALS

More than half of all galaxies are ellipticals.
In other words, they are ball- or egg-shaped
masses of stars with no trace of the curved
arms of spirals. Ellipticals contain little gas
and dust, so there isn't much star formation
taking place inside them. They are made up
mostly of old stars. Some of the smallest and
largest galaxies are ellipticals. Galaxy NGC
4881 (above) is a giant elliptical galaxy
in Coma Berenices.

Galaxies NGC 4038 and NGC 4039

‹ GALAXY BIRTH ›

The first galaxies were probably born
less than a billion years after the Big
Bang created the Universe. They may
have formed out of collisions and mergers
between the clouds of gas that were then
scattered around in space. Collisions
between small galaxies produced larger
ones. This can be seen happening in the
Hubble Deep Field image, which shows
galaxies as they were more than
10 billion years ago. 142 ›

*Remote galaxies in
the Hubble Deep Field*

Irregulars
While most galaxies are spirals or
ellipticals, some have no definite
shape at all. Astronomers
call them irregulars (Irr
for short). In general,
irregulars are rich in gas
and dust, with much
star formation taking
place. Galaxy M82 (left)
is an irregular galaxy
in Ursa Major.

Galaxy M82

LET'S EXPERIMENT
SPIRAL GALAXY

A SPIRAL GALAXY, SUCH AS THE MILKY WAY, keeps its shape for
billions of years as the stars inside it orbit the galactic centre. Make
a spiral in this simple experiment. **You will need:** an adult to help
you; cup; coffee; cream; spoon.

1 Ask an adult to make a cup
of black coffee. Then
gently lower a spoonful of
cream into it, and stir
round and round in
the same direction.

2 The cream
should form
a spiral shape,
rather like a
spiral galaxy.
When the
spiral is
turning
steadily,
stop stirring.
See how the
spiral keeps
its shape.

COLLISION COURSE

Many galaxies are on a collision course with one another.
When they collide, a great celestial fireworks display
takes place. The picture above shows two spiral galaxies
colliding, or interacting. Giant clouds of gas in the
galaxies are crashing into each other, triggering outbursts
of star formation. During the collision, some stars have
been flung out into space, leaving bright streamers.

ACTIVE GALAXIES

MOST GALAXIES GIVE OUT the amount of energy you might expect from groupings of billions of shining stars. But about one galaxy in ten gives out exceptional energy, usually from a tiny region at its centre. We call these active galaxies. They may emit their energy as light, and as invisible radiation, such as radio waves and X-rays. Active galaxies fall into four main types called radio galaxies, Seyferts, blazars, and quasars, depending on their distance from us and the angle at which they face us. At the heart of each lurks a massive black hole – the source of the galaxy's power.

Radio image of Centaurus A

Visible part of galaxy

Galaxy's centre is obscured by dust lanes.

CENTAURUS A

A broad, dark band of dust cuts across the middle of galaxy NGC 5128 in Centaurus (left). Also known as Centaurus A, the galaxy is the third strongest source of radio waves in our skies. It was one of the first radio galaxies to be discovered, and at a distance of about 15 million light years, is the nearest active galaxy to us. In its centre is a colossal black hole with a mass of about 100 million Suns. A radio image of Centaurus A (inset) shows radiation coming from regions known as lobes, which extend thousands of light years out from the centre.

Jet emerges from hot core of accretion disc

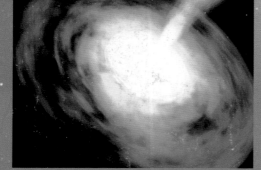

POWER ENGINE

An active galaxy is powered by the enormous energy released as matter disappears into a black hole. A structure builds up around the hole that is common to all active galaxies. Matter attracted by the hole's ultra-strong gravity forms into a doughnut-shaped ring called a torus. Towards the core, the matter flattens into an intensely hot and rapidly rotating accretion disc before being sucked into the hole. The disc emits X-rays and shoots out jets of gas and charged particles. From Earth, we see the torus, disc, and jets at different angles depending on which way the active galaxy is facing.

Torus at centre of galaxy NGC 4261 in Virgo

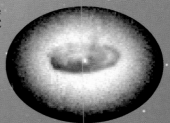

Dusty torus
This torus of gas and dust in an active galaxy was photographed by the Hubble Space Telescope. It is lit up by a hot accretion disc surrounding a black hole in the centre. Astronomers believe that this hole has the mass of about 1.2 billion Suns.

Radio galaxies

We see an active galaxy as a radio galaxy when we view the torus side-on. The jets of gas and particles shoot out to either side, giving off radio waves. They are fast-moving and extend for thousands or even millions of light years. They expand to form bubble-like lobes, which produce the most radiation.

Radio galaxy 3C 296; red shows radio waves, blue shows visible light

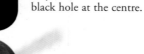

View of active galaxy showing the torus side-on

Blazars

When we view the torus face-on, the jet points directly towards us and we can look straight into it. Then we see the active galaxy as a blazar. Like quasars, blazars are intensely bright and therefore visible over great distances. They also vary rapidly in brightness as jet material accelerates out of the accretion disc.

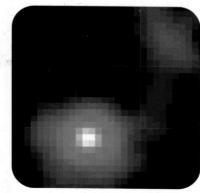

Blazar 3C 279, viewed by the intense gamma radiation it gives out

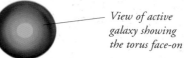

View of active galaxy showing the torus face-on

Seyferts

Seyfert galaxies are spiral galaxies with a very bright spot of light at the centre. We see an active galaxy as a Seyfert galaxy when we view the torus at an angle and look at the bright central region. Seyferts are probably similar to quasars, but appear fainter because they have a less massive black hole at the centre.

Seyfert galaxy NGC 7742; core is about 3,000 light years across

View of active galaxy showing torus at angle

Quasars

Quasars are the most distant objects we can see. Although very far away, these active galaxies are so powerful that they were named quasi-stellar objects (quasars for short) because they look like faint stars. They emit radio waves, X-rays, infrared, and light. Like Seyferts, we view quasars at an angle so that we can see part of the brilliant core.

The energy of quasar PG 1012+008, seen in radio waves

View of active galaxy showing torus at angle

LET'S EXPERIMENT
QUASAR BRIGHTNESS

QUASARS ARE AMONG the brightest and most remote objects in the Universe. In this experiment, we compare the brightness of distant quasars with nearby stars. **You will need:** bright desk lamp with 40 or 60 watt bulb; small pocket torch.

1 Place the "quasar" lamp on a table and point it towards you. Switch it on. Switch on the "star" torch too. Now turn off the room lights. Stand about 3–4 m (10–13 ft) away from the lamp. Hold the torch pointing towards you.

2 Move the "star" torch towards you until it appears just as bright as the "quasar" lamp. This tells you that to be as bright as the nearby star, the quasar must be very bright indeed, because it is so much further away.

OUR GALACTIC NEIGHBOURS

MOST OF THE GALAXIES in the Universe lie extremely far away from us, but a few are just close enough to see with the naked eye. These are some of our galactic neighbours, and we see them as hazy patches in the sky. Two of the closest ones, called the Large and Small Magellanic Clouds, are visible in the Southern Hemisphere. The other is found in the constellation Andromeda in the Northern Hemisphere. It is amazing that we can see the Andromeda Galaxy at all, because it lies 2.4 million light years away. This is the furthest object that we can see in space with the naked eye.

SKYWATCHING
ANDROMEDA

THE ANDROMEDA Galaxy is easy to find because it lies roughly halfway between two prominent Northern Hemisphere star patterns – the W-shape of Cassiopeia and the Square of Pegasus. Though visible to the eye, it is better seen through binoculars.

Satellite galaxy NGC 205

ANDROMEDA GALAXY

The Andromeda Galaxy (M31) is one of the largest spiral galaxies known, with a diameter of about 150,000 light years. It is one and a half times larger than our own Galaxy, and contains two to three times more stars, maybe as many as 400 billion. We see the Andromeda Galaxy nearly edge-on, so we can't easily make out its spiral structure. The galaxy travels through space with two close companions, the satellite galaxies M32 and NGC 205, which orbit around it. Both are small elliptical galaxies.

Satellite galaxy M32

THE MAGELLANIC CLOUDS

The Magellanic Clouds are named after the Portugese navigator Ferdinand Magellan, who first spotted them when he sailed the South Pacific in 1519. The Large Magellanic Cloud (LMC) is the closest major galaxy to us, at a distance of about 160,000 light years (right). It is about 30,000 light years closer than the Small Magellanic Cloud (SMC). With a diameter of about 30,000 light years, the LMC is one and a half times larger than the SMC. The main feature of the LMC is a broad band of old stars. However, there are also regions containing young, hot stars, and bright, star-forming nebulas like the Tarantula.

Tarantula nebula
A spidery-looking nebula called the Tarantula is the LMC's brightest feature. This Hubble picture shows (at bottom right) a cluster of brilliant, massive old stars. Some have already exploded as supernovas, blasting clouds of matter into the surrounding space.

About 250 million years ago, the Clouds passed close to the Galaxy; some stars are pulled out .

About 500 million years ago, the Clouds started to close in on the Galaxy.

Today, the Clouds are heading outwards again, away from the Galaxy, trailing a stream of gas.

Clouds in orbit
The Magellanic Clouds are satellite galaxies of the Milky Way. They orbit around our Galaxy about once every 1.5 billion years. Sometimes they travel so close that the gravity of our Galaxy starts pulling them apart. In time it will swallow them up.

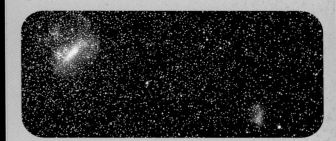

SKYWATCHING
MAGELLANIC CLOUDS

THE LARGE AND SMALL Magellanic Clouds appear quite close together in the far Southern Hemisphere. The LMC can easily be found by looking south of the bright star Canopus in the constellation Carina. The SMC is found south of the bright star Achernar in the constellation Eridanus.

NGC 604

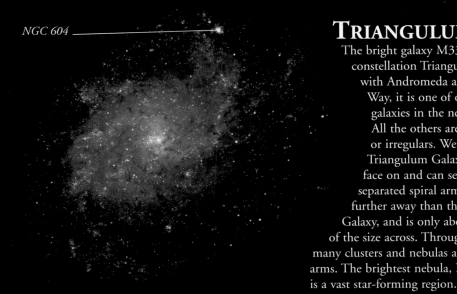

TRIANGULUM

The bright galaxy M33 lies in the constellation Triangulum. Along with Andromeda and the Milky Way, it is one of only three spiral galaxies in the neighbourhood. All the others are ellipticals or irregulars. We view the Triangulum Galaxy nearly face on and can see its widely separated spiral arms. It lies a little further away than the Andromeda Galaxy, and is only about a quarter of the size across. Through telescopes, many clusters and nebulas are visible in its arms. The brightest nebula, NGC 604, is a vast star-forming region.

Star birth in M33
This colourful cloud is nebula NGC 604 in the Triangulum Galaxy. The hundreds of young, hot stars in this great stellar nursery give out intense ultraviolet radiation, which lights up the surrounding gas and produces a spectacular glow.

GALAXY CLUSTERS

THE MILKY WAY and its galaxy neighbours all belong to a larger collection, or cluster, of galaxies. We call this cluster the Local Group. The more distant galaxies are also found gathered together in clusters. Some clusters contain just a few galaxies, others may contain thousands. On a larger scale still, even the clusters group together into superclusters. The Local Group of galaxies forms part of the Local Supercluster, centred on the gigantic Virgo cluster. On the largest scale of all, the superclusters are strung together to form the Universe.

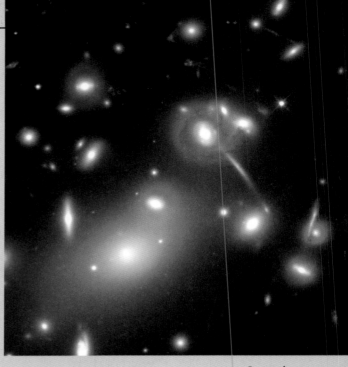

Large cluster
Abell 2218

LOCAL GROUP

The cluster of galaxies in our corner of the Universe, the Local Group, contains about 30 members. They are scattered over a region of space about three million light years across. The Andromeda Galaxy, the Milky Way, and Galaxy M33 (in Triangulum) are by far the biggest galaxies in the group and are all spirals. The other, smaller members are either ellipticals or irregulars. The diagram (right) shows how the main members of the Local Group are spread out in space. Both the Milky Way and Andromeda have close satellite galaxies circling around them. In time, gravity may pull all the galaxies together into a single supergalaxy.

LARGE CLUSTERS

Elsewhere in the Universe, galaxies such as the ones shown above gather together in their hundreds and even in their thousands. The nearest large cluster to us is the Virgo cluster, which is about 50 million light years away. It is a collection of some 2,000 galaxies, scattered over a region of space about 10 million light years across. About 300 million light years away is the Coma cluster, which contains half as many galaxies again. Most large clusters have one or more giant-sized elliptical galaxies at their centre, which probably grew over time by swallowing up other galaxies in the cluster.

Elliptical giants

Three giant elliptical galaxies are found in the middle of the Virgo cluster – M84, M86, and M87 (shown right). Like many giant ellipticals, M87 is a powerful source of radio waves. It is classed as a radio galaxy, one type of active galaxy (p. 130).

NGC 185
NGC 147
NGC 205
Andromeda
M32
M33

Local Group galaxies

Newborn stars

The dwarfs

The galaxy Sextans A (above) is one of about ten irregular dwarf galaxies in the Local Group. Typically, they are just a few thousand light years across. But the smallest galaxies of all are the dwarf ellipticals, some of which are only about 500 light years across. These tiny galaxies may contain fewer than a million stars and do not shine very brightly.

NGC 6822
Ursa Minor
Draco
Milky Way
Sextans
Leo II
Sculptor
Fornax
Large Magellanic Cloud (LMC)
Small Magellanic Cloud (SMC)
Carina
Leo I

Hot stuff
Galaxy clusters seem to be filled with masses of very hot gas, which we can detect by the X-rays it gives out. Gas temperatures reach 100 million °C (180 million °F). The X-ray image (right) shows strange gas plumes within the Centaurus cluster.

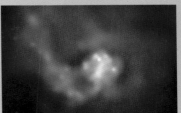

X-ray image of
Centaurus cluster

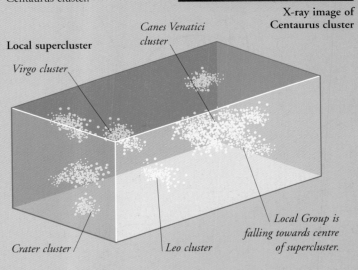

Local supercluster

Virgo cluster

Canes Venatici
cluster

Crater cluster

Leo cluster

Local Group is
falling towards centre
of supercluster.

SUPERCLUSTERS

The Local Group of galaxies and the clusters in Virgo, Crater, Leo, and Canes Venatici are all linked by gravity to form our Local Supercluster. This supercluster, which is dominated by the vast Virgo cluster, measures more than 100 million light years across. Astronomers know of about 50 other superclusters, which take many different shapes. In some, the galaxies are strung out like paper streamers, while in others they form flattish, sheet-like structures. The largest supercluster we know is a flat sheet named the Great Wall, which is about 750,000 light years across.

WE CAN SEE that the galaxies are not spread evenly through space. They cluster together in a random, uneven pattern. In this experiment, we see how matter naturally clusters together.
You will need: old newspaper; large piece of dark card; coarse sea salt.

1 Cover a table with the newspaper to protect it. Place the dark card on the table. Pour some sea salt into the palm of your hand. Holding your hand about 1 m (3 ft) above the card, gradually sprinkle the salt over it. Repeat once or twice.

2 When you look at the grains of salt on the card, you'll see that they are not spread evenly. In some places, they cluster together. In others, they are more spread out. This type of pattern mimics how the galaxies are distributed in space.

Salt grains form
clusters on card.

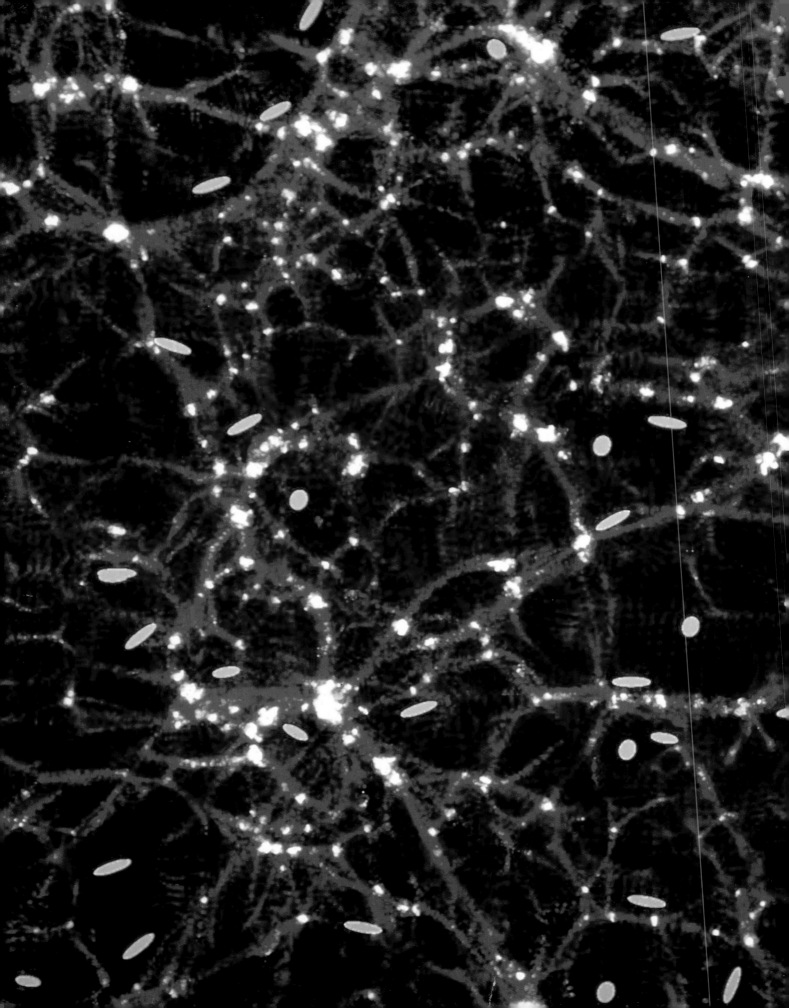

MYSTERIOUS UNIVERSE

Picture: *This computer model shows the distribution of invisible dark matter (red) between distant galaxies (blue).*

THE SHAPE OF THE UNIVERSE

THE LARGEST STRUCTURES in the Universe are the clusters and superclusters of galaxies, millions of light years across. But the Universe itself is far, far bigger still – so big that we cannot, and never will, see it all. The study of the Universe – its nature, origins, and fate – is called cosmology and involves some of the weirdest ideas in science. Questions about the Universe have puzzled the human mind since ancient times. Did the Universe have a beginning? Will it come to an end or last forever? Is ours the only Universe, or are there many? Today's scientists are beginning to answer some of these questions with ingenious theories.

THE BEGINNING

Most astronomers now think that the Universe came into being about 14 billion years ago in one almighty explosion called the Big Bang. The best evidence for this is that the Universe is still expanding rapidly in every direction. Whichever way we look in space, we see distant galaxies rushing

For the first fraction of a second after the Big Bang, the Universe would have been so tiny, hot, and dense that the normal laws of physics can't explain what happened.

away from us. Further evidence came when astronomers detected the lingering, cooled-down radiation left over from the immense explosion, still heating the Universe to roughly three degrees above absolute zero. In one cataclysmic instant, the Big Bang created space, all the matter in the Universe, and time itself. It makes no sense to ask what came before the Big Bang, because there was no space and no time. There was nothing in a sense so profound that it's hard for us to imagine.

EVERYTHING'S RELATIVE

Because everything else in the Universe seems to be moving away from our Galaxy, it would be easy to think that there is something special about our position – that maybe we are at the centre of the Universe. This was the mistaken belief of the ancient Greeks, who put Earth at the centre of the cosmos. But, as the great German-American scientist Albert Einstein established with his principle of relativity, the Universe looks much the same to any observer anywhere within it. The Universe has no measurable centre and, as we shall see, no observable edge. Relativity shows

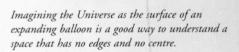

Imagining the Universe as the surface of an expanding balloon is a good way to understand a space that has no edges and no centre.

that the movement of galaxies is best explained if space as a whole is expanding, and everything within the Universe is moving away from everything else like currants in a rising bun.

LOOK BACK IN TIME

Because light travels at a fixed speed, we can only see objects and events whose light has had time to reach us. The further away we look in space, the further back we look in time, since light must have left distant galaxies billions of years ago in order to

C. AD 150 Ptolemy summarizes ancient view of an Earth-centred Universe in his *Almagest*.

1543 Nicolaus Copernicus suggests that the Universe is centred on the Sun rather than Earth.

1609 Observations by Galileo Galilei and calculations by Johannes Kepler confirm Copernicus's ideas.

1785 William Herschel produces first map of our Galaxy, at that time thought to be the entire Universe.

1838 The Michelson-Morley experiment shows that speed of light is constant.

1905 Albert Einstein produces his *Special Theory of Relativity*.

1915 Albert Einstein produces his *General Theory of Relativity*.

arrive at Earth now. This is one reason why violent objects such as quasars are some of the most distant in the cosmos. We are looking back to a time when the young Universe was much more active than it is today. Fourteen billion light years away, our Universe is surrounded by an invisible wall – objects further away than this are invisible because their light has not had time to reach us since the Big Bang.

SPACE AND TIME

The sphere of space extending for 14 billion light years around us marks the boundary of our observable Universe, but it is far from the whole Universe.

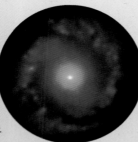

Barred spiral galaxy NGC 1097 lies 65 million light years away. We are seeing it now as it was when the dinosaurs died out.

Alien astronomers on a planet 14 billion light years away would have their own observable Universe the same size as ours, and so on. Humans will never cross such distances unless they can somehow find shortcuts through space and time. Some scientists speculate that there may be quick routes between the Universe's distant parts via black holes, but for the time being this remains the stuff of science fiction.

Space and time ("spacetime") provide the clue to the Universe's physical shape. According to Einstein, the two are intimately bound up with each other, and both can be distorted by the gravity of massive objects. A crucial question in cosmology, therefore, is how much mass the Universe contains. Enough mass and gravity will curve spacetime right round on itself, creating a "closed" Universe. Too little mass and spacetime won't curve – the Universe is then said to be open, or "flat". If you imagine spacetime as a grid, and you follow two parallel lines for long enough, they might eventually join (as on the surface of a globe) or never join (as on a flat sheet).

FATE OF THE UNIVERSE

The shape of spacetime is linked to the eventual destiny of the Universe. A bubble-like, closed Universe means that the gravity of all the matter it contains will eventually slow down and stop its expansion. The Universe would then start shrinking, eventually imploding out of existence in a "Big Crunch". An open, flat Universe, without enough gravity to stop the expansion, would keep growing forever.

For decades, astronomers have tried to measure the mass of the Universe – both its visible matter and its mysterious "dark matter". Dark matter has never been seen, but we know it exists because galaxies have much more mass than can be accounted for by their glowing stars and gas. It always seemed as though the Universe was on

The visible galaxies seen here probably contain large amounts of dark matter, because they do not have strong enough gravity to contain the hot gas between them (coloured pink in this X-ray image).

the borderline between Big Crunch and eternal expansion.

Then something changed all that. In 1999, astronomers discovered that the most distant galaxies are further away than they should be if the Universe had always grown at its current rate. In other words, the expansion of the Universe is accelerating. Space itself seems to be stretching, powered by some type of "dark energy" that we know very little about. Our current understanding of the Universe is, therefore, that it is indeed flat and will expand forever, until the last stars burn out and space becomes cold and dark.

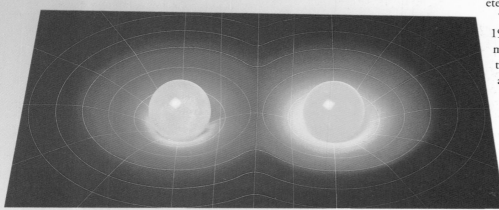

The gravity of massive objects such as stars causes spacetime to curve around them.

SPACETIME AND RELATIVITY

EVERYTHING IS RELATIVE. This was the insight of a young genius called Albert Einstein in 1905. Einstein transformed the way we see the Universe by abandoning what seemed like the soundest law of nature – that space and time were absolute fixed quantities. He argued instead that space and time are relative – they appear differently to people moving at different speeds. Einstein also realized that space and time interact to form a four-dimensional "spacetime", which could be warped by the presence of matter. He published his revolutionary ideas in the special and general theories of relativity.

Albert Einstein

German-born Einstein (1879–1955) is best remembered for his theories of relativity. These showed, among other things, that nothing moves faster than the speed of light, that this speed is always constant, and that objects become more massive as they move faster. He also found that mass is equivalent to energy. In what has become the most famous equation in the world, Einstein stated that energy (E) was equal to mass (m) times the speed of light (c), squared: $E=mc^2$.

GENERAL RELATIVITY

According to Einstein, time and space are closely connected. This "spacetime" has a shape – it can be curved and warped by the gravity of massive objects, such as stars. To take a two-dimensional example, imagine space as the surface of a rubber sheet dented in the middle by a bowling ball. Because the ball has mass, it makes a distortion, or "dent", in the sheet. A marble rolling past would not follow a straight path but would go around the dent made by the ball, pulled in by the ball's "gravitational well". The planets move around the Sun in the same way. Our example, however, doesn't show the effect on time. Because space and time are bound up with each other, the ball not only curves space but curves time as well.

Position of star

Apparent position of star

Proof of relativity

The new theory of curved spacetime was proved spectacularly in 1919. During a total solar eclipse, British astronomers saw that the stars nearest the Sun had shifted from their normal positions. Rays of starlight passing close to the Sun had somehow been deflected. However, since light has no mass, it should not have been affected by gravity according to Newton's theories. The only explanation was that the light's path – the spacetime through which it was travelling – had been warped by the Sun's gravity. This produced a shift in the stars' apparent positions as seen from Earth (diagram, left).

A massive object, such as a star, curves spacetime around it, creating a gravitational well.

A passing object, such as a planet, is deflected by the curved spacetime and goes around the star's gravitational well.

Craft appears contracted from viewpoint of Earth and its clocks seem slower.

Diagram A

Diagram B

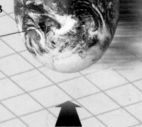

Earth appears contracted from viewpoint of craft and its clocks seem slower.

The laws of physics feel the same for the craft's crew as they do for people on Earth, regardless of the relative motion of each.

SPECIAL RELATIVITY

The special theory of relativity contains some bizarre conclusions about the way space and time behave at very high speeds. In this example, a spacecraft is passing Earth at a speed approaching the speed of light. From the viewpoint of Earth, time seems to be running slowly on board the spacecraft, its mass has increased, and its length has contracted (diagram A). However, for the crew of the spacecraft nothing has changed, and it is Earth's shape that appears contracted, and Earth's clocks that have slowed (diagram B). The laws of physics are the same on board the craft as they are on Earth. Both viewpoints are relative. The constant speed of light means it is impossible to tell which viewpoint is the correct one.

EXPANDING UNIVERSE

The consequence of relativity was that the Universe must either be expanding or contracting – pulled back by its own gravity. In the early 1900s, everyone, including Einstein, thought the Universe was unchanging, and so he fudged his theory to fit what he thought were the facts. However, by the 1920s scientists proved that the Universe was indeed expanding. This led to new ideas about its origin. Instead of existing forever, the Universe must originally have been concentrated in just one tiny point in space and time from which it exploded outwards.

Expansion of Local Supercluster galaxies

75 million light years

100 million light years

115 million light years

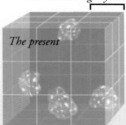

Three billion years ago

The present

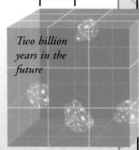

Two billion years in the future

Clusters were 15% nearer each other.

Clusters will be 15% further apart

LET'S EXPERIMENT
UNIVERSAL EXPANSION

ALTHOUGH GALAXIES are moving away from us in every direction, we are part of the movement, not the still centre of it. This is illustrated in a simple experiment using bread dough and currants. **You will need:** mixing bowl; 5 tbspn flour; 1 tsp dried yeast; water; currants.

1 Put the flour in the mixing bowl, add the yeast and 2 tbspn warm water, and mix into a dough. Then sprinkle a small amount of flour on a warm, dry surface. Place the dough on the surface and shape. Push the currants into the top.

2 As the yeast reacts with the flour, the dough will expand. You'll see the currants all moving apart from each other, like galaxies in an expanding space.

Increasing redshift and speed

Increasing distance

Redshift and distance

The expansion of the Universe is revealed by redshifts in the light from distant galaxies. Redshift is the Doppler shifting of light towards the red end of the spectrum, caused by an object's movement away from us (p. 102). The more the light is redshifted, the higher the speed. A galaxy twice as distant as another will have double the redshift. This means that redshift itself can be used as a measure of distance.

THE BIG BANG

THE MOMENT WHEN THE UNIVERSE began is known as the Big Bang. About 14 billion years ago, space and time were born in a tiny, condensed speck, which was smaller than an atom and almost infinitely hot and dense. A few trillionths of a second later, the infant Universe exploded with unimaginable violence and began to expand in a fireball of such concentrated energy that matter spontaneously started to appear. It's meaningless to ask where the Big Bang happened, or what came before it. There was no "where", because space did not exist. There was no "before", because time had not begun to flow.

Fuelled by the release of the fundamental forces, the Universe suddenly inflated. It doubled in size every 10 quadrillion quintillionths of a second.

IN THE BEGINNING

Scientists cannot answer the question of what triggered the Big Bang in the first place. That may always remain a mystery. We can use the laws of physics to trace the history of the Universe back to a fraction of a second after the Big Bang, but these laws do not apply in the extreme conditions that existed at the very instant of creation. Trillionths of a second after the first moment, the temperature dropped to about 10,000 trillion trillion degrees and energy transformed into particles of matter. This became the future building material of stars, planets, and galaxies.

The evidence of creation

In the early 1960s, American physicists Arno Penzias and Robert Wilson were testing a sensitive new antenna when they found a faint and inexplicable background noise, apparently coming from all over the sky. After dismissing everything from design faults to pigeon droppings, they finally realized that they had stumbled upon the lingering afterglow of the Big Bang itself. Today, this weak radio noise is called the Cosmic Background Radiation.

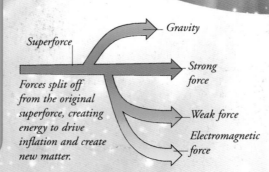

Gravity

Superforce

Strong force

Forces split off from the original superforce, creating energy to drive inflation and create new matter.

Weak force

Electromagnetic force

Fundamental forces

The four fundamental forces – electromagnetism, gravity, and the two nuclear forces (p. 16), formed in the Big Bang as a single superforce. As the temperature dropped, they separated, releasing huge amounts of energy that caused the Universe to balloon faster than the speed of light. In less than a second, the Universe grew from smaller than a pinhead to the size of a galaxy.

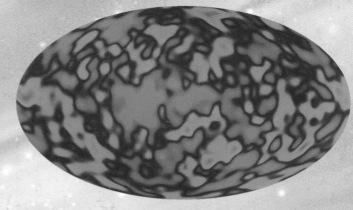

Particle soup

All the matter in the Universe was created in the first few seconds of the Big Bang, as raw energy turned into a wide variety of particles. Conditions would have been rather like those in a particle accelerator (above), with particles whizzing around, colliding, and disintegrating. As the temperature dropped, only some of these particles survived to make matter.

Between the denser clouds of gas (blue in the COBE map)...

THE FOG CLEARS

The infant Universe was opaque, like a thick fog. Particles were so densely packed that light simply bounced around between them. Then, after about 300,000 years, the temperature dropped low enough for atoms to form and remain stable. Most of the particles in the Universe were absorbed into atoms, and space suddenly became transparent – an event called "decoupling". Radiation from this period is the earliest and most distant thing we can see in the Universe. The Cosmic Background Explorer (COBE) satellite produced this map of it, showing tiny ripples.

...low density (pink) regions expand to become empty voids.

Early structure

How did the Universe transform from a dense fog of matter into the galaxies we see today? The ripples in the COBE map show that structure was already developing very early in the Universe. Blue patches mark regions that were slightly denser, while pink regions were slightly emptier. Over about 300 million years, material concentrated in the denser areas, forming long narrow filaments with huge voids between them. Gas within the filaments condensed to form galaxy clusters and superclusters.

Quasars and megasuns

After decoupling, the Universe entered a dark age from which it did not emerge for millions of years. The first objects to light up the darkness may have been quasars – violent, bright galaxies that are the most distant objects we can see today. There may also have been megasuns – a theoretical, early generation of supersized stars that exploded in "hypernovas". These scattered the heavier elements throughout the Universe and helped the formation of galaxies.

A quasar is the brilliant, tiny core of a very young, active galaxy.

Three hundred million years later, the Universe consisted of huge empty voids, surrounded by filaments of denser gas. The gas pulled together into galaxies.

DARK MATTER

HOW MUCH MATTER is there in the Universe? The answer to this question is very important to our understanding of the past, present, and future. Astronomers believe that only a fraction of the total material in the Universe can be detected through telescopes. The rest of the Universe is made up of invisible "dark matter" that can only be detected by the effects of its gravity on known objects in space. The precise quantity of this dark matter holds the key to the fate of the Cosmos. Will the Universe continue to expand, or will gravity eventually cause it to contract?

WHAT IS DARK MATTER?

The Big Bang created far more matter than that which is visible in the Universe today. This dark matter exists all over the Universe. Because it is invisible, our only clues to its existence come from visible matter. For example, some galaxy clusters, such as the Coma cluster shown here, seem to have a gravitational pull that is too strong to be caused only by the galaxies' visible stars and gas. There must be more mass that is creating the extra gravity – dark matter. Astronomers have some ideas about what dark matter might be. These include MACHOs, WIMPs, and neutrinos.

MACHOs and WIMPs

The MACHO (Massive Astrophysical Compact Halo Object) theory involves large, dark objects orbiting the halos around galaxies. They may include burnt-out stars, brown dwarfs, and black holes. Because MACHOs contain densely packed matter, their gravity can distort light, causing gravitational lensing that can sometimes be seen. Scientists are currently trying to prove the existence of WIMPs (Weakly Interacting Massive Particles). They believe that WIMPs are subatomic (smaller than an atom), with significant mass. Although WIMPs are tiny, there may be so many of them that they could make up a large part of dark matter.

Visible mass in galaxy cluster Abell 2218 equals roughly 50 trillion Suns. Lensing reveals 10 times more than that in dark matter.

GRAVITATIONAL LENSING OCCURS when a massive object lies in front of a faintly luminous, more distant visible object, causing a brightening of the visible object or a distorting of its image. This happens because the gravity of the nearer object bends and focuses the light of the more distant one. This experiment shows how gravitational lensing works. **You will need:** an adult to help you; candle with holder; glue stick; clear plastic drinks bottle.

1 Ask an adult to light the candle. Stand the glue stick (or something of a similar shape) upright in front of the candle so that it completely hides your view of the flame.

2 Fill the drinks bottle with water, stand it in front of the glue stick and look through it. The bottle shows the effects of gravitational lensing, as it bends the light from the candle, giving you a distorted image.

LET'S EXPERIMENT
GRAVITATIONAL LENSING

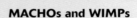

The candle represents a visible object, the glue stick represents a dark object, and the bottle acts as a gravitational lens.

When a dark object (glue stick) passes in front of a visible object (candle), its gravity distorts, and may also brighten, the image.

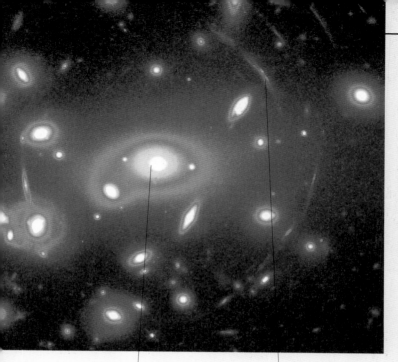

Super-Kamiokande neutrino telescope in Japan

Neutrinos

Neutrinos are known to exist in huge quantities. They are produced by the Sun and other stars. With very little mass and no electric charge, they can only be detected by highly sensitive instruments, such as this special telescope in the underground water tank shown above. Astronomers once thought that neutrinos had zero mass, but recent discoveries indicate a tiny mass, in which case neutrinos may account for at least some dark matter.

Bright galaxies in Abell 2218 cluster, 3 billion light years away

Distorted image of galaxy 10 billion light years away

UNIVERSAL DESTINY

According to Einstein's theory of relativity, large amounts of matter distort spacetime, causing it to curve around on itself. The amount of visible matter can be worked out, so it is the amount of dark matter that could decide the shape and fate of the Universe. Recent discoveries suggest that another force, "dark energy", is accelerating the expansion of the Universe, possibly forcing space to curve in the opposite direction. The precise balance of dark matter and dark energy will determine the form of curve. Measurements currently suggest that our Universe is flat.

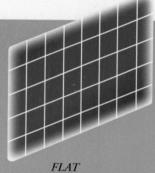

FLAT SPACE

With exactly the right balance between dark matter and dark energy, the forces that cause the Universe to curve will cancel each other out and the Universe will remain completely flat.

POSITIVELY CURVED SPACE

If large amounts of dark matter overpower the effect of dark energy, the Universe will curve around on itself, perhaps eventually resulting in a closed, bubble-shaped Universe that can no longer expand.

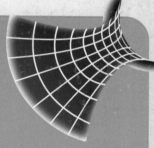

NEGATIVELY CURVED SPACE

If there is not enough dark matter to counteract the effect of dark energy, then the stretching forces will curve the Universe outwards, creating an infinite, saddle-shaped space.

Open or closed?

The Universe is still expanding after the Big Bang (p. 142). But if the total mass of the Universe is great enough, gravity will eventually slow the expansion, forming a closed Universe and possibly even causing it to collapse in a Big Crunch. Some scientists believe that the presence of dark energy indicates an open Universe that will continue to expand indefinitely, only to die as space gradually becomes emptier. Other scientists believe that the power of dark energy will fade as the Universe grows older, and the empty Universe will eventually be replaced by another Big Bang trillions of years from now.

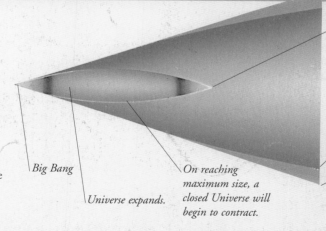

If the Universe is closed, it may end in a Big Crunch.

If the Universe is open, it may continue to expand, but at a slower rate.

Alternatively, an open Universe may expand at the same rate forever.

Big Bang

Universe expands.

On reaching maximum size, a closed Universe will begin to contract.

SPACE AND TIME TRAVEL

ALTHOUGH HUMANS HAVE left Earth and journeyed into space, so far we have gone no further than the Moon. In the next century or more it's unlikely that we'll even reach the edge of our Solar System. However, one day humans may travel to the stars and colonize other worlds in the Galaxy. At the moment, rockets are not powerful enough to propel us across these great distances at practical speeds, so new methods of propulsion will be needed. Some physicists even predict that there are shortcuts, known as wormholes, which lead from one area of space and time to another.

Daedalus *could reach nearby stars within a human lifetime.*

STAR TRAVEL

Even the fastest rocket-propelled spacecraft would take thousands of years to reach the nearest stars. This is because rockets cannot continue to speed up once their initial fuel supply has been used up. To reach the speeds needed to make star travel practical, we will require far more efficient propulsion, capable of accelerating a spaceship for years, not seconds. The *Daedalus* project (above) is a blueprint for a spacecraft propelled by exploding small pellets of radioactive fuel. In theory, it could reach one-tenth the speed of light.

Alternative propulsion
Ion engines use solar cells to split apart the atoms of gas fuel. Although the spacecraft would experience only a small amount of thrust, it could still reach very high speeds. Solar sails (left) would need no fuel at all – they are vast membranes propelled by the force of solar winds blowing away from the Sun and other stars. Both of these methods could help spacecraft reach speeds that are a significant proportion of the speed of light.

If one of a pair of identical twins sets off on a long, high-speed space journey, while his brother remains on Earth...

TIME TRAVEL

Humans aboard a spacecraft capable of travelling close to the speed of light would experience an amazing consequence of relativity – "time dilation". Time would slow down for the crew relative to the outside Universe (p. 141). A spacecraft may set off on a journey that takes 50 years in Earth time, but only five years pass for the crew. Time on Earth would continue at the normal pace, so that when the crew returned they would have travelled 45 years into the future. This would give rise to the "twin paradox" illustrated above.

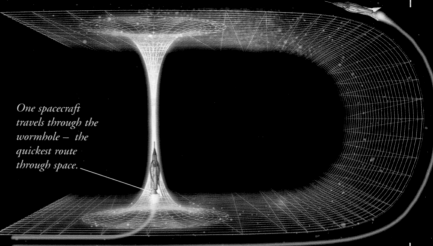

One spacecraft travels through the wormhole – the quickest route through space.

SHORTCUTS THROUGH SPACE

Wormholes are hypothetical (not yet proven) objects linking two points in space and possibly even in time. From the outside, a wormhole might seem like a black hole, but instead of leading to a singularity (p. 19), the wormhole would open out again in another part of space. Some astronomers think that the structure of spacetime itself may be made of tiny natural wormholes. If one could be made large enough, it might be possible to take shortcuts across the Universe. By carrying the other end of such a wormhole back to its starting point at high speed, and taking advantage of time dilation, it could be possible to use a wormhole as a time machine.

Kip S. Thorne and the wormhole theory

Using a wormhole as a shortcut across space was first suggested by Kip S. Thorne, a theoretical physicist who helped describe the formation of black holes. He initially came up with the idea as a favour to his friend, the planetary scientist Carl Sagan, who was writing the science-fiction novel *Contact*. Sagan needed a way to send his heroine 25 light years across space to the star Vega without breaking the laws of physics. Although Thorne's theory was used for fiction, it may turn out to be fact.

Kip Thorne
(1940–)

1 the astronaut returns, he would hardly have aged, while
n has grown old. Yet both were born at the same time!

The grandfather paradox

The old science fiction idea of travelling back in time and accidentally killing your own grandfather before your father is conceived points to an intriguing paradox – backwards time travel could violate the basic principle of cause and effect. If your father never existed, then neither would you, so who exactly travelled back in time to kill your grandfather? The theoretical physicist Stephen Hawking proposed a "Chronology Protection Principle" which states that, somehow, the laws of physics would not allow a machine such as the wormhole time machine to be built. Hawking suggests that nature might find an obstacle to prevent a machine travelling back to a time before it was built.

He was never in time for his classes... He wasn't in time for his dinner...
Then one day... he wasn't in his time at all.

STEVEN SPIELBERG Presents

"BACK TO THE FUTURE" ... MICHAEL J. FOX
CHRISTOPHER LLOYD · LEA THOMPSON · CRISPIN GLOVER
... ROBERT ZEMECKIS & BOB GALE ... ALAN SILVESTRI ... BOB GALE ... NEIL CANTON
... STEVEN SPIELBERG · KATHLEEN KENNEDY ... FRANK MARSHALL
... ROBERT ZEMECKIS ... A UNIVERSAL Picture

In the classic time-travel film Back to the Future, *Marty McFly's trip back to the 1950s almost prevents his parents meeting, and hence his* ...

How many stars in the galaxy are born with the right mass and composition to remain stable over the billions of years it takes for life to evolve?

How many of these stars give birth to stable planetary systems around them?

How many of these planetary systems contain worlds with suitable conditions for life to evolve?

On how many of these planets does life actually begin and take hold?

On how many of these planets does life become intelligent and able to communicate?

How many of the planets with intelligent life also have the right conditions to create technology suitable for interstellar communication?

How many potentially advanced civilizations are wiped out by natural or self-inflicted disaster?

CHANCES OF LIFE

The Drake Equation (named after the American radio astronomer Frank Drake) is a way of working out the chances of intelligent life existing elsewhere in our Galaxy. Each of the elements in the equation is an obstacle that must be overcome for intelligent life to evolve on another world and to survive long enough to start communicating with the rest of the Universe. Unfortunately, with only one example of such a planet to work from (our own), many of the variables are hard to estimate. As a result, optimistic astronomers can predict a million civilizations in our galaxy, while pessimists say that even our own is a fluke!

LIFE IN THE UNIVERSE?

EARTH IS THE ONLY known world capable of sustaining life. However, each year, dozens of new planets, orbiting stars far beyond our Solar System, are being discovered. What are the chances that intelligent life has evolved on these planets? Although most scientists don't believe that UFOs (Unidentifiable Flying Objects) are alien spaceships visiting Earth, the SETI program (Search for Extraterrestrial Intelligence) is a serious scientific pursuit. Radio telescopes are constantly monitoring our skies for intelligent signals coming from deep space.

Finding other Earths
Since the mid-1990s, dozens of planets have been found orbiting other stars. As our methods improve for detecting these "exoplanets", working out their orbits, and even analyzing the chemicals in their atmospheres, we will gradually be able to narrow down some of the factors in the Drake Equation (far left). The artist's impression above shows a blue world orbiting the star Tau Boötis – the first exoplanet to have its colour measured.

Alien forms
There is no way of knowing what aliens may look like, since even life on Earth could have evolved in many different directions. It's very unlikely that aliens will look like the "little green men" seen in old films – such creatures are far too humanoid. All we can say is that airborne and water-dwelling animals might have roughly the same shapes as those on Earth, and any alien creatures would probably have sense organs with the same functions as our own.

FOR YEARS, SETI ASTRONOMERS had to concentrate on just a few wavelengths because they were swamped with Earth's radio signals and had limited computer power. Now the search has been revolutionized by the internet. Millions of people are helping to analyze radio signals from space, and you can help too. **You will need:** computer with internet connection.

1 Visit the SETI@Home webpage at: http://setiathome.berkeley.edu to download and install the program. SETI@Home sifts through packets of radio data looking for potential signals. You can configure it to run when your computer has spare processor power.

2 Once SETI@Home has analyzed a packet of data, it reconnects to the website, returns its results for the SETI scientists to check, and downloads a new chunk of data.

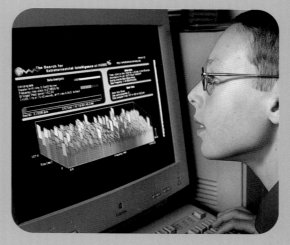

SETI@Home shows you its progress via a screensaver activated when you stop using your computer.

LISTENING FOR E.T.

Since the 1960s, astronomers have been searching for radio signals broadcast by alien civilizations. However, the huge range of possible wavelengths means that this is like looking for a needle in a haystack. Radio signals are a logical way for aliens to announce their presence, because radio waves can travel for long distances without interference. Using some of the world's largest radio telescopes, astronomers have even sent a signal towards a distant cluster of stars.

Dish antenna of a 43-m (140-ft) radio telescope at Greenbank, West Virginia, USA, one of several used for SETI.

Blue stragglers (ringed in yellow)

Alien spotting

Radio telescopes are only able to pick up deliberate signals sent from space. Some astronomers believe we should also look for other signs of alien life, including those from civilizations much further advanced. These might include stars with lifespans that may have been artificially prolonged – such as the blue stragglers in this globular cluster. These form when two old stars collide and merge. Some astronomers speculate that these may have been deliberately merged by aliens to create new energy sources.

SPACE DATA

SOLAR SYSTEM

	Diameter km (miles)	Mass (Earth=1)	Surface gravity (Earth=1)	Average surface temperature °C (°F)	Length of a day – sunrise to sunrise (hours)	Length of a year (Earth days)	Average distance from Sun million km (miles)	Average speed around Sun km/s (miles/s)	Tilt of axis (degrees)	Number of known moons
Sun	1,392,000 (865,000)	332,950	28.0	5,500 (9,900)	–	–	–	–	–	–
Mercury	4,879 (3,032)	0.055	0.38	167 (333)	4,223	88	58 (36)	48 (30)	0.01	0
Venus	12,104 (7,521)	0.82	0.91	464 (867)	2,802	225	108 (67)	35 (22)	177	0
Earth	12,756 (7,926)	1	1	15 (59)	24	365	150 (93)	30 (19)	23	1
Mars	6,794 (4,222)	0.11	0.38	-65 (-85)	25	687	228 (142)	24 (15)	25	2
Jupiter	142,984 (88,846)	318	2.36	-110 (-166)	10	4,331	779 (484)	13 (8)	3	39
Saturn	120,536 (74,897)	95.2	0.92	-140 (-220)	11	10,747	1,434 (891)	10 (6)	27	30
Uranus	51,118 (31,763)	14.5	0.89	-195 (-319)	17	30,589	2,873 (1,785)	7 (4)	98	20
Neptune	49,528 (30,775)	17.1	1.12	-200 (-328)	16	59,800	4,496 (2,794)	5 (3)	28	8
Pluto	2,390 (1,485)	0.002	0.06	-225 (-373)	153	90,588	5,870 (3,647)	5 (3)	123	1

BRIGHTEST STARS

Star	Constellation	Distance from Earth (light years)*
Sun	–	0.000015
Sirius A	Canis Major (the Great Dog)	8.6
Canopus	Carina (the Keel)	313
Alpha Centauri A	Centaurus (the Centaur)	4.3
Arcturus	Boötes (the Herdsman)	36
Vega	Lyra (the Lyre)	25
Capella	Auriga (the Charioteer)	42
Rigel	Orion (the Hunter)	773
Procyon	Canis Minor (the Little Dog)	11
Achernar	Eridanus (River Eridanus)	144
Betelgeuse	Orion (the Hunter)	427

*One light year = 9.46 trillion km (5.88 trillion miles)

ANNUAL METEOR SHOWERS

Name	Constellation	Peak dates
Quadrantids	Boötes (the Herdsman)	3–4 January
Lyrids	Lyra (the Lyre)	20–22 April
Eta Aquarids	Aquarius (the Water Carrier)	4–6 May
Southern Delta Aquarids	Aquarius (the Water Carrier)	28–29 July
Northern Delta Aquarids	Aquarius (the Water Carrier)	6 August
Southern Iota Aquarids	Aquarius (the Water Carrier)	6–7 August
Perseids	Perseus (Perseus)	12 August
Orionids	Orion (the Hunter)	20–22 October
Taurids	Taurus (the Bull)	3–5 November
Leonids	Leo (the Lion)	17–18 November
Geminids	Gemini (the Twins)	13–14 December
Ursids	Ursa Minor (the Little Bear)	23 December

MAJOR PLANETARY MOONS

Moon	Planet	Average distance from planet in million km (miles)	Orbital period (Earth days)	Diameter km (miles)
Moon	Earth	0.38 (0.24)	27	3,476 (2,159)
Io	Jupiter	0.42 (0.26)	2	3,642 (2,262)
Europa	Jupiter	0.67 (0.42)	4	3,130 (1,944)
Ganymede	Jupiter	1.07 (0.66)	7	5,268 (3,272)
Callisto	Jupiter	1.88 (1.17)	17	4,806 (2,985)
Tethys	Saturn	0.29 (0.18)	2	1,058 (657)
Dione	Saturn	0.38 (0.24)	3	1,120 (696)
Rhea	Saturn	0.53 (0.33)	5	1,530 (950)
Titan	Saturn	1.22 (0.76)	16	5,150 (3,199)
Iapetus	Saturn	3.56 (2.21)	79	1,440 (894)
Ariel	Uranus	0.19 (0.12)	3	1,160 (720)
Umbriel	Uranus	0.27 (0.17)	4	1,170 (727)
Titania	Uranus	0.44 (0.27)	9	1,580 (981)
Oberon	Uranus	0.58 (0.36)	13	1,520 (944)
Triton	Neptune	0.35 (0.22)	6	2,706 (1,681)
Charon	Pluto	0.02 (0.01)	6	1,186 (737)

TOTAL SOLAR ECLIPSES UNTIL 2020

Date	Where visible
23 November 2003	Indian Ocean, Antarctica
8 April 2005	Central America
29 March 2006	Central Asia, Africa
1 August 2008	China, Russia, Greenland
22 July 2009	Pacific Ocean, China, India
11 July 2010	South America, Pacific Ocean
13 November 2012	Australia, South Pacific Ocean
20 March 2015	Svalbard Arctic Islands
9 March 2016	Indonesia, Pacific Ocean
21 August 2017	USA
2 July 2019	South America, South Pacific Ocean
14 December 2020	South America

SPACE WEBSITES

NASA Homepage
www.nasa.gov

Hubble Space Telescope
http://hubblesite.org

Exploratorium Observatory
www.exploratorium.edu/observatory

Amazing Space web-based activities
http://amazing-space.stsci.edu

The nine planets of the Solar System
www.seds.org/nineplanets/nineplanets

Galaxy guide
http://stardate.org/resources/galaxy

Search for extra-terrestrial life
www.seti.org

Space rocks
www.nearearthobjects.co.uk

GLOSSARY

Absolute magnitude: See *Magnitude.*

Absolute zero: lowest possible temperature: –273°C (–459°F).

Absorption line: a dark line in a spectrum, caused by atoms absorbing radiation of a certain wavelength. Astronomers use absorption lines to identify elements in stars and galaxies.

Accretion disc: disc of hot material that forms around a spinning object. Accretion discs may form around black holes.

Active galaxy: galaxy with a black hole at its centre that is generating huge amounts of energy.

Antimatter: matter made of subatomic particles with equal and opposite properties to normal matter. Positrons (positively charged) are the antiparticles of electrons (negatively charged).

Aphelion: point in an object's orbit at which it is furthest from the Sun.

Apparent magnitude: See *Magnitude.*

Arc second: unit used by astronomers to measure the size or separation of objects in the sky. One arc second is equal to 1/3,600 of a degree.

Asteroid: small rocky object in the Solar System. Asteroids vary in size from grains of dust to more than 1,000 km (600 miles) across. Most are in a belt between Mars and Jupiter.

Astrolabe: ancient astronomical instrument used to measure the position and movement of objects in the sky.

Astronomical unit (au): average distance between Earth and the Sun – 149.6 million km (92.9 million miles).

Astronomy: the study of celestial objects beyond Earth's atmosphere and of the physical Universe as a whole.

Atmosphere: layer of gas held around a planet by its gravity. Also the outer layers of a star, beyond its photosphere.

Atom: smallest part of an element, made up of three types of subatomic particles – protons, neutrons, and electrons.

Aurora: green and red glow seen in the sky near the polar regions. Auroras are caused by electrically charged particles from the magnetosphere colliding with gases in Earth's atmosphere.

Axis: imaginary line that passes through the centre of a planet or other body, around which the object rotates.

Barred-spiral galaxy: galaxy with spiral arms linked to a central bulge by a straight bar of stars and gas.

Barycentre: the centre of mass between a pair or group of bodies that move around each other.

Big Bang: violent explosion that gave birth to the Universe about 14 billion years ago.

Billion: one thousand million.

Binary system: pair of stars in orbit around each other.

Black hole: collapsed object with gravity so strong that nothing can escape it, not even light.

Blazar: active galaxy angled in such a way that when viewed from Earth we see radiation coming straight from its core.

Blue shift: a shortening of the wavelength of electromagnetic radiation emitted from an object when it is moving towards us, so that its spectrum is shifted towards the blue end. The shift is caused by the Doppler effect.

Brightness: See *Luminosity, Magnitude.*

Brown dwarf: object less massive than a star but more massive than a planet. It produces heat, but little light.

Carbon: one of the most common elements in the Universe, produced by stars. Carbon is the basis of all life.

CCD: See *Charge-coupled device.*

Celestial object: any object seen in the sky, including planets, stars, and galaxies.

Celestial sphere: imaginary sphere of sky that surrounds Earth and on which celestial objects appear to lie. Astronomers measure star positions according to their declination (celestial latitude) and right ascension (celestial longitude) on the celestial sphere.

Cepheid variable: type of variable star that changes in brightness and size. The length of the cycle of change is linked to the absolute magnitude of the star. Astronomers use Cepheids to measure distances in space.

Chandrasekhar limit: upper limit for core mass of stars, which determines whether they become white dwarfs or explode as supernovas.

Charge-coupled device: light-sensitive electronic device used for recording images in telescopes.

Chromosphere: lower layer of the Sun's atmosphere. It has a pinkish shine, but can be seen only when the brighter photosphere is blocked out, as in a total eclipse.

Circumpolar star: any star that does not appear to set from an observer's location on Earth, but instead appears to circle the celestial pole.

Cluster: See *Galaxy cluster. Star cluster.*

Coma: envelope of dust and ionized gas surrounding the nucleus of a comet.

Comet: body made of ice and rocky dust. When a comet nears the Sun, the Sun's heat melts the ice, creating a glowing head of gas with tails of dust and ionized gas.

Compound: substance formed by the combination of two or more different elements in fixed proportions.

Conjunction: alignment in the orbits of two bodies in the Solar System when they appear to be in the same place in the sky as seen from Earth.

Constellation: pattern of stars in the sky, often named after a mythological person or creature. Astronomers define constellations as areas of sky around traditional star patterns.

Copernican system: model described by Polish astronomer Nicolaus Copernicus (1473–1543) in which Earth and the other planets orbit the central Sun.

Core: the innermost part of a star or planet. In a star, the region where nuclear reactions take place.

Corona: the Sun's very hot upper atmosphere, visible as a halo during a total solar eclipse.

Coronal mass ejection (CME): high-speed eruption of material from the Sun's corona. CMEs affect the solar wind and cause magnetic storms on Earth.

Cosmic background radiation: faint radio signal emitted by the entire sky – the remnant of radiation from the Big Bang.

Cosmological constant: hidden property of space, first proposed by Albert Einstein, that may be stretching space and accelerating the expansion of the Universe.

Cosmos: another word for the Universe.

Crater: circle-shaped basin blasted into the surface of a moon or planet by the impact of a meteorite, or caused by volcanic eruption.

Crust: rocky surface layer of a planet or moon.

Dark energy: hypothetical repulsive force thought to be causing the expansion of space. The true nature of dark energy is not yet understood.

Dark matter: invisible matter that is thought to make up 90 per cent of the Universe's mass. Dark matter may include brown dwarfs, MACHOs, WIMPs, and neutrinos.

Deep-sky object: collective term for nebulas, star clusters, and galaxies.

Degree: basic unit for measuring angles – 1/360 of a full circle.

Doppler effect: the change in the frequency of waves (of sound or radiation) that reach an observer when the source is moving closer or further away.

Double star: two stars that appear close together in the sky. They may or may not actually be close together. See *Binary system.*

Dust grains: microscopic grains in space that absorb visible light.

Eclipse: effect caused by one celestial object casting a shadow on another. A lunar eclipse happens when Earth's shadow falls on the Moon. A solar eclipse occurs when the Moon passes between Earth and the Sun, casting a shadow on Earth.

Eclipsing binary: pair of stars in orbit around each other in such a way that the stars periodically pass in front of and behind each other as seen from Earth.

Ecliptic: imaginary line around the sky along which the Sun appears to move through the year, and near which most of the planets are seen. This line is a projection onto the sky of Earth's orbit around the Sun. *See also Zodiac.*

Edgeworth-Kuiper Belt: area of the Solar System containing millions of icy, comet-like objects. It extends from the orbit of Neptune to the inner edge of the Oort Cloud.

Electromagnetic radiation: waves of energy, carried by photons, that can travel through space and matter. They travel at the speed of light, and range from gamma rays (shortest wavelength) to radio waves (longest wavelength).

Electron: *See Atom.*

Element: any of the basic substances of nature which cannot be broken down into simpler substances by chemical reactions. Each element has unique properties.

Elliptical galaxy: galaxy with an oval or round shape, and no spiral arms. Elliptical galaxies are made mostly of old stars, and contain very little dust or gas.

Elliptical orbit: orbit that is oval in shape. Orbits are elliptical or circular.

Emission line: bright line in a spectrum caused by atoms giving out energy of a certain wavelength. Hot gas in a nebula often produces emission lines.

Escape velocity: the speed at which one object must travel to escape from another's gravity.

Event horizon: the area surrounding a black hole from within which light cannot escape.

Extrasolar: not belonging to the Sun – outside the Solar System.

Extraterrestrial: not belonging to Earth.

Filament: descriptive term given to string-like structure of galaxy superclusters. Filaments are the largest structures in the Universe, and are separated by immense voids.

Frequency: number of waves of electromagnetic radiation that pass a point every second.

Galaxy: any family of millions of stars, and gas and dust, held together by gravity and separated from other galaxies by space. The Galaxy, with a capital G, is our own galaxy, the Milky Way.

Galaxy cluster: group of galaxies held together by gravity.

Gamma rays: electromagnetic radiation with very short wavelengths. All stars and galaxies emit some gamma rays.

Gas giant: *see Giant planet.*

Giant planet: planet that is much larger than the rocky planets, has a lower density, and is composed mainly of hydrogen. The bulk of a giant planet is liquid. Jupiter, Saturn, Neptune, and Uranus are the giant planets of the Solar System.

Giant star: A star that has reached the late stage of its evolution, has swollen in size and increased in brightness. Sunlike stars become red giants. Stars with more than 10 times the mass of the Sun become supergiants, which are the most luminous stars in the Universe.

Globular cluster: *See Star cluster.*

Gravitational lensing: distortion of light from a distant object as it passes through a region of powerful gravity.

Gravitational well: distortion of space and time caused by the gravity of a massive object, such as a star.

Gravity: force of attraction between any objects with mass, such as the pull between Earth and the Moon.

Greenhouse effect: rise in temperature caused by gases – such as carbon dioxide and methane – trapping the heat that a planet's surface should be reflecting back into space.

Halo: vast, unseen spherical region surrounding a spiral galaxy. A halo contains dark matter and globular star clusters.

Heliosphere: space within 100 astronomical units of the Sun, where the solar wind still has an effect.

Helium: second lightest and second most common element in the Universe after hydrogen. Produced in the Big Bang and by nuclear fusion in stars.

Hertzsprung-Russell diagram: diagram showing how a star's brightness and colour are related. The diagram shows that stars fall into just a few main types. It can be used to trace the life cycle of stars.

Hubble constant: measure of the rate at which the Universe is expanding, measured in kilometres per second per million parsecs.

Hydrogen: most common and lightest element in the Universe – the main component of stars and galaxies.

Ice dwarf: small planetary body composed mainly of rock and ice. Pluto belongs to this category.

Inferior planet: planet in the Solar System that orbits closer to the Sun than Earth. The inferior planets are Mercury and Venus.

Inflation: period of extremely rapid expansion that occurred less than a second after the Big Bang.

Infrared: type of electromagnetic radiation with wavelengths just longer than visible light, but shorter than radio waves. It can be felt as heat.

Intergalactic: between galaxies.

Interstellar: between stars.

Interstellar matter: atoms and molecules in the space between the stars. Includes dust.

Ionosphere: electrically charged region of the Earth's atmosphere between 50 and 600 km (30 and 370 miles) above the surface.

Irregular galaxy: galaxy with no obvious shape. Irregular galaxies are generally small, full of gas, and contain a mix of young and old stars.

Kuiper belt: *See Edgeworth-Kuiper belt.*

Latitude: distance north or south of the equator of a spherical body, such as Earth. Latitude is measured in degrees and is shown on globes as lines running parallel to the equator.

Lava: molten rock released from the interior of a planet.

Lepton: any of three types of negatively charged subatomic particles created in the Big Bang. Only the electron and neutrino still exist. *See also Atom.*

Libration: an effect of the Moon's orbit that allows observers on Earth to see slightly more than half of its surface.

Light: electromagnetic radiation with wavelengths that are visible to the human eye.

Light pollution: glow in the sky, caused by streetlights and atmospheric pollution, that blocks astronomers' views of faint objects.

Light year: unit of astronomical measurement, based on the distance light travels in one year – roughly 9.5 million million km (5.9 million million miles)

Local arm: also Orion Arm – the spiral arm of the Milky Way Galaxy in which the Solar System is located.

Local Group: cluster of about 30 galaxies to which the Milky Way belongs.

Longitude: distance measured in degrees around a spherical body such as Earth, east or west from an imaginary line.

Low-Earth orbit: orbit of a few hundred kilometres above Earth's surface. Low-Earth orbits are used by space shuttles, space stations, and many satellites.

Luminosity: true brightness of a star expressed as the total radiation given off each second.

MACHOs: Massive Astrophysical Compact Halo Objects. MACHOs are unseen, star-sized objects thought to make up a portion of a galaxy's invisible mass. *See also Dark matter.*

Magnetic field: magnetism generated by planets, stars, and galaxies that extends into space.

Magnetosphere: bubble around a planet where the magnetic field is strong enough to act as an obstacle to the solar wind.

Magnetotail: the side of Earth's magnetosphere that is pushed away from the Sun, like a comet tail, due to the flow of the solar wind.

Magnitude: brightness of a celestial object, denoted on a scale of numbers. Bright objects have low (sometimes negative) numbers. Dim objects have high numbers. Apparent magnitude is a measure of brightness as seen from Earth. Absolute magnitude is a measure of an object's real brightness.

Mantle: rocky layer that lies between the crust and the core inside a planet or moon.

Mare: large, dark marking on the Moon, originally thought to be a lunar sea but now known to be huge depressions flooded with lava. (Plural: maria)

Mass: a measure of the amount of matter in an object. The greater the mass of an object, the greater its gravity.

Matter: anything that has mass and occupies space.

Messier objects: catalogue of about one hundred of the brightest star clusters, nebulas, and galaxies, denoted with the prefix "M".

Meteor: streak of light across the sky caused by a speck of rock burning up as it enters Earth's atmosphere. Also known as a shooting star or falling star.

Meteoroid: fragment of rock and dust from asteroids and comets.

Meteorite: a meteor that has fallen to the surface of a planet or moon. Where it hits the surface, it may form a crater.

Meteor shower: numerous meteors that appear to radiate from a single point in the sky over a few hours or days. A meteor shower occurs when Earth passes through a stream of dust deposited by a comet around its orbit.

Methane: gas made of carbon and hydrogen.

Microgravity: very low gravity, as experienced in orbit. Microgravity is a more accurate term than zero gravity. This is because a spacecraft's movements are usually creating

gravity in one direction.

Micrometre: one-millionth of a metre.

Microwave: type of radio wave, which has the shortest of the radio wavelengths.

Microwave background: *See Cosmic background radiation.*

Milky Way: the galaxy in which we live. Also the pale band of stars running across the sky when we look along the plane of our Galaxy.

Molecular cloud: interstellar cloud made up of molecules such as hydrogen and carbon monoxide.

Molecule: collection of atoms linked by chemical bonds so that they act as a single unit.

Moon: a planet's natural satellite. Earth's satellite is called the Moon. Those of other planets have unique names, such as Jupiter's moon, Io.

Multiple star: three or more stars held in orbit around each other by gravity.

Naked eye: unassisted human eyesight. The term naked eye is used for any object that should be visible to an average observer in good conditions.

Nanometre: one-billionth of a metre.

Nebula: cloud of gas and dust in space. Nebulas are visible when they reflect starlight or when they block out the light behind them. *See also Planetary nebula.*

Neutrino: extremely common subatomic particle produced by nuclear fusion in stars and by the Big Bang. Neutrinos are thought to have a tiny mass and may make up dark matter.

Neutron: *See Atom.*

Neutron star: collapsed star composed mainly of neutrons – the most common aftermath of a supernova explosion.

Nitrogen: gas that makes up 78 per cent of Earth's atmosphere.

Nova: faint star that suddenly becomes thousands of times brighter. It is a white dwarf star in a binary system that pulls material off its companion star and collects an atmosphere. It flares up when nuclear processes take place in this atmosphere and release energy.

Nuclear fusion: combining of

nuclei of atoms at very high temperatures and pressures. Nuclear fusion is the energy source of stars.

Nucleus: central part of an atom, where nearly all its mass is contained. The nucleus is made up of protons and neutrons. (Plural: nuclei)

Observatory: place where astronomers make observations of celestial objects and phenomena.

Occultation: the passing of one celestial object in front of another – for example, when the Moon blocks the view of a distant star.

Oort Cloud: huge spherical cloud, about 1.6 light years wide, that surrounds the Sun and planets. It contains billions of comets.

Open cluster: *See Star cluster.*

Opposition: point in the orbit of a planet when it appears directly opposite the Sun for an observer on Earth. This is when the planet is best viewed.

Orbit: path of one object around another, more massive object in space. Satellites, planets, and stars are held in orbit by the pull of gravity of a more massive body.

Orbital period: time taken for one object to complete its orbit around another.

Oxygen: element vital to the development of advanced life, and widespread in the Universe. Oxygen makes up 21 per cent of the Earth's atmosphere.

Parallax: shift in a nearby object's position against a more distant background when seen from two separate points. Parallax is used to measure the distances of nearby stars.

Parsec: distance at which a star or other object has a parallax of 1 arc second, equivalent to 3.26 light years.

Particle: *See Subatomic particle.*

Payload: cargo carried into space by a launch vehicle or on an artificial satellite.

Penumbra: outer, lighter part of a sunspot. Also the ring of partial shadow surrounding the full shadow, or umbra, cast by an object.

Perihelion: the point in an object's orbit in which it is closest to the Sun.

Phase: size of the illuminated portion of a planet or moon, as seen from Earth.

Photon: particle of electromagnetic radiation. Photons are the most common particles in the Universe.

Photosphere: star's visible surface, from which its light shines out into space.

Planet: spherical object made of rock or gas that orbits a star. A planet does not produce its own light but reflects the light of the star. *See also Brown dwarf.*

Planetary nebula: shell of gas puffed off by a red giant star before it becomes a white dwarf.

Planetary rings: ring-shaped structures composed of small bodies of dust, rock or ice surrounding Jupiter, Saturn, Uranus, and Neptune.

Plasma: state of matter in the interior of stars, consisting of ionized gas.

Pole star: the star Polaris, in the constellation Ursa Minor, around which the northern sky appears to rotate.

Positron: antimatter equivalent of an electron. It has the same mass as an electron, but a positive, rather than negative, charge. *See Atom.*

Precession: apparent "wobble" in Earth's rotational axis over a period of 25,800 years caused by the gravitational pull of the Sun and Moon. During the course of the wobble, Earth's poles trace circles in the sky causing stars to move across the celestial spheres.

Prominence: huge arc of gas in the Sun's lower atmosphere.

Proplyd: contraction of the term protoplanetary disc. The cloud of gas and dust around a newborn star that may give rise to a planetary system.

Proton: *see Atom.*

Protoplanetary disc: *See Proplyd.*

Protostar: young star that has not yet started nuclear fusion in its core.

Ptolemaic system: model of the Universe described by the Greek astronomer Ptolemy

(c. AD 100–170) in which a stationary Earth is orbited by the Sun, Moon, and planets.

Pulsar: spinning neutron star that sends beams of radiation across space.

Quadrillion: one thousand million million.

Quark: basic subatomic particle, created in the Big Bang. Three quarks combined can produce a proton or a neutron.

Quasar: distant active galaxy, releasing enormous amounts of energy from a small central region. Quasars are some of the most distant galaxies in the Universe.

Quintillion: one million million million.

Radiation: energy released by an object in the form of electromagnetic waves.

Radio galaxy: active galaxy that emits radiation at radio wavelengths. Most of its radiation comes from huge clouds on either side of the main galaxy.

Radio telescope: telescope that detects radio waves from objects in space.

Radio waves: electromagnetic radiation with very long wavelengths, produced by gas clouds and energetic objects.

Red giant: *See Giant star.*

Red shift: lengthening of the wavelength of electromagnetic radiation emitted from an object when it is moving away from us, so that its spectrum is shifted towards the red end. The shift may be caused by the Doppler effect or by the expansion of the Universe as a whole. *See also Blue shift.*

Reflecting telescope: telescope that gathers light with a concave mirror.

Refracting telescope: telescope that gathers light with a combination of several lenses.

Relativity: theory devised by Albert Einstein that describes how objects behave at very high speeds or in a powerful gravitational field.

Retrograde motion: apparent backwards movement of a superior planet in the sky, as Earth

overtakes it on its journey around the Sun.

Rings: *See Planetary rings.*

Roche limit: the minimum distance from a planet at which a liquid or gaseous satellite can survive without being destroyed by tidal disturbances. Rocky satellites can survive within the Roche limit.

Rocky planets: the four inner terrestrial planets of the Solar System – Mercury, Venus, Earth, and Mars.

Satellite: any object held in orbit around another object by its gravity. Includes moons and artificial satellites in orbit around planets, as well as small galaxies in orbit around larger ones.

SETI: abbreviation for Search for Extraterrestrial Intelligence. SETI involves searching for intelligent radio signals coming from space.

Seyfert galaxy: spiral galaxy with an unusually bright centre – a type of active galaxy.

Singularity: region of spacetime where normal physical laws don't apply because quantities such as heat and density may be infinite. The Big Bang may have originated in a singularity.

Solar flare: huge explosion above the surface of the Sun, occurring when two loops of the Sun's magnetic field touch.

Solar System: everything trapped by the Sun's gravity, from planets to comets.

Solar wind: stream of high-speed particles blowing away from the Sun.

Spacetime: framework that allows for a description of reality common to all observers in the Universe regardless of the speed of their relative motion.

Space weather: variation in physical conditions between Earth and the Sun caused by changes in solar activity.

Spectral analysis: study of spectral lines to reveal information about the composition of a star or galaxy, or to find its red shift.

Spectral lines: bright or dark lines in the spectrum of a body emitting radiation. *See also Absorption line, Emission line.*

Spectral type: method of classifying stars according to their colour and surface temperature.

Spectroscope: instrument used for splitting starlight into a spectrum and revealing spectral lines.

Spectrum: band of radiation split up into different wavelengths. The rainbow is a spectrum produced by splitting sunlight. (Plural: spectra)

Speed of light: measure of how far a ray of light travels in one second – nearly 300,000 km/second (186,000 miles/second). Nothing travels faster than this speed.

Spiral galaxy: galaxy with spiral arms emerging from a smooth central hub. Spiral galaxies have a mix of old and young stars, and are rich in star-forming regions.

Star: hot, massive, and luminous ball of gas that makes energy by nuclear fusion.

Starburst galaxy: galaxy that has undergone a sudden period of star formation, often as the result of colliding with another galaxy.

Star cluster: group of stars held together by gravity. Open clusters are loose groups of a few hundred young stars. Globular clusters are dense balls containing many thousands of old stars.

Star system: *See Multiple star.*

Steady state theory: discredited theory arguing that the Universe had no beginning and will have no end, but will remain the same forever.

Subatomic particle: particle smaller than an atom. Protons, neutrons, and electrons are the main subatomic particles that make up atoms.

Sunspot: cool, dark spot on the Sun's surface, created by the Sun's magnetic field, that stops the normal circulation of gases.

Sunquake: wave-like disturbances on the Sun's surface caused by erupting solar flares.

Supercluster: group of galaxy clusters held together by gravity.

Supergiant: *See Giant star.*

Superior planet: planet whose orbital path is further from the Sun than Earth's.

Supernova: enormous stellar

explosion. Supernovas happen when a white dwarf explodes (type I), or when a supergiant star runs out of fuel (type II).

Tidal force: distorting force on one object caused by the gravity of a nearby object.

Trillion: one million million.

Ultraviolet: electromagnetic radiation with a wavelength just shorter than visible light.

Umbra: inner, darker region of a sunspot. Also the darkest part of a lunar eclipse shadow, where the Moon is completely eclipsed.

Universe: the entirety of everything in existence.

Van Allen belts: regions of radiation around Earth, where Earth's magnetic field traps particles from the solar wind.

Variable star: star that changes in brightness. Many variable stars also regularly change size.

Visible light: *See Light.*

Voids: immense empty regions of space, separating the filaments of galaxies.

Wavelength: distance between the peaks or troughs in waves of electromagnetic radiation.

Weightlessness: *See Microgravity.*

White dwarf: collapsed core of a Sunlike star that has stopped generating energy.

WIMP: Weakly Interactive Massive Particle created in the Big Bang. Dark matter is thought to include WIMPs.

Wormhole: hypothetical tunnel in the fabric of spacetime, which may connect separate regions of space and time.

X-rays: radiation with a very short wavelength produced by hot gas clouds and stars, and around black holes.

Zero gravity: *See Microgravity.*

Zodiac: an imaginary band in the heavens, on either side of the ecliptic through which the Sun, Moon, and planets appear to move.

INDEX

Numbers in **bold** refer to main entries; numbers in *italic* refer to experiments and demonstrations.

ACKNOWLEDGEMENTS

The publishers would like to thank the following for their kind permission to reproduce their photographs:
Abbreviations key: t=top, b=bottom, r=right, l=left, c=centre

1 NASA c; 3 NASA: PIRL/ University of Arizona tr; Science Photo Library: BSIP CHAIX c, Celestial Image Company tc, Jack Finch cl, Jerry Schad cr; 4 NASA: COBE cr; SOHO & ESA cl; STScI tc, tr; 5 NASA: tr, br; 6–7 NASA: PIRL/University of Arizona c; 7 Science Photo Library: br, David Nunuk tr, Royal Observatory, Edinburgh cr; 8–9 Science Photo Library: David Nunuk; Science Photo Library: Jean Loup Charmet bl; 10–11 Robert Harding Picture Library: A. Woolfitt t; 11 Science Photo Library: David Parker tr, Hale Observatories bl; NASA br; 12 Bruce Coleman Ltd: Astrofoto cr; NASA: JPL, U.S. Geological Survey; Science Photo Library: M-Sat Ltd tl; 13 European Southern Observatory: c; NOAO /AURA/NSF: David Talent tr, Mike Pierce (Indiana) br; The Solar And Heliospheric Observatory: ESA & NASA tl; 14 NASA: FORS Team, 8.2-meter VLT, ESO cl, The Solar And Heliospheric Observatory br; 14–15 Corbis: Richard A. Cooke t; 15 CERN: br, NASA: TRACE, Stanford-Lockheed ISR cr; 16 Science Museum bl; 16–17 NASA: cl; Science Photo Library: Kent Wood c; 17 Corbis: cr, Tim Wright tc; 18 NASA: br;, CXC/SAO bl, CXC/SAO/HST/J. Morse/K.Davidson crb; 19 Corbis: Jonathan Blair bc; NASA: CXC/SAO/ATCA (S. white el al) br, CXC/SAO/E.Polomski, U. Florida/ CTIO cl; 20 European Southern Observatory: t; 21 Corbis: Roger Ressmeyer br; European Southern Observatory cl; NASA: Margarita Karovska (Harvard-Smithsonian Center for Astrophysics) bc; Science Photo Library: Dr Fred Espenak tl, Royal Greenwich Observatory cb; 22 Galaxy Picture Library: Howard Brown-Greaves bl, Robin Scagell bc, 22–23 Science Photo Library: Jack Finch tc; 23 Popperfoto: Paul Hackett/Reuters br; Science Photo Library: National Snow and Ice Data Center bl; 24 Galaxy Picture Library: Robin Scagell tr; 25 Science Photo Library: David Parker br; 26 Galaxy Picture Library: Robin Scagell cl; Science Photo Library: Julian Baum br; 27 NASA: br; 28 Corbis: Bettmann tr; Galaxy Picture Library: Robin Scagell cl; Science Photo Library: Celestial Image Co bc; Luke Dodd crb; 29 Science Photo Library: bl, Royal Observatory, Edinburgh br; 30 Corbis: Bojan Brecelj bl; Science Photo Library: John Sanford tr; 31 Galaxy Picture Library: Robin Scagell tl, tc; 32 NASA: tc, cb, bc; Science Photo Library: NASA cl; 32–33 Corbis: NASA b; 33 NASA: cr, clb; Science Photo Library: NASA tr; 34–35 NASA: ESA & SOHO; 36 NASA: cb, bl, 36–37 NASA: t; 37 NASA: br; Science Photo Library: Jerry Schad bl; 38 Popperfoto: Kamal Kishore/Reuters bc; 39 Galaxy Picture Library: Robin Scagell tc; Science Photo Library: br, Claus Lunau/Foci/Bonnier, Publications clb; Sheila Terry cr; 40 Science

Photo Library: Mark Garlick br; National Optical Astronomy Observatories bl. 40–41 Science Photo Library Claus Lunau/Foci/Bonnier Publications tc; 41 Natural History Museum cr; Science Photo Library: John Sanford br, Mark Garlick cl; 42 Science Photo Library: Mark Garlick cl; 44 NASA: bl, Geological Survey cl, Johnson Space Center bc; 45 Corbis: James A Sugar tl; NASA: tr, clb; 46 NASA: tl, c; Science Photo Library: David Weintraub bl; 46–47 Corbis: NASA; 47 Science Photo Library: Anthony Howarth tr; 48 Galaxy Picture Library: Bob Garner cb; Science Photo Library: br; NASA cr; 49 Science Photo Library: NASA cr, t; 50 NASA: US Geological Survey br; Science Photo Library: Detlev Van Ravensswaay cl; 51 Galaxy Picture Library: David Jewitt cl, clb; NASA: bc, U.S Geological Survey t; 52 Corbis: Jonathan Blair bl; Science Photo Library: Claus Lunau/Foci/Bonnier Publications cl; 53 NASA: JPL cl; Science Photo Library: Jerry Lodriguss tr; 54 Science Photo Library: cr; 54–55 Science Photo Library: A. Behrend/Eurelios; 55 The Natural History Museum, London: tr, cla, cr; Science Photo Library: David Nunuk tl, David Parker bl, br, Detlev Van Ravensswaay c; 56 NOAA: cl; Science Photo Library: John Reader bl; Peter Menzel c. 56–57 Science Photo Library: NASA c; 57 Science Museum tr; Science Photo Library: NASA cl; 58–59 Galaxy Picture Library: Arne Danielsen; 60–61 NASA; 62–63 NASA: USGS; 63 Galaxy Picture Library: JPL cl; Science Photo Library: John Sanford br; 64 Science Photo Library: NASA cr; 64–65 NASA; 65 NASA: bl; Science Photo Library: John Sanford bl; 66 Science Photo Library: cr; 67 NASA: cl; Science Photo Library: NASA tl; 68 Corbis: Bettmann br; Marie Tharp: br; 68–69 Jim Sugar Photography c; 69 Artic Images: Ljosmyndasafn RTH ehf tr; Science Photo Library: NASA ca; 70 Planet Earth Pictures bl, br; 70–71 Science Photo Library: Rev Ronald Royer tc; NASA: all planets; 72 Science Photo Library: Joe Tucciarone tr; John Heseltine bl; 72–73 NASA: bl; 73 NASA: tl, cl, cr; 74 Galaxy Picture Library: Robin Scagell br; 74–75 NASA: Photojournal; 75 NASA: Photojournal tr, c; Science Photo Library: Detlev van Ravensswaay cr; 76–77 NASA: JPL/Caltech b; 77 NASA: JPL/Caltech: bc; NASA: tl, cla, cl, cr; Science Photo Library: Julian Baum tr; 78 NASA/John Clarke, University of Michigan bc; Galaxy Picture Library: Robin Scagell bl; 78–79 NASA c; 79 Corbis: cr; Science Photo Library: MSSSO, ANU tr; 80 NASA: br; DLR (German Aerospace Center) c;. 80–81 NASA: CICLOPS/Uiversity of Arizona (background), PIRL/University of Arizona tc; 81 Mary Evans Picture Library: br; NASA: DLR cl, PIRL/ University of Arizona cr, U.S, Geological Survey tr; 82 Science Photo Library: BSIP CHAIX br; 82–83 NASA; 83 Science Photo Library: cr, bc; 84 NASA: cr; 85 Science Photo Library: US Geological Survey tr; 86 NASA cl, br; 86–87 Corbis: NASA/ Roger Ressmeyer c; 87 Liverpool

Astronomical Society cla; NASA: tr; Science Photo Library: Mark Garlick br; 88 Corbis: Scheufler Collection cr; NASA: tr, br; Galaxy Picture Library: Lowell Observatory cl; Science Photo Library: cb; 89 Corbis: Dean Conger tr; NASA. cl (pluto), Eliot Young (SwRI) et al bc; U.S. Geologial Survey cl (mercury); 90–91 Science Photo Library: Royal Observatory Edinburgh; 92 NASA: SOHO; STScI br; 93 NASA: STScI cl, br, t; 94–95 NASA: Soho; 95 Science Photo Library: Jerry Loriguss br, Professor Jay Pasachoff c; 96 NASA: Soho tr, cr, b, b (inset); 97 NASA: br; Soho tr, c (all); 98 NASA cb; 98–99 Science Photo Library: Jack Finch (background); 99 Corbis: Lowell Georgia tr; NASA: cr; Science Photo Library: bl; 100 NASA: c; Science Photo Library: Eckhard Slawik cl; 101 Science Photo Library: John Sandford bc; 102 NASA: STScI tr; Science Photo Library: David Parker cl; 104 Space Telescope Science Institute/NASA crb; 104–105 Science Photo Library: Celestial Image Co c; 105 NASA: C.R. O'Dell and S.K. Wong (Rice University) tc; K.L Luhman; G. Schneider, E. Young, G. Rieke, A.Cotera, H.Chen; M.Rieke, R.Thompson tr; Science Photo Library: Tony and Daphne Hallas cr; 106 Galaxy Picture Library: bl; NASA: tl; 107 Galaxy Picture Library: NOAO/ AURA/NSF t; Science Photo Library: Maptec International Ltd tr; 108 Science Photo Library: D. Ermakoff/ Eurelios cr; Space Telescope Institute/ NASA bl; 109 Royal Greenwich Observatory br; NASA: Jet Propulsion Laboratory bl; JPL/ University of Arizona tr; 110 Bridgeman Art Library, London / New York: Jean Loup Charmet Collection cr; 110–111 Science Photo Library: Celestial Image Co c; 112 Royal Greenwich Observatory bl; NASA: Nigel Sharp (NOAO), NSF, AURA br.; Science Photo Library: Celestial Image Co tr; 113 NASA: tr; 114 NASA: bc; 115 NASA: tl; 116 Science Photo Library: bl; 117 Corbis: Dave Bartruff tr; NASA: cr; 118 NASA: cr; 119 Science Photo Library: James King Holmes br; 120–121 NASA; 122 NASA: COBE cr; Science Photo Library: Tony & Daphne Hallas bl; 123 NASA: STScI tl, tr, cr, bl; 124 NASA: STScI bc; Science Photo Library: Jerry Schad bl; NASA cr; 124–125 Mark Garlick tc; 125 Jodrell Bank Observatory, University of Manchester br; NASA: STScI tr; Science Photo Library: Max–Planck–Institut fur Radroastronomie cr; 126 A. Steere bl; J.Morse (U.Colorado), K. Davidson (U. Minnesota) et al, WFPC2, HST br; National Radio Astronomy Observatory: tr; 127 Anglo Australian Observatory: Royal Observatory, Edinburgh tr; Science Photo Library: Jean-Charles Cuillandre/Canada-France-Hawaii Telescope br, Tony & Daphne Hallas cl; 128 European Southern Observatory: br; NASA: STScI bl; NOAO/AURA/NSF c; Science Photo Library: Hale Observatories tr; 129 NASA: STScI tr, cl; NOAO/AURA/NSF: N.A Sharp cr; 130 European Southern Observatory: c; NASA: tr, STScI br; Science Photo Library: Space Telescope Science

Institute/NASA bl; 131 NASA: tl, cl, cr; CGRO tr; 132 NOAO/AURA/NSF: Bill Schoening, Vanessa Harvey/REU Program b; Science Photo Library: George East tr; 133 NASA: tl, br; NOAO/AURA/NSF: tr, Bill Schoening bl; Science Photo Library: Eckhard Slawik cr; 134 Anglo Australian Observatory: David Malin cr; NASA: S.D Van Dyk (IPAC/Caltech) et al, KPNO 2.1-m Telescope, NOAO bl; 134–135 NASA: A. Fruchter and the ERO Team (STScI, ST–ECF) t; 135 NASA: CXC/SAO c; 136–37 Science Photo Library: Yannick Mellier/IAP; 138 Science Photo Library: Chris Butler bl; 139 NASA: Richard Mushotzky (GSFC/NASA), ROSAT, ESA tr; NOAO/AURA/NSF: Gemini Observatory/ Abu Team cl; 140 NASA: tr; 141 NASA: tl, tc; 142 Corbis: Roger Ressmeyer bl; Science Photo Library: Mehau Kulyk cr; 143 Science Photo Library: NASA tr, Patrice Loiez tl, Space Telescope Science Institute/NASA bl; 144 NASA: c; 144–45 Science Photo Library: W. Couch & R. Ellis/NASA tc; 145 ICRR (Institute for Cosmic Ray Research), The University of Tokyo tr; 146 Science Photo Library: Julian Baum cl, Mark Garlick bl; 147 Ronald Grant Archive: br; 148 Science Photo Library: David A. Hardy/PPARC cr, Victor Habbick Visions bc; 149 NASA: Rex Saffer(Villanova University) and Dave Zurek (STScI) cr; Science Photo Library: David Parker tr, Dr Seth Shostak tl; 150–51 NASA: ESA & SOHO; 152–53 NASA; 154–55 Science Photo Library: NASA.

All other images © Dorling Kindersley. For more information see;
www.dkimages.com

Artworks:
Abreviations; Tim Brown=TB; Darren Holt=DH; Robin Hunter=RH; John Kelly=JK; Martin Wilson=MW

15 c DH; 17 bc MW; 18–19 c RH; 18 MW; 20 bl, br RH; 26 tr TB; 38 c RH; 40–41 c RH; 40 bl RH; 41 r MW; 44 tr RH; 47 tl RH; 52 t RH; 62 tc, tr MW; 66 tr RH; 62 cl MW; 70 c DH; 71 cl DH; 74c DH; 84 cl RH; 88–89 c TB; 88 bl RH; 94 bl DH; 98–99 tc JK; 101 tl, bl, br DH; 102 bl, br DH; 103 br DH; 104 bl TB; 105 br TB; 106 tl–r RH; 107 bl RH; 108 br TB; 108–9 tc TB; 110 tr RH; 113 cr RH; 114 c RH; 115 cl RH; 116 c RH; 116–117 c TB; 119 tr, bl TB; 126 c DH; 127 c DH; 131 tl–cr DH; 133 cr DH; 134 br DH; 135 cl DH; 138 c DH; 140–141 RH; 140 c RH; 141 bl DH; 146–147 c JK; 147 tr JK; 148 tr–cr RH;

Dorling Kindersley would like to thank the following people for their contributions to the making of this book:
Proof reading: Caryn Jenner;
Chris Bernstein for the index;
Kate Bradshaw for hand modelling;
Alex O'Reilly for editorial assistance;
Roger Langston at King's College London, University of London, for kindly loaning scientific equipment